Palgrave Studies in Theatre and Performance History is a series devoted to the best of theatre/performance scholarship currently available, accessible, and free of jargon. It strives to include a wide range of topics, from the more traditional to those performance forms that in recent years have helped broaden the understanding of what theatre as a category might include (from variety forms as diverse as the circus and burlesque to street buskers, stage magic, and musical theatre, among many others). Although historical, critical, or analytical studies are of special interest, more theoretical projects, if not the dominant thrust of a study, but utilized as important underpinning or as a historiographical or analytical method of exploration, are also of interest. Textual studies of drama or other types of less traditional performance texts are also germane to the series if placed in their cultural, historical, social, or political and economic context. There is no geographical focus for this series and works of excellence of a diverse and international nature, including comparative studies, are sought.

The editor of the series is Don B. Wilmeth (Emeritus, Brown University), PhD, University of Illinois, who brings to the series over a dozen years as editor of a book series on American theatre and drama, in addition to his own extensive experience as an editor of books and journals. He is the author of several award-winning books and has received numerous career achievement awards, including one for sustained excellence in editing from the Association for Theatre in Higher Education.

Also in the series:

Undressed for Success by Brenda Foley
Theatre, Performance, and the Historical Avant-garde by Günter Berghaus
Theatre, Politics, and Markets in Fin-de-Siècle Paris by Sally Charnow
Ghosts of Theatre and Cinema in the Brain by Mark Pizzato
Moscow Theatres for Young People: A Cultural History of Ideological Coercion and Artistic Innovation, 1917–2000 by Manon van de Water
Absence and Memory in Colonial American Theatre by Odai Johnson
Vaudeville Wars: How the Keith-Albee and Orpheum Circuits Controlled the Big-Time and Its Performers by Arthur Frank Wertheim
Performance and Femininity in Eighteenth-Century German Women's Writing by Wendy Arons
Operatic China: Staging Chinese Identity across the Pacific by Daphne P. Lei
Transatlantic Stage Stars in Vaudeville and Variety: Celebrity Turns by Leigh Woods
Interrogating America through Theatre and Performance edited by William W. Demastes and Iris Smith Fischer
Plays in American Periodicals, 1890–1918 by Susan Harris Smith
Representation and Identity from Versailles to the Present: The Performing Subject by Alan Sikes
Directors and the New Musical Drama: British and American Musical Theatre in the 1980s and 90s by Miranda Lundskaer-Nielsen
Beyond the Golden Door: Jewish-American Drama and Jewish-American Experience by Julius Novick
American Puppet Modernism: Essays on the Material World in Performance by John Bell

On the Uses of the Fantastic in Modern Theatre: Cocteau, Oedipus, and the Monster by Irene Eynat-Confino
Staging Stigma: A Critical Examination of the American Freak Show by Michael M. Chemers, foreword by Jim Ferris
Performing Magic on the Western Stage: From the Eighteenth-Century to the Present edited by Francesca Coppa, Larry Hass, and James Peck, foreword by Eugene Burger
Memory in Play: From Aeschylus to Sam Shepard by Attilio Favorini
Danjūrō's Girls: Women on the Kabuki Stage by Loren Edelson
Mendel's Theatre: Heredity, Eugenics, and Early Twentieth-Century American Drama by Tamsen Wolff
Theatre and Religion on Krishna's Stage: Performing in Vrindavan by David V. Mason
Rogue Performances: Staging the Underclasses in Early American Theatre Culture by Peter P. Reed
Broadway and Corporate Capitalism: The Rise of the Professional-Managerial Class, 1900–1920 by Michael Schwartz
Lady Macbeth in America: From the Stage to the White House by Gay Smith
Performing Bodies in Pain: Medieval and Post-Modern Martyrs, Mystics, and Artists by Marla Carlson
Early-Twentieth-Century Frontier Dramas on Broadway: Situating the Western Experience in Performing Arts by Richard Wattenberg
Staging the People: Community and Identity in the Federal Theatre Project by Elizabeth A. Osborne
Russian Culture and Theatrical Performance in America, 1891–1933 by Valleri J. Hohman
Baggy Pants Comedy: Burlesque and the Oral Tradition by Andrew Davis
Transposing Broadway: Jews, Assimilation, and the American Musical by Stuart J. Hecht
The Drama of Marriage: Gay Playwrights/Straight Unions from Oscar Wilde to the Present by John M. Clum
Mei Lanfang and the Twentieth-Century International Stage: Chinese Theatre Placed and Displaced by Min Tian
Hijikata Tatsumi and Butoh: Dancing in a Pool of Gray Grits by Bruce Baird
Staging Holocaust Resistance by Gene A. Plunka
Acts of Manhood: The Performance of Masculinity on the American Stage, 1828–1865 by Karl M. Kippola
Loss and Cultural Remains in Performance: The Ghosts of the Franklin Expedition by Heather Davis-Fisch
Uncle Tom's Cabin *on the American Stage and Screen* by John W. Frick
Theatre, Youth, and Culture: A Critical and Historical Exploration by Manon van de Water
Stage Designers in Early Twentieth-Century America: Artists, Activists, Cultural Critics by Christin Essin
Audrey Wood and the Playwrights by Milly S. Barranger
Performing Hybridity in Colonial-Modern China by Siyuan Liu
A Sustainable Theatre: Jasper Deeter at Hedgerow by Barry B. Witham

The Group Theatre: Passion, Politics, and Performance in the Depression Era
by Helen Chinoy and edited by Don B. Wilmeth and Milly S. Barranger

Cultivating National Identity through Performance: American Pleasure Gardens and Entertainment by Naomi J. Stubbs

Entertaining Children: The Participation of Youth in the Entertainment Industry
edited by Gillian Arrighi and Victor Emeljanow

America's First Regional Theatre: The Cleveland Play House and Its Search for a Home
by Jeffrey Ullom

Class Divisions on the Broadway Stage: The Staging and Taming of the I.W.W.
by Michael Schwartz

The New Humor in the Progressive Era: Americanization and the Vaudeville Comedian
by Rick DesRochers

The New Humor in the Progressive Era

Americanization and the Vaudeville Comedian

Rick DesRochers

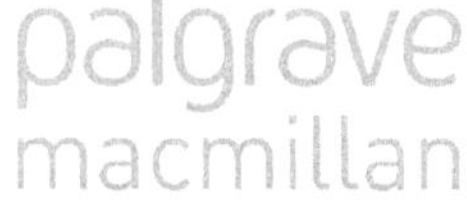

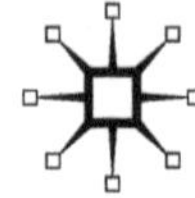

THE NEW HUMOR IN THE PROGRESSIVE ERA

Softcover reprint of the hardcover 1st edition 2014 978-1-137-35742-7

First published in 2014 by
PALGRAVE MACMILLAN®
in the United States—a division of St. Martin's Press LLC,
175 Fifth Avenue, New York, NY 10010.

Where this book is distributed in the UK, Europe and the rest of the world, this is by Palgrave Macmillan, a division of Macmillan Publishers Limited, registered in England, company number 785998, of Houndmills, Basingstoke, Hampshire RG21 6XS.

Palgrave Macmillan is the global academic imprint of the above companies and has companies and representatives throughout the world.

Palgrave® and Macmillan® are registered trademarks in the United States, the United Kingdom, Europe and other countries.

ISBN 978-1-349-47074-7 ISBN 978-1-137-35718-2 (eBook)
DOI 10.1057/9781137357182

Library of Congress Cataloging-in-Publication Data

DesRochers, Rick.
The new humor in the Progressive Era : Americanization and the vaudeville comedian / Rick DesRochers.
pages cm—(Palgrave studies in theatre and performance history)
Includes bibliographical references and index.

1. Vaudeville—United States—History—20th century. 2. Vaudeville—Social aspects—United States. 3. Stand-up comedy—United States—History—20th century. 4. Comedians—United States—History—20th century. I. Title.

PN1968.U5D38 2014
792.70973'09041—dc23 2014003219

A catalogue record of the book is available from the British Library.

Design by Newgen Knowledge Works (P) Ltd., Chennai, India.

First edition: July 2014

10 9 8 7 6 5 4 3 2 1

For Ashley and Lucy—à la folie
In memory of Dan Gerould

Contents

Illustrations

Preface

At the turn of the twentieth century, the United States saw an unprecedented wave of immigration. It began in the mid-nineteenth century, coming mostly from northern and western Europe. From the 1880s to 1900s, however, a new influx began, and by the 1920s, about 13 million "new" immigrants had entered, most of them from eastern and southern Europe.[1] In 1902, Woodrow Wilson, then a professor of political science at Princeton University, noted in his *History of the American People* that the census of 1890 was marked by "students of affairs" with "uneasiness." He went on to remark that the "sturdy stocks of the north of Europe" were being overtaken by "multitudes of men of the lowest class from the south of Italy and men of meaner sort out of Hungary and Poland, men out of the ranks where there was neither skill nor energy nor any initiative of quick intelligence."

According to Wilson, "the countries of the south of Europe were disburdening themselves of the more sordid and hapless elements of their population."[2] Wilson's views were not far from those of Prescott Hall, secretary of the Immigration Restriction League and a Harvard graduate, who bluntly asked if Americans wanted their country "to be peopled by British, German, and Scandinavian stock, historically free, energetic, progressive, or by Slav, Latin, and Asiatic races, historically downtrodden, atavistic, and stagnant."[3] The League was founded in 1894 in Boston with branches in New York, Chicago, and San Francisco. It opposed the influx of the new immigrants who were threatening the "American" way of life. That no less than Wilson, later the twenty-eighth US president and known as a leader of the Progressive movement, made such comments is a telling indication of how these new immigrants were received in the American "melting pot." Indeed, Anglo-American xenophobia touched on all aspects of how the new immigrants, and the culture they brought with them, were treated and interpreted.

Of primary concern for this study is that the new immigrants brought with them a sense of humor that could produce subversive laughter. The playwright and librettist Edward "Ned" Harrigan, author of the popular *Mulligan Guard* series of light comedy revues, warned in 1900 that "there's been a great change in the sense of humor in New York, the great influx of Latins and Slavs—who always want to laugh not with you but at you—has brought about a different kind of humor."[4] Harrigan echoed the pronouncements of associations like the Immigration Restriction League, which denounced these immigrant humorists for appealing to the prurient interests of the underclasses and for introducing comic popular entertainments that would infect middle-class Anglo-Americans with their vulgarity.[5] Vaudevillians were cast as lowbrow, ribald, and a threat to the American way of life; popular comedians in particular were perceived as dangerous, immoral, and hazardous to the process of Americanization. Many established Americans—some of them from an earlier immigration of Irish, Germans, and Scandinavians during the middle to late nineteenth century—felt that their "Americanness" was coming under attack with the advent of what I call the "new humor."

According to Edward Harrigan, this insurgent new form of laughter was created by the new southern and eastern European immigrants, "who always want to laugh not with you but at you."[6] Confirming Harrigan's xenophobia was Stanford University Professor Ellwood Cubberley, whose *Changing Conceptions of Education* (1909) posited what made these same new immigrants inferior to their northern and western European brethren:

> About 1882, the character of our immigration changed in a very remarkable manner... Illiterate, docile, lacking in self-reliance and initiation and not possessing Anglo-Teutonic conceptions of law, order, and government, their coming has served to dilute tremendously our national stock, and to corrupt our civic life.[7]

Harrigan, who is best remembered for his turn-of-the-twentieth-century musical comedies with collaborator Tony Hart, went on to clarify that "it isn't native, it isn't New York," by way of explaining the un-Americanness presumably espoused by these new immigrants.[8] Reformers, critics, and authorities who wanted to define Americanness through middle-class Anglo traditions and morals came into direct conflict with these new humorists, who were depicting an alternative definition of what it meant to be American on the comic vaudeville stage. The irony was that the new humor of the new immigrants would become a distinctly American form of popular entertainment in vaudeville.

Part of the effort to create a distinctive Americanness was through the performing arts, and in particular, the theater. In stark contrast to the vaudeville stage was the legitimate theater. It distinguished itself from lowbrow genres like musical revues, burlesque, and vaudeville, as critics and aesthetes alike canonized this presumably more serious and literary art form, represented by playwrights like Elmer Rice, Sophie Treadwell, Clifford Odets, and Eugene O'Neill, who confirmed that Americans had created their own literature for the theater, one that rivaled that of Continental authors.[9]

Whereas the legitimate theater was perceived to promote a quiet and thoughtful response to a play of literary merit, the comic vaudeville stage conversely encouraged audience response and participation. The rowdiness in a vaudeville house should have been discouraged, according to reformers and critics, because it incited spectators to shun polite and disciplined appreciation for the performing arts. It also stimulated the violent outbursts and crude behaviors that had characterized nineteenth-century popular entertainments. The new humor in particular was found to offend so-called sophisticated artistic sensibilities. These comic stage acts came under attack by social reformers and cultural critics to promote a standard for Anglo-American, middle-class cultural identity in the United States during the Progressive era.

The New Humor in the Progressive Era defines this brand of humor and how it was practiced by comic vaudevillians from the 1880s to the early 1920s, vaudeville's golden era. It focuses on the various forms of vaudeville performances, including ethnic acts, family acts, and school acts, as well as on the comedians who excelled at writing and producing them. In order to provide a comprehensive and wide range of comic vaudevillians, including the celebrated along with more obscure artists who trafficked in traditional acts in a distinctive and provocative way, a special emphasis is placed on the comedy team and ethnic act of Joe Weber and Lew Fields; the family act of the Three Keatons;

the school act of the Marx Brothers; the combination ethnic and family act of Kate and May Elinore, known as the Elinore Sisters; and the burlesque-inspired comedy of May Irwin, Eva Tanguay, and Marie Dressler. This diverse array of performers will be considered in relationship to Progressive-era reformers, cultural critics, and moral authorities, and their attempts to control, censure, and regulate popular comic entertainments on the vaudeville stage.

Progressive activists and politicians felt that the nationalist ideals of loyalty and patriotism were coming under attack through popular entertainments. They began to agitate for reforms and censorship in support of a national agenda of Americanization through moral, educational, and civic-minded diversions and recreations. I discuss the new humorists with regard to their engagement with this agenda and its proponents, including the reformers Jane Addams, John Dewey, Elbridge Thomas Gerry, Frances Kellor, and Belle Israels Moskowitz, as well as cultural critics like Caroline Caffin, Mary Cass Canfield, H. L. Mencken, and Sime Silverman. I also consider cultural theorists and public intellectuals of the era, including Randolph Bourne, Walter Lippmann, and Benjamin Parke De Witt, placing them in counterpoint with the reformers and critics to examine how arguments for and against Americanization, its benefits and detriments, were conceived.

This analysis illustrates how the new humor of vaudeville comedy intentionally unsettled Anglo-American middle-class values, even as the crusaders sought to promote Americanization by exploiting sociocultural divides. Comic vaudevillians created their art in a clear relationship to the reformers, critics, and authorities, using physical and verbal types that mocked Americanness and its relationship to class, gender, and ethnicity to disrupt the propriety of what constituted an American. In this regard, the new humor in vaudeville was unassumingly subversive. The performers' control over the masks of ethnicity and gender allowed them to become anyone at any time—in 1922 critic Mary Cass Canfield perceptively called vaudeville a "Protean miracle."[10] Vaudeville comedians became quite successful in portraying the ethnic types that they brought with them from the "old country" as they melded them with parodies of how immigrants and the new working classes attempted to assimilate into and infiltrate the Anglo-American way of life. But the comic actors' portrayal of ethnic and native roles not their own provoked fear among some Anglo-Americans, who worried that the new humor could reach a wide variety of audiences. As a result, vaudeville comedy was subjected to Progressive-era reform and censure.

This book uniquely examines the popular stage's comic forms in the context of suppression, an area that needs further scrutiny. By examining iconic as well as lesser-known comedic performers from this era of cultural and political ferment, this study seeks to reclaim an important part of American theatrical and sociocultural history, one that needs more attention in US performance studies and in sociocultural evaluations of Americanization in the early twentieth century.

Chapter 1, "Americanization: Progressive-Era Reformers, Cultural Critics, and Popular Comic Entertainments," examines a diverse range of reformers and critics, their arguments for and against Americanization, and the conflicts among them in the context of the Progressive-era agenda of Americanization. These reformers and critics are seen in relationship with the new immigrants and their progeny, who were often targeted at the turn of the twentieth century as corrupting the aesthetics and culture of the American middle class.

Chapter 2, "Putting It Over in American Vaudeville," defines the new humor as it evolved from comic vaudeville performers and their roots in nineteenth-century American theatrical forms such as minstrel shows, concert saloons, variety theater, and burlesque comedy. This chapter examines the transition and separation of these earlier popular forms from vaudeville as they became marginalized entertainments for the lower classes and as select comic performers attempted to upgrade to the "cleaned up" and more respectable vaudeville stage. Key to this transition was the development of "putting it over," or the notion of connecting with audiences through ethnic- and gender-coded comic acts. To avoid overtly offending unsuspecting audience members, comic vaudevillians hid their intentions with masked physical and vocal language that traded in double entendres and hidden meanings, including references that only certain spectators from the underclasses could appreciate.

Chapter 3, "The New Humor: Ethnic Acts and Family Acts," examines the conflicts between Progressives and vaudeville comedians through ethnic acts and family acts. The vaudeville impresarios Joe

Weber and Lew Fields, who began as a "Double Dutch" act; the Three Keatons and their faux-Irish family who trafficked in domestic strife; the family act of the Marx Brothers and their ethnic mix of German, Italian, and Irish character types; and the Elinore Sisters' mistress–servant act, which enacted the Irish–British conflict—all these would confront the notion of Americanness, often dramatizing the new humor's clash with the reformers' campaigns. One such campaign was undertaken in the early 1900s by John Dewey, Edgar Gardner Murphy, and E. A. Ross, who sought to reform public education and regulate child labor and welfare.

Chapter 4, "The Marx Brothers Go to School," examines how the Marx Brothers—as first-generation children of eastern European Jewish immigrants—commented on the American public school system and satirized the reformers. Years before their international success in Hollywood films, the brothers' first successful vaudeville routine was "the school act," originally titled *Fun in Hi Skule* (1910)—the intentional misspelling indicated how poorly public school had educated this trio of comedians. The failure of the public schools for the Marx boys, and their resistance to the American formal education system, paved the way for their school act. *Fun in Hi Skule* and its later incarnations—*Mr. Green's Reception* (1912), *Home Again* (1914), and the film *Horse Feathers* (1932)—serve as a lens through which to view how the Marx Brothers used the new humor to satirize and critique Progressive-era education reform at the beginning of the twentieth century.

Chapter 5, "The New Woman and the Female Comedian as Social Insurgent," will look at the new women on the comic vaudeville stage in relationship to class, ethnicity, and body image. Female comic performers considered here include May Irwin and her comic persona as staged through her "coon" numbers (racially charged comic songs); Eva Tanguay, whose comically wild and unruly sexualized singing and dancing made her the "Queen of Vaudeville"; and Marie Dressler, whose unconventional body image was featured in her "Big Girl" portrayals and led her to be described as a grotesque female comedian and later a dowager comic film star. The chapter concludes with an evaluation of how these comedians embodied the characterization of sexualized wild women. The class confrontations of these working-class "tough girls" are contrasted with Florenz Ziegfeld's glorified image of the "all-American girls." These contradictory images of the female performer combined to create the new woman as a social insurgent in her early comic appearances in burlesque, vaudeville, and eventually the commercial worlds of Broadway and Hollywood. All three of the comedians discussed here share a common Canadian immigrant background as well as an affinity for issues of class simply because of their chosen profession; as working-class women in the male-dominated world of comedy, they challenged the conventional notion of womanhood, especially as it related to ethnicity, immigration, and sexual permissiveness.

Together, the chapters in this book explore the new humor's historical influence and its challenge to Progressive-era reformers and definitions of Americanness. They examine how the popular forms of vaudeville comedy combined to create an alternative place for new immigrants and new women, through ethnic acts, family acts, school acts, stump speeches, and burlesque acts. Studying the new humor in vaudeville thus provides an understanding of how comedy became a significant art form in the Progressive era, one that critiqued the divisions of class, ethnicity, and gender in the United States.

Acknowledgments

First and foremost to Robyn Curtis, Erica Buchman, and Don Wilmeth, for their stewardship of this book for the Palgrave Studies in Theatre and Performance History Series. Many thanks are due to several mentors and colleagues at the CUNY Graduate Center who were influential in guiding my research interests and process including Morris Dickstein, Lynn Gibson, Jean Graham-Jones, Judy Milhous, and James Wilson. A special tribute is in order for the late Daniel Gerould whose support of my scholarship at the Graduate Center was paramount in making this project possible.

And to my colleagues at Long Island University Post—Jon Fraser, Cara Gargano, David Hugo, Maria Porter, Robert Wildman, Noel Zahler, and the many students over the years that have sustained my passion for the practice and scholarship of theater. I want to thank Paul Meshejian for the endless hours we have spent talking theater and collaborating on amazing new theater projects for the past ten years for the PlayPenn New Play Development Conference; Pablo Morales for his excellent editorial feedback; and to T. J., Vera, and Keifer at Du Jour Bakery, Brooklyn, who indulged my endless hours at their "coffice."

I need to acknowledge the generous support of the Long Island University Post research grant committee who provided much needed funding, especially professors Nancy Frye and Heather Parrott, as well as the American Travel Research Fund (the CUNY-sponsored Tackel Grant), and the multiple CUNY Graduate Center Salk Travel Grants, and several Long Island University Post Travel Grants that made it possible to do the archival research for this book.

And finally I want to extend my deepest gratitude and love to my family—my sister Elaine—my daughter, Lucy Frances, who keeps me smiling and laughing in the darkest moments when I think I can't go on—I go on—and the love of my life and partner in crime—Ashley Semrick DesRochers.

1. Americanization: Progressive-Era Reformers, Cultural Critics, and Popular Comic Entertainments

In 1921, "the Four Marx Brothers and Company" presented a "musical revuette" titled *On the Balcony*.[1] The theatrical poster billed the show as "the comedy hit of the age; quaint characterization; humorous episodes; every type of vaudeville talent." The opening scene, simply called the "The Theatrical Agency," features the four brothers trying to persuade an agent to hire them for his latest vaudeville show. The scene was repeated for a film trailer with this added exchange featuring Groucho Marx: Speaking in a heavy Russian accent, Groucho entreats the theatrical manager with, "I vant to play a dramatic part, the kind that toucha a woman's heart, to make her cry for me to die." Chico Marx, portraying his now-iconic Italian-immigrant peasant character, cuts Groucho off in accented English: "Did you ever get hit with a cocoanuts [sic] pie?" Groucho, dropping character and his accent, turns to the camera and says, "There's my argument. Restrict immigration."[2] The seemingly absurd commentary on immigration inserted into a vaudeville scene—later re-created for the trailer of their 1931 Hollywood film *Monkey Business*—speaks to vaudeville comedians' ability to comment directly on their status as ethnic immigrants, and to the xenophobia that attended Americanization during the early twentieth century.

Groucho was always aware of his status as the son of eastern European Jewish immigrants. This seeming non sequitur about restricting immigration was an overt criticism of the bigoted and hypocritical

US immigration policies during the Progressive era. Groucho was directly affected by these restrictions that contradicted the very notion of "Give me your tired, your poor, your huddled masses, yearning to breathe free," emblazoned on the Statue of Liberty.[3] While traveling from England to the United States in 1931, Groucho joked that he was a smuggler to a customs officer. After a lengthy search of his family, his belongings, and himself, and several hours of detainment, Groucho was enraged at how he was treated and that he had been suspected as a criminal simply for telling a joke. He let loose his ire on immigration and customs officials, saying: "How about the Pilgrims, were they bothered with all this landing card and visa business? Did a guard stand on Plymouth Rock waiting for them?"[4]

Groucho Marx's humor stemmed from his self-conception as an outsider in his own country. He pointed out the hypocrisy of discrimination and the marginalization of ethnic immigrants and their families, who had to prove that they were as American as their Anglo-American neighbors. The irony is that Groucho and the Marx Brothers would achieve unprecedented success on the comic stage as well as in the new media of film, radio, and television, becoming internationally famous examples of fulfilling the American dream of success, even through they did not fit the dominate ideal of Americanness.

It was during the Progressive era that a particular ideal of Americanness came to dominate middle-class ideals, thanks to the attempt by reformers, cultural critics, politicians, and local authorities to Americanize the newest citizens of the United States. How did Americanization take hold so successfully? Why was it deemed so essential in the formation of American identity during the first two decades of the twentieth century?

It began with the formation of a new middle class of Americans, precipitated by the expansion of a nonmanual working class and the repurposing of manual labor under the increasing advances in industry away from an agricultural and artisanal culture. This shift in the workforce created many factory-based, unskilled jobs that increased tedium in the workplace as well as leisure time and disposable income. Coupled with the unprecedented immigration of some 13 million new immigrants from 1886 to 1925, divisions between the working and middle classes arose along with the social marginalization attributed to ethnic heritage. This restructuring of the American workplace and the subsequent economic disparity raised questions with regard to cultural inclusion and national belonging.[5]

Before 1880 the vast majority of European immigration came from its northern and western countries. A major shift, however, occurred between the 1880s and 1900s, and the dominant immigrant groups now came from southern and eastern European nations. Until the early 1880s, almost 63 percent of European immigrants came from Belgium, Britain and Ireland, France, Germany, the Netherlands, Scandinavia, and Switzerland, compared to only about 37 percent from the southern and eastern regions. In 1882, almost 650,000 European immigrants entered the United States, with more than 13 percent coming from Austria-Hungary, Greece, Italy, Montenegro, Poland, Portugal, Romania, Russia, Serbia, Spain, and Turkey—countries that were then relatively unknown to Americans. By 1907, more than 80 percent of some 1.2 million European immigrants had come from these countries.[6] The fear attending this new influx of immigrants was characterized by Massachusetts senator Henry Cabot Lodge, who was quick to point out that the new immigrants were responsible for the "greatest relative increase from races most alien to the body of the American people," and that "the shifting of the sources of the immigration" was "unfavorable," bringing people who were "very difficult to assimilate" and did "not promise well for the standard of civilization in the United States—a matter as serious as the effect on the labor market."[7]

In addition to this new wave of immigration from these "unfavorable" countries, major paradigm shifts occurred during the first two decades of the twentieth century that contributed to the anxieties of a nation in flux and experiencing revolutionary changes in composition and character. Referring to a visit to the United States in 1900, an Englishman remarked, "Life in the States is one perpetual whirl of telephones, telegrams, phonographs, electric bells, motors, lifts, and automatic instruments."[8] From 1900 to 1910, Americans were inundated with new technologies and innovations with the advent of electric sewing machines, fans, washing machines, and vacuum cleaners. In addition they could purchase new inventions like irons, stoves, heaters, and phonographs. Telegraphs and telephones, with their instantaneous messaging, connected people all over the country. Movies began in earnest to attract mass audiences, and electric trolleys and elevated trains allowed consumers efficient and faster travel from rural and residential areas to enjoy new forms of leisure and entertainment in the urban core. By 1920, over eight million automobiles were sold, and the percentage of Americans living in cities increased dramatically from 35 percent in 1890 to more than 50 percent in 1920.

The post–Civil War era had given rise to large corporations and with them conflicts between management and labor. Resentments and anxieties were exacerbated when industrialists displaced independent small businessmen, farmers, and craftsmen. In response, the reforms of the Progressive movement began to influence local government in the 1890s, later expanding its influence to state and national government by the turn of the twentieth century. In 1915, Benjamin Parke De Witt, professor of English and government at New York University, wrote in his book *The Progressive Movement* that beginning in the late nineteenth century, "complex conditions that were bringing wealth to the magnate and the railroad king were bringing difficult social and economic problems to the masses of people... The individual could not hope to compete with the wealthy corporation which employed him." He also noted with grim finality that "men became economic slaves... Slowly, Americans realized that they were not free."[9] Thus began an antagonism between capital and labor, working and bourgeois classes, new immigrants and nativist Americans.

De Witt, a member of the original Progressive Party, clearly articulated its agenda and that of the movement that took its name. Progressive-era reformers, he argued,

> propose to regulate the employment of women and children in factories; to impose a maximum number of hours of work a day for men under certain conditions; to provide for workingmen in their old age and for their widows and orphans when their support is taken from them; to reduce or remove the tariff and substitute in its stead a system of taxation which will fall most heavily on those best able to bear it; to adopt a minimum wage law to strengthen the needy against temptation; to strike at poverty, crime, and disease; to do everything that government can do to make our country better, nobler, purer, and life more worth living.[10]

This political agenda, which countered that of the dominant Democratic and Republican parties, was noble in its intentions. It advocated for the underclasses of ethnic immigrants, as well as for women and children, and promoted the ideal of equal rights and treatment under the law for all American citizens regardless of their class, ethnicity, or gender. It should be noted that race and the rights of African Americans were not considerations for most Progressives.

At the turn of the twentieth century, a fundamental shift took place from small-town American cultural values of the 1880s to those of the new urban middle class. Industrialization and incorporation created a new bureaucratic, white-collar middle class that enforced productivity and the practical concerns of business and raising a family. The Progressive movement, according to social historian Robert H. Wiebe, produced "the need for a government of continuous involvement" and an emphasis on executive administration and regulation.[11] This need for a paternalistic government was reflected in the many reform organizations that developed during this period of middle-class ascendency. The values of the rural farms and small towns of the nineteenth century were being replaced by those of an urban, professional class of managers and supervisors. Reformers, cultural critics, and politicians, with the aid of law enforcement, called for changes in social and moral structures and legislation that would support industry and discourage individualism. The "company man" became the socioeconomic ideal of "making it" in America, along with moving from the working classes to the middle classes. Loyalty to bosses, corporate interests, and the bureaucracy that sustained this new "productive" system became more important than the pride in individual ownership and craftsmanship that characterized the US economic ethos only a few decades earlier.

Progressive-era reformers were members of this forward-looking new middle class who were touting their beliefs in the progress of America as a leader in industry, and economic prosperity in a "classless" society where opportunity was available to all. This idealized United States was meant to become a role model for the rest of the world. Progressive-era presidents—Theodore Roosevelt and later Woodrow Wilson—were determined to bring this moral and social authority to other nations under the guise of progress, which would become more and more like imperialism. The new immigrants would pose a threat to this Progressive agenda with their Old World values and customs. The new wave of immigrants was thought to undermine a forward-looking American culture with their presumed ignorance and backwardness.

In reaction, a nativist movement began to permeate American middle-class society that appeared to have the new immigrants' best interests at heart. Paternalism, however, began to set in as an effort to elevate and transform these new Americans began in earnest. Israel Zangwill, an Englishman who directed an emigration society for Russian Jews from Britain, wrote a play, *The Melting-Pot,* in 1908 that promoted the assimilationist ideal of Americanization. As Progressive-era historian John Higham notes, the moral of the play was that America was "God's fiery crucible, consuming the dross of Europe and fusing all of its warring peoples into 'the coming superman.'" In 1907, University of Wisconsin sociologist E. A. Ross wrote, in *Sin and Society*, that American culture must "establish righteousness" through an activist government. His tract would become a call for immigration restriction and the Americanization of already-established immigrants.[12]

A more benevolent attitude toward immigration and the future of Americans came in the form of Randolph Bourne and Walter Lippmann, who would become the intellectual spokesmen of liberal and Progressive politics and culture in the United States during the early twentieth century. As Lippmann's fellow cofounder of the *New Republic*, Herbert Croly, recommended in *The Promise of American Life* (1909), America's future "will have to be planned and constructed rather than fulfilled of its own momentum."[13] Bourne and Lippmann attempted to construct that plan.

One of the central conflicts of the Progressive era was the concept of Americanization and how it was to be achieved. From Bourne and Lippmann, we can examine the notion of the constrained and confined social values that were part of the Americanization process promoted by Progressive-era reformers and authorities. The public intellectuals' response to sociocultural paradigm shifts before World War I was to form a new vision of politics and a new culture for Americans. As cultural conditions changed with the development of corporate trusts, the new labor movement, and the continued domination of institutional needs over that of individuals, theorists like Bourne and Lippmann began to formulate new philosophies of politics and culture that would embrace a progressive liberal agenda.

Such thinkers came out of the upheaval that would produce a pragmatic philosophy through progressive education. Various schools of thought emerged, including the Chicago school of sociology led by John Dewey, the Chicago school of architecture, the new liberalism as articulated by the founders of the *New Republic*, and the "new paganism" of *The Masses*. All originated as a conscious rejection of outmoded traditions and beliefs. Intellectuals embraced the idea that a new society needed a new cultural philosophy. Through the *Seven Arts* magazine, an attempt was made to create an aesthetic forum for such a culture to develop. The magazine was established on the premise that the United States required a literature, music, architecture, painting, philosophy, and performing arts that reflected the changes of the Progressive era and that it would help provide the United States with an "indigenous culture." Randolph Bourne wrote, "whatever American nationalism turns out to be, it is certain to become something utterly different from the nationalism of twentieth-century Europe—not a nationality but a transnationality." America was to become a federation of cultures that went beyond mere nationalism or ethnic identifications, with a cosmopolitanism unique to the United States. Bourne was interested in not only the immigrants who were content to remain on the bottom rungs of the socioeconomic ladder, but also those who were the "acclimatized" sons of immigrants who worked at becoming "citizen[s] of a larger world."[14]

Randolph Silliman Bourne was born in Bloomfield, New Jersey, in 1886. He was a graduate of Columbia University and best known for his many essays on the pragmatic implementation of Progressive ideals and his anti-imperialist stance against the policies of presidents Roosevelt and Wilson. Bourne rejected the Americanization agenda. He insisted, however, that left to themselves the new immigrants and middle classes would become "detached fragments of people" who would devolve into "the flotsam and jetsam of American life, the downward undertow of our civilization with its leering cheapness and falseness of taste and spiritual outlook, the absence of mind and sincere feeling which we see in our slovenly towns, our vapid moving pictures, our popular novels, and in the vacuous faces of the crowds on the city street." Americans' cultural identity was a response to the social and political changes that attended the Progressive era, and that response was not to be left up to the "vacuous faces of the crowds." Nor certainly was it, as this statement makes clear, to be found in popular entertainments.[15]

But nineteenth-century cultural values were not the answer either, according to Bourne, because "the ruling class, descendent of those British stocks which were the first permanent immigrants," had come to dictate the standards and the process of Americanization without consulting the new immigrants of eastern and southern Europe.[16] It resulted in a destruction of the "national cultures" of ethnic immigrants and their progeny. Bourne wished to see a pluralistic "federation of cultures," which would in turn make America an "international nation."[17]

Striving for a melting pot of cultures that would create an alternative American culture, Bourne insisted that the performing arts be called upon to develop the creative impulses of the immigrant classes, which had the potential to break away from the conditioning of Anglo- bourgeois Americanization. As Bourne wrote in 1918, "The jealous old individual arts with their formal techniques and their tight little categories of critical norms get broken up...The solitary artist bores. We like group-art. And we are tired of seeing artistic expression stereotyped, sophisticated, artificially segregated into subjects."[18] Bourne would call for the integration of the arts through a communal "pageantry" created from "the outburst of Pagan expressiveness." This process of creating American culture was "far more revolutionary than any other social change we have been making," Bourne wrote, "a New Freedom that really liberates and relaxes the spirit from the intolerable tensions of an over-repressed and mechanized world."[19]

Bourne's idealistic assumption, that all Americans had a tacit understanding of morality, misled him into believing that Progressives were moving in the same direction regardless of their class, ethnicity, or gender. This implicit agreement was predicated on a value system that was not necessarily to everyone's benefit, and certainly not to the new immigrants who became comic vaudevillians. Bourne simply re-created his own vision of what American culture should become—described as the general "we"—replacing the nineteenth century's individualized, western European concept of the artistic "genius" with an amalgamation of all arts under one ideal, community-oriented "pageant" of performance.

Another central theorist of American political and cultural values was Walter Lippmann, who from the mid-1910s to his death in 1974 was extremely prominent in decisions in public policy and international politics. The author of ten books on social theory, including *Public Opinion* (1922), *The Phantom Public* (1925), and *A Preface to Morals* (1929), a cofounder of the *New Republic*, and the author of an influential column, "Today and Tomorrow," Lippman was a policy adviser to politicians, powerbrokers, and presidents. He was born to German-Jewish parents in 1889 on New York's affluent and prestigious East Side. After graduating from Harvard with distinction, he was tutored in journalism by Lincoln Steffens—the legendary muckraker—then wrote *A Preface to Politics* (1913) and *Drift and Mastery* (1914) before he was twenty-five.

Lippmann's *Public Opinion* recognized the differences between "the world outside and the pictures in our heads."[20] He discussed in vivid detail the limiting reliance on "stereotypes" that Americans used to cope with the complexity and chaos of quotidian existence. In this oversimplified way, people could divide ethnic groups into easy-to-grasp categories such as "Germans," "southern Europeans," "Slavs," "Negroes," "anarchists," and "Reds." These stereotypes gave a continuity and linear organization to ever-shifting realities at the turn of the twentieth century. It was especially useful to qualify and quantify the mass immigration of southern and eastern Europeans who defied normative identification when it came to social behaviors, cuisines, languages, and seemingly incomprehensible belief systems. Reducing the ethic immigrant to stereotypical roles was a way to put people in their place and keep them there. Rather than add to a rapidly changing and overly complicated world, established Americans clung to categories that assuaged their fears.

Lippmann called these fears "bogeys," the terrors that attended the era's overwhelming changes in social and economic status, employment opportunities, and competition for resources. These bogeys, Lippman contended, drove the Progressive reformers and critics to create cultural and aesthetic criteria for their conception of a more civilized Americanness. For Lippmann, "a great deal can be done by exorcising bogeys—by refusing to add the terrors of the imagination to the terrors of fact... For the breakdown of absolutism is more evident than the way to mastery."[21] Conquering fears of the extreme changes in America through a mastery of one's bogeys was a way of combating the destructiveness of bigotry.

Lippmann, like Bourne, was highly critical of Americanization. In 1922, he wrote:

> Americanization, for example, is superficially at least the substitution of American for European stereotypes. Thus the peasant who might see his landlord as if he were the lord of the manor, his employer as he saw the local magnate, is taught by Americanization to see the landlord and employer according to American standards. This constitutes a change of mind, which is, in effect, when the inoculation succeeds, a change of vision. His eye sees differently.[22]

Lippmann goes on to cite Edward Hale Bierstadt, writing for the *New Republic*, who referred to the threat that "average" middle-class, Anglo-American citizens felt from recent European immigrants:

> One kindly gentlewoman has confessed that the stereotypes are of such overweening importance, that when hers are not indulged, she at least is unable to accept the brotherhood of man and the fatherhood of God: "we are strangely affected by the clothes we wear. Garments create a mental and social atmosphere. What can be hoped for the Americanism of a man who insists on employing a London tailor? One's very food affects his Americanism. What kind of American consciousness can grow in the atmosphere of sauerkraut and Limburger cheese? Or what can you expect of the Americanism of the man whose breath always reeks of garlic?"[23]

The fear of ethnic immigrants is couched in their offensive appearance and strange, distasteful behaviors, particularly those of the working classes who "reek of garlic" and are unwashed and uncouth.

Lippmann forcefully argued against the perceived need for censoring the arts, which was provoked by the anti-immigrant xenophobia and part of the Americanization agenda. "We are told about the world before we see it," he wrote. "We imagine most things before we experience them. And those preconceptions...govern deeply the whole process of perception." This statement can also apply to audience reception, as he continued: "All history is antiseptic in this fashion. It enables us to know what fairy tale, what school book, what tradition, what novel, play, picture, phrase, planted one preconception in this mind, another in that mind." He argued against the idea that entertainment, and the stage in particular, can influence impressionable young people as well as the vulnerable working and middle classes. "Those who wish to censor art do not at least underestimate this influence," he wrote. "They generally misunderstand it, and almost always they are absurdly bent on preventing other people from discovering anything not sanctioned by them."[24]

For Lippmann, setting the agenda for normative values was purely subjective, for "at the core of every moral code there is a picture of human nature, a map of the universe, and a version of history."[25] By presenting their philosophy as if for a general public, Lippmann excoriated such sanctimonious improvements, noting that given the state of education, a public opinion was "primarily a moralized and codified version of the facts."[26] Progressives, not unlike the conservatives of the late nineteenth century, operated on the assumption that their principles of morality and behavior were ubiquitous and unwavering. Their positive angle was that popular entertainments, if they were "well regulated," could be a tool to assimilate recent immigrants. By challenging the new reform movement, however, one ran the risk of being labeled anti-Progressive and, according to Lippmann, reformers and their advocates had "made civilization which provides them who made it with what they feel to be ample satisfaction in work, mating, and play... The pattern has been a success so nearly perfect in the sequence of ideals, practice, and results, that any challenge to it is un-American."[27]

Lippmann underwent a profound change in his thinking that, by 1925 with the publication of *The Phantom Public*, and even more radically by 1929 with *A Preface to Morals*, he embraced a wholly pragmatic view of reform. He eschewed the idea that reformers and experts with a "mastery" of sociocultural issues could be disinterested enough to make social policy that reflected "the will of the people." With *A Preface to Morals*, Lippmann contended that Americans needed to distance themselves from "the tyranny of public opinion" as well as from the force of their own desires. "Disinterestedness, detachment, asceticism, discipline, and disillusion" were his watchwords. By the late 1920s and early 1930s, Lippmann was convinced that neither the general public nor its expert elites could practice disinterestedness. People's self-interests would always rule their decision making, and this led him to reject the belief that Progressivism could improve social conditions, particularly when it came to cultural, political, and educational reforms.[28]

Lippmann might have looked to the comic vaudeville stage to see the challenges that stereotyped images of ethnicity could pose to the Anglo-American moral hierarchies he had rejected. Vaudeville comedy challenged the segregation of high- and lowbrow, as well as insider and outsider, by including all audiences for a reasonable price and catering to a multiplicity of tastes.[29] Although Lippmann never directly addressed popular entertainments, his confrontation of the "bogeys" of the new immigrants, the new women, and the impoverished classes born of the Industrial Revolution can shed light on the fear of the new humor that Progressive-era reformers, authorities, and politicians felt.

Fears of the foreign and un-American bogey were exacerbated by reformers looking for terrors that were not there, whether in dance halls, nickelodeons, burlesque houses, or vaudeville theaters. The new immigrants, new women, and working-poor Americans on the comic vaudeville stage could be said to have trafficked in absurd stereotypes of ethnic and gender behaviors to satirize and perhaps even exorcise, as Lippmann suggested, the bogeys of modernist urban living. What appeared to be foreign, incomprehensible, and threatening to conventional Anglo-American wisdom could be laughed at, as well as with, to dispel fears of the foreign invasion and social insurgency of women. By confronting these uncertainties on the comic stage—as Sigmund Freud suggested in his seminal *The Joke and Its Relation to the Unconscious* (1905)—stereotypes born of fear and ignorance would lose their authority through the exorcising power of laughter.[30] The new humor posed a special problem for Progressive-era reformers and critics in that it could not be managed because of its troubling nature—not being able to discern if one was being laughed at, or with.

Combined with the elusive nature of the new humor, the double-edged sword of Americanization was lurking in the Progressive agenda. It promoted civil rights politically and economically but was more conservative on cultural issues. The Progressive era saw an unprecedented shift in the demand for popular entertainments and fine arts. Alongside this flourishing new entertainment industry, the basic categories of human existence, and the patterns of thought and belief that structured that existence, appeared to be collapsing in the first two decades of the twentieth century. The architect Frank Lloyd Wright was to reinforce this perception of collapse, and set about with what he termed "the destruction of the box" that had been the Victorian house. Artists like Edward Steichen and Georgia O'Keefe would begin experiments in abstract art, all of which encouraged the deconstruction of boundaries in painting, photography, and sculpture. Jazz and its popular cousin ragtime would develop in tandem with vaudeville and embrace the synthesis of classical, blues, and improvisation, along with nontraditional rhythms and chord structures, by musicians like W. C. Handy, Jelly Roll Morton, and Louis Armstrong. Vaudeville was formed by using a fragmented and inclusive format to fuse a variety of entertainments, one that rejected the boundaries of conventional narrative theater with its emulation of the highbrow western European stage.

Artists of the Progressive period, led by innovators like Wright, upheld "the sovereignty of the individual" that was being discouraged by aesthetic cultural authorities.[31] The modernist sensibility in the performing arts promoted the theory that nothing was stable and that any idea or morality could be challenged. As American expatriate novelist and art doyenne Gertrude Stein stated: "the American thing is the vitality of movement...This generation does not connect itself with anything...That is why it is American."[32] Frederic Thompson, creator of Coney Island's Luna Park and the New York Hippodrome theater—both of which offered popular entertainment to a variety of classes—corroborated this idea of the "vitality of movement" in his 1908 article "Amusing the Million," saying: "Speed has become an inborn American trait. We as a nation are always moving, we are always in a hurry, we are never without momentum."[33] *Vitality*, *speed*, and *forward motion* would become the watchwords of popular entertainment, as seen with the slapstick silent short films produced by Mack Sennett at Keystone Pictures Studio and with vaudeville comedians (soon to be sound-film stars) such as the Marx Brothers, Buster Keaton, and Charlie Chaplin, all of whom would bring the intensity of these changes to their comedy worldview.

These instincts toward breaking down the borders of the box, coupled with the frantic energy that accompanied this reimagining of categories, would find their way onto the comic vaudeville stage. For Progressive-era critic and playwright Edmund Wilson, one of the reasons that vaudeville's new humor became a vital reflection of the complex and changing times was that "it relieves some anxiety for people to watch acts or listen to stories that are completely inconsecutive and pointless, because that is the way the world is beginning to seem, the way their own minds are beginning to work." Wilson observed that Americans "have to think about too many things and the relation between all these things is not in the least clear...our laughter both confesses and dismisses our fears."[34] Vaudeville was an art form that could both reveal and alleviate the anxieties of life in the early twentieth century.

Vaudeville promoted acts that avoided narrative structures and discarded the rules of the legitimate theater, drawing on popular forms of the nineteenth century like minstrelsy, concert saloons, variety theater, and burlesque. It sought to create an amalgamation of these various entertainments that would run parallel with the innovations of other popular arts. These comic performance forms brought unconventional ideas and the rejection of conformity to middle-class audiences, who were sheltered from and fearful of new concepts, cultures, and ethnicities at the beginning of twentieth-century America. They crossed sociocultural boundaries and challenged the authority of political, cultural, and religious leaders. The behaviors, customs, ethics, and appearances associated with the new immigrants were contradicted and confused further in ethnic acts and comic burlesque revues. The hierarchies and structures of domestic life, along with the role of women in the household, the workplace, and the bedroom, also came in for satirical critique.

All manner of middle-class American life appeared to be under attack, especially the morality that had characterized the Victorian era. As Lippmann pointed out, "Under the term moral codes I include all kinds: personal, family, economic, professional, legal, patriotic, international. At the center of each there is a pattern of stereotypes about psychology, sociology, and history."[35] Therefore, those who embraced these stereotypes reasoned, "since my moral system rests on my accepted version of the facts, he who denies either my moral judgments or my version of the facts, is to me perverse, alien, dangerous."[36] The seemingly perverse, alien, and dangerous were reinforced by stereotypes in public life and, as I contend here, dispelled on the comic stage. Reformers and critics were quick to condemn the popular stage for causing the collapse of civilized behavior and middle-class propriety, which now was coming to define "Americanness."

To further explore the cultural aesthetics of popular entertainments and how they affected comic vaudevillians, cultural theorist Stuart Hall's essay "Notes on Deconstructing 'the Popular'" is of particular interest. Hall proposes that there has always been a need to both appropriate and police popular culture for sociological purposes:

> There is a more or less continuous struggle over the culture of working people, the laboring classes and the poor . . . The changing balance and relations of social forces throughout that history reveal themselves, time and again, in struggles over the forms of the culture, traditions and ways of life of the popular classes.[37]

We can use this concept of a "struggle over the culture of working people" to analyze the juxtaposition of legitimized performing arts with popular entertainments that, as elements of working-class culture, were categorized as lowbrow—not to be considered anything more than sheer diversions from quotidian drudgery. In contrast, Hall asserts that popular entertainments perpetually struggle against, and diverge from, the dominant culture, since they are established in and formulated by the "excluded classes," as they exist as a "culture of the oppressed."[38] The point I wish to emphasize is that popular culture—and specifically comic vaudeville entertainment—is based on the structural relationship between class and the aesthetic form it takes within the performing arts. Therefore, "popular" is defined here by the material conditions of the lower classes and their new immigrant aesthetic and cultural heritages, together with the legacy of first-generation ethnic Americans.

Weren't these "popular" vaudeville artists producing socially relevant cultural critique, since they were the very artists who were struggling with issues of class and Americanization as representatives of the "oppressed" classes? Why did cultural critics and Progressive thinkers, like Bourne and Lippmann, assume it necessary to create an American social aesthetic in the arts when they were already being produced in the popular entertainments like comic vaudeville? Echoing Hall's theory, comic vaudevillians refused to be kept in their place. The control over popular entertainments that reformers sought caused comic performers to circumvent their confines, as well as use them as fodder for their acts in defiance of Anglo-American authority. Progressives and cultural critics meant to be benevolent and even embraced popular entertainments as a way to elevate the tensions and anxieties of the working and middle classes. Reformers like Jane Addams encouraged young people of the underclasses to attend the theater, which she saw as a necessary relief from the tedium and exhausting routines of their work schedules—especially since many of them would enter the workforce as early as age fourteen. "'Going to a show' for thousands of young people in every industrial city is the only possible road to the realms of mystery and romance," she wrote; "the theater is the only place where they can satisfy that craving for a conception of life higher than that which the actual world offers them."[39] Addams was born into an upper-middle-class family from northern Illinois in 1860. In Chicago, she cofounded the Hull House, which began the US settlement-house movement. Addams created the template for American social work and authored several books on the subject. Her primary focus while at Hull House focused on the needs of mothers and children as well as public health. As a leader in the women's suffrage movement, Addams encouraged other middle-class women to become moral role models for their local communities. In 1931, she became the first American woman to be awarded the Nobel Peace Prize.

Addams was convinced that edifying, uplifting theater performances would help enrich the underclasses. When it came to theatergoing, she and other reformers focused on educational entertainments and plays with a strong ethical content that provided this "conception of life higher." Therefore dance halls, nickelodeons, and vaudeville houses were to be monitored for their content, as restrictions and regulations were put in place, to ensure that the quality of the shows matched the expectations of the reformers and critics who had designated mass entertainments as too lowbrow.

Addams set the tone for the conflict between entertainments that cultivate middle-class values and those such as "vaudeville shows" and "five-cent theaters" that were "full of the most blatant and vulgar songs." For Addams, offensive behavior and language on the comic stage was a direct result of "trivial and obscene words" and "meaningless and flippant airs" that combined "to incite that which should be controlled, to degrade that which should be exalted, to make sensuous that which might be lifted into the realm of the higher imagination." The intensity and movement of urban life were reflected on the popular stage, and according to Addams, it was "nothing short of cruelty to over-stimulate [the] senses as does the modern city."[40]

Belle Israels Moskowitz was another turn-of-the-twentieth-century reformer who advocated the regulation of popular amusements. She began working at the New York City settlement called the Educational Alliance in 1900, afterward joining the Council of Jewish Women. While she was with the Council, she organized the Committee of Amusements and Vacation Resources for Working Girls. Moskowitz and her colleagues amassed statistics and anecdotes that affirmed their conviction that public entertainments had to be controlled and used their influence to implement their own standards.[41] Although Moskowitz was the daughter of ethnic immigrants herself, she serves as a non-Anglo example of Progressive reformers who also wanted to control and regulate what was considered "popular."

She was born Belle Lindner on October 5, 1877, in Harlem, New York, to Esther (Freyer) and Isidor Lindner. Her parents had emigrated from East Prussia in 1869. She was educated at Horace Mann High School for Girls and briefly at Teachers College at Columbia University. Belle trained to become a "dramatic reader" and taught drama to children. While working at the Educational Alliance, she organized monthly exhibits, orchestral and choral performances, and dramatic events, and coached youth groups in drama. In New York, Moskowitz would dedicate herself to improving the quality of the performing arts, especially for children and young adults. She, like Addams, applied a set of criteria to popular entertainments that came from an educated, upper-middle-class perspective.

In an effort to tame public dancing in New York City, Moskowitz noted that the unchaperoned girls and young women were in danger of predatory males who frequented dance halls, particularly those that served alcohol. She was instrumental in getting a 1911 state law passed that banned the sale of liquor in "dancing schools" and that was soon applied to dance halls by association. Moskowitz also promoted the "substitution" of alternative dance halls that discouraged the more lascivious popular dances and that required female dancers to be chaperoned. Dance partners had to keep a "decent" distance between each other. No unsavory body movements were tolerated by supervisors, especially those considered sexually suggestive or that involved touching below the waist. What constituted this "dirty dancing" would be left entirely to dance hall monitors and managers. Moskowitz knew that trying to ban dance halls and other public amusements like movie theaters would be near impossible. Therefore, she focused on regulating these popular forms of entertainment. They were to be under the watchful gaze of moral authorities who used their own standards of ethnical behavior as principal guidelines for reform.[42]

Some reformers encouraged the outward trappings of popular entertainments to entice audiences to their "wholesome" divertissements. "We have gone in for confetti showers, prize waltzes and various kinds of wholesome vaudeville features," explained Moskowitz, and "we expect to go into every type of novelty that will compete with the man next door."[43] Reformers like Addams and Moskowitz wanted to restrict mass entertainments to what was normal and educational, as they perceived it, and adjusted them to fit their criteria of decency in the effort to Americanize immigrants in their image. They were certainly not alone in their assessment that comic and satiric songs and dances were ripping apart the social fabric. Michael M. Davis, an official from New York's Child Welfare Committee, also perceived the "hyper-stimulus" of popular stage entertainment in combination with the "kaleidoscopic stimuli" of modernist urban living as a fatal mixture that unleashed his fears of the bogeys of the vaudeville stage, producing "stimulating but disintegrating" consequences.[44]

In addition, reform committees and associations were fueled by fears that the new immigrants had brought with them their corrupted tastes and desires for lowbrow amusements. These anxieties were coupled with the fact that many of these immigrants and subsequently their children—now first-generation Americans—did bring their unique forms of popular entertainments to their communities. As a consequence, bigoted and xenophobic reformers and cultural critics sought to control these lowly performers, who were suspected of enticing and degrading decent Americans with their underclass culture.

In addition to reforms and censures, there was a backlash from sociologists and religious leaders against cultural and aesthetic shifts brought about by the new immigrants. Therefore the importance of outwardly declaring one's US citizenship and fidelity to America became extremely important, as seen with the Pledge of Allegiance's introduction to the public school system. Francis Bellamy, Christian socialist and author of the pledge, made the following xenophobic and bigoted remarks in an editorial for the *Illustrated American* in 1892, not long after writing this jingoistic oath of American loyalty:

> A democracy like ours cannot afford to throw itself open to the world... where all classes of society merge insensibly into one another and every alien immigrant of inferior race may bring corruption to the stock. There are races more or less akin to our own whom we may admit freely and get nothing but advantage by the infusion of their wholesome blood. But there are other races, which we cannot assimilate without lowering our racial standard, which should be as sacred to us as the sanctity of our homes.[45]

The danger of ethnic immigrants and their questionable ethics that were feared to challenge the values of true Americans during this era of Progressive reform were, through Bellamy's pledge, thought to counteract disloyalty and un-Americanness.[46]

Social workers were key players in creating the reform platform. They encouraged Americanization through integration. Sociologist and Americanizing crusader Lillian Wald pointedly argued that the main task of reform was "fusing these people who come to us from the Old World civilization into... a real brotherhood among men."[47] Presenting two sides of the efforts of Americanization, reformers like Wald created a binary contradiction, creating a sense of "real brotherhood" through assimilation, on the one hand, while fostering fear of ethnic immigrants and their foreignness, on the other. Another sociologist and the original director of the Young Men's Christian Association, Peter Roberts, embraced the ethnic immigrant in theory, but only if "redeemed and uplifted."[48] If not guided and advised in the process of Americanization, however, the immigrant and his family could be a threat to Americanness. A rallying cry to maintain American ideals by reformers and authorities was often interspersed with a counterintuitive appeal to benevolent service for all mankind.[49]

A social reformer of the Progressive era who was a central architect for the Americanization movement was Frances Alice Kellor. Kellor was born on October 20, 1873, in Columbus, Ohio. In 1897, she earned her law degree from Cornell Law School and continued her studies at the University of Chicago and the New York Summer School of Philanthropy. Kellor served as secretary and treasurer of the New York State Immigration Commission in 1909 and as chief investigator for the Bureau of Industries and Immigration of New York State from 1910 to 1913. During World War I, she directed the National Americanization Committee, the most important private organization promoting Americanization during this time. She felt that social reform could be interwoven with an allegiance to American nationalism. For many advocates of Americanization like Roberts and Kellor, social welfare was analogous to national pride and loyalty, echoing Bellamy's Pledge of Allegiance, which was so paramount to setting new citizens on the path to Americanization. Kellor set up the Committee for Immigrants in America as a bureaucratic agency, designed to support, guide, and coalesce public and private institutions throughout the United States. It required "a national policy...to make of all these people one nation," and a central federal bureau to enforce this unification.[50] Kellor's committee persuaded affluent Anglo-American backers—like railroad president Frank Trumbull, banker Felix Warburg, and the wife of another railroad magnate, Mrs. E. H. Harriman—to establish a Division of Immigrant Education within the US Bureau of Education.[51] The committee staffed this new division with workers instructed to publicize the necessity of teaching ethnic immigrants the virtues and ideals of Americanization through educational organizations. The committee's five-year history shows consistent pressure by the well-subsidized Division of Immigrant Education that Kellor dominated to Americanize ethnic immigrant youth through public and private schooling. (Public education reform is examined through the lens of the vaudeville school act as performed by the Marx Brothers in chapter 4.)

To promote Americanization, patriotic societies demanded not only allegiance but also humility in the face of their self-created

American values. The Anglo-nationalist organization the Daughters of the American Republic (DAR)—whose members claim ancestry to the founders of the United States—"taught obedience to law, which is the groundwork of true citizenship." Their objective was to be self-appointed arbiters of Americanness to stave off the dangers associated with "immigrant radicalism or discontent." Their weapon of choice was the press, which they used to promote xenophobia and create smear campaigns.[52]

Reformers often pursued the collusion of critics and journalists to promote their agenda. The popularity of vaudeville at the beginning of the twentieth century could be seen in newspapers such as the *New York Times*, *New York Clipper*, *New York Dramatic Mirror*, and *Variety*, offering daily reviews and articles about performers and their stage acts. The critics of vaudeville also became respected and influential. Founder and chief entertainment critic for *Variety* Sime Silverman, for example, published reviews that were often instrumental for the booking of new acts on the vaudeville circuit. His tastes were well known to be extremely conservative. Silverman and his fellow critics often set the tone as to what was respectable and noteworthy stage fare, and what was of interest only to the lower classes that could not, in his estimation, discern aesthetic value. While praising the Marx Brothers' family act in 1912, he appreciated their vaudeville performance of *Fun in Hi Skule*, remarking, "there is little rough stuff in this 'school act,' and it will be liked on almost any bill."[53] Silverman and other critics of the period gave a show credit for being clean (no "rough stuff") in addition to its comic merits. Mae West would suffer at the hands of *Variety* when Silverman reviewed her 1912 act, writing, "The girl is of the eccentric type. She sings rag melodies and dresses oddly, but still lacks that touch of class that is becoming requisite nowadays in the first-class houses."[54] The concern for "class" that this review points out is typical of vaudeville criticism from this period, when being "clean" was as important as being funny.

Popular entertainment entrepreneur Benjamin Franklin Keith, and later his partner Edward F. Albee, took advantage of this nativist attitude toward Americanization during the turn of the twentieth century. In a bid to make the new form of popular entertainment appear respectable, Keith gave it a French-sounding name—vaudeville. Albee added the notion that this new vaudeville provided "something for everyone."[55] Keith and Albee were intent on appealing to men, women, and children in an effort to sell more tickets for this "cleaned up" form of cheap amusement. Popular entertainment historian Robert Snyder makes the case that vaudeville was indeed for everyone with his theory that the term "vaudeville" was a corruption of *voix de ville*, or "voice of the city," echoing *vox populi*. This "voice of the people" reinforces the basic tenet of democracy that voting—which was legally open to every American citizen regardless of origin—is an inalienable right. Sadly enough, half the population of the United States would not receive this right until 1920, when women's suffrage was constitutionally adopted as the Nineteenth Amendment. Much as it was in politics, the *voix de ville* was in the process of being curbed by reformers and cultural critics at the same time as it was promoted as something for everyone.

Critics were often mystified that people were drawn to the lowbrow vaudeville theater. "Don't you think we have had enough of the cheapest and poorest form of entertainment ever slung over the apron of the stage into the face of a self-respecting and unoffending audience?" begins a 1911 review by Louis Reeves Harrison in the *Moving Picture World*. Not understanding why audiences did not desire more "high-class" entertainment, Harrison goes on to say, "I went back to the more pretentious [vaudeville] theater, and, noticing it was only about half full, I asked the proprietor why he handed out such indigestible stuff as 'vodeveal.'" The reply from the manager was "'I don't like it, but the people want it and I have to give it to 'em.'" Harrison ends with the admonition of the manager: "That is what *he* thinks. It is quite possible that a number of people are really drawn into his place by the variety entertainment, but I doubt if they equal the number driven away by it. Those driven away are the most desirable patrons; they are the steadies who have acquired the habit; in this case they have acquired the habit of going elsewhere."[56]

The question of discernment and by whose standards was always a subjective matter at best when it came to vaudeville criticism. Rather than reviewing the act in question, critics often commented on the decency or tastefulness of any given bill. In 1905, journalist Hartley Davis commented that vaudeville acts "may not be your standards nor mine, but evidently they are accepted by the millions that support this form of show."[57] The pejorative "this form of show" tipped the hand of this seasoned writer and reviewer who condemned vaudeville in and of itself, regardless of the content and quality of the acts or their performers. Three years later *American Magazine* was very clear in its condemnation of vaudeville, noting that the "Cheap and Wholesome" slogan promoted by Keith and Albee had "been so well advertised by the vaudeville dealers and so innocently swallowed" by those who ought to have known better "that fathers and husbands" had "come to take it for granted that any vaudeville show in a 'first-class' theatre" was "a perfectly safe environment for the women and children of their families."[58] This criticism considers the producers of popular entertainment to be "dealers," no better than criminals who pedal illicit pleasures. The audience is treated paternalistically as unsuspecting innocents who need the protection of cultural critics and authorities who will expose to them vaudeville's insidious, lowbrow nature. Women are given no credit for their power of judgment.

Toward the end of the vaudeville era in the mid-1920s, critic Rob Wagner offered an assessment of why vaudeville comedy was on the wane:

> That the great majority of those whose lives are gray, love color, skill, and sheer beauty in preference to sophisticated smart-cracking and the jaded thrills of sex-perversion jokes... When the hard-boiled, rough-neck critics of *Variety* are shocked at the very stuff they are supposed to celebrate [in comic vaudeville acts], perhaps there is a touch of Puritanical decency in the worst of us.[59]

The belief in "decency" pervaded the conception of Americanness. But rather than condemning and trying to close popular entertainments, reformers began a campaign of creating parameters to promote the morals and ethics that characterized Americanization, targeting popular entertainment. A special emphasis was placed on children and young adults who were the most vulnerable to vaudeville's so-called corruption. The culture editors of *Outlook* (1905–16), for example, expressed their concerns that recently arrived immigrants and first-generation Americans, as well as other "undeveloped people," were too vulnerable to the myriad salacious and debasing influences of modern urban existence. The journal discussed concern over "the more or less rudderless human being whom we must educate into a good citizen, the child of alien parents who too often is contemptuous of the habits and maxims of his parents and ignorant of anything American but the hybrid life of a polyglot city."[60] The primary problem with the Progressive reform movement in popular culture of the first decades of the twentieth century was the assumption of what ethnic immigrants and working-class audiences wanted from their entertainment and what in fact they actually enjoyed.

Turn-of-the-twentieth-century popular entertainment entrepreneur Frederic Thompson summed up the contrast between what reformers wished for and what the general public actually wanted in entertainment: "The difference between the theater and the big amusement park is the difference between the Sunday-school and the Sunday-school picnic. The people are the same; the spirit and the environment are wholly different."[61] Thompson, who had spent many years as a carny and self-proclaimed showman, stated: "The one thing absolutely necessary is the carnival spirit. Without that no show in the open, nothing that has to do with people in the mass, can hope to succeed."[62] The carnival spirit according to Thompson took the audience away from its troubles and the drudgery of the workweek. According to him, what the public wanted was a sense of excitement and anticipation that "there will be things doing, to get emotional excitement into the very air."[63] Popular entertainment was a way to experience the joy and sensuality that was withheld from their daily lives. According to Thompson, one of the keys to getting an audience to respond and embrace a performer and his act was laughter. "When people go to a park or an exhibition," he noted, "and admire the buildings, the exhibits and the lights without having laughed about half the time until their sides ached, you can be absolutely sure that the enterprise will fail."[64] Creating a public space for uninhibited laughter, as the new humorists understood, was an important way of forgetting about the hardships of daily life and a release from restrictive authority.

By respecting the audience's intelligence and appealing to their sense of humor, Thompson was convinced that they would respond in kind. The moralizing and social-improvement agendas that reformers and critics advocated were the wrong way to approach public amusements. "It is foolish to make people serious or point a moral, for you *are* [emphasis added] dealing with a moral people, nor is it worthwhile to try to educate the amusement-seeking public. It is better to take it for granted that they are educated, and if you start to amuse them, stick to that."[65] Thompson asserted that if the audience were treated in a condescending or paternalistic way, they would know they were being spoken down to and would reject any attempt to edify them. The Anglo-American upper middle class of Progressive reformers assumed an ethical superiority over their presumed inferiors who needed their form of salvation. That the underclasses of working men and women had the capacity to make their own aesthetic and ethical decisions did not seem to occur to these reformers, whose privileged socioeconomic backgrounds distanced them from the very masses with whom they claimed to empathize.

The background and upbringing of the Progressive reformers themselves was a stimulus to fears of underclass bogeys—particularly stage performers. Progressive reformers' good intentions toward the public and its assumed need for protection from unsavory purveyors of commercial entertainments masked the privileged social class and access to higher education that divided them from the working poor who patronized these amusements. Many reformers were white, upper-middle-class men and women from "good" families, well meaning but condescending toward their socioeconomic inferiors. They appeared oblivious to the circumstances that produced variations in the demand for popular theatrical performances. The reformers' determination to improve and inform popular audiences' tastes with their own criteria clouded the fact that cleaned-up mass entertainments simply did not appeal to their sensibilities.

There was a need to create a sharp division between lowbrow popular entertainment and highbrow aesthetics in the performing arts in order to establish a singular American aesthetic on par with the celebrated culture of western Europe. Once this separation was established by cultural forces during the industrial transformation of the United States, a need to distinguish between edifying entertainments and frivolous ones for pure pleasure focused on drawing a line between the ethnic working class and Anglo-American middle class, especially in the performing arts. According to reformers, this divide would improve the moral and aesthetic values for assimilation into the Anglo-American hierarchical dream of success through upward mobility. As discussed by popular entertainment historians Lawrence Levine and David Savran, for aesthetes this potential assimilation could be found in highbrow cultural institutions like the legitimate theater—the plays of Shakespeare or Eugene O'Neill being primary examples—and inherited European performance forms like opera and classical symphonic music, all of which paradoxically began as popular entertainments themselves.[66] These Eurocentric studies in art and culture were juxtaposed by reformers against the lowbrow, new-immigrant-driven burlesque theater, folk music and dance, and vaudeville comedy, derived from popular amusements of the nineteenth century. Before the transition to film as the dominant form of popular amusement, vaudevillians began to use their comedy to challenge those reformers who wished to ban offensive stage entertainments that promoted the self-criticism of Americanization.

By 1912, many of the new immigrant Americans, feeling hemmed in by the rules, regulations, and regimented life of conformity to middle-class values and lifestyles, enjoyed the satire and critique that popular comic entertainments like vaudeville provided. Certain Progressive reformers, who meant to be advocates for the subjugated underclasses, were now dictating to them morals and behaviors. However, many popular entertainers and their audiences scorned the Progressive movement's focus on reforming entertainments that purportedly promoted the "sins" of those Americans who did not subscribe to middle-class cultural authority.

One of the factors that exacerbated the class conflicts in popular comic entertainments was that most of the vaudeville comics were from working-poor backgrounds. These were the very artists whom Progressive reformers (like Jane Addams and Frances Kellor) and cultural critics (like Randolph Bourne and Walter Lippmann) ignored as the "socially conscious" creative artists who reflected a culture with "something for everyone." I argue in the following chapters that these new humorists, ranging from May Irwin to the Marx Brothers, created comedy that reacted against Bourne's "over-repressed and mechanized world."

By considering the comic vaudevillians who disrupted the attempts at Americanization, we can see why popular entertainments were a source of American cultural identity at the same time as they refused

Anglo-American, middle-class concepts of cultural aesthetics. Chronicling comic vaudeville's history, structures, and acts is necessary to see how it developed and to understand that great comic artists revolutionized the vaudeville aesthetic by rejecting the moral codes and precepts of reformers, critics, and cultural authorities. Closely assessing vaudeville's ethnic and family acts will allow a window into how the new humor was able to stem the tide of Americanization for the new immigrants of the Progressive era.

2. Putting It Over in American Vaudeville

The October 1905 issue of *Midway*, a monthly periodical for amusement park professionals, claimed that vaudeville was "the acme of variegated theatrical entertainment"[1] and served as a superior model of good business practices for all performers. According to *Midway*, vaudeville's success derived from the "joyously, frankly absurd," and represented "the almost universal longing for laughter, for melody, for color, for action and for wonder-provoking things." More importantly for this study, the article asserts that vaudeville

> strikes directly at the heart [of the] interests and the foibles of the day. Vaudeville is creative and progressive. The mind of the vaudeville creator runs, lightning-like, ahead of the public craving for the ever "new"; and his voyage of discovery leads him into strange haunts... [where] human nature parades all her eccentricities and moods, at his beck, for the delectation of legions of pleasure seekers.[2]

The "new" in all its permutations was the watchword in America's early twentieth century. Vaudeville embodied the "new" onstage and reflected the arrival of the new immigrants, the new middle class, and the new woman. The new was a harbinger of the industrial age, when machines, factories, automated assembly lines, and offices with white-collar middle managers began to dominate daily life. This was especially true of major urban centers like New York, Boston, and Chicago. The industrialization of American life also created new leisure time for the middle class, along with the disposable income to devote to this newly created free time, which became accessible to an ever-increasing number of Americans.

One of the many manifestations of the "new" was the new humor. It first appeared during the 1880s as a boldly burlesque entertainment tailored for a new audience that enjoyed a more openly antagonistic, physicalized form of comedy. Vaudeville historian Albert McLean Jr. was one of the first to identify the modernist era's "change in the sense of humor" and called it the "New Humor" (capitalized in the original). According to McLean, it "indicated a humor that was more excited, more aggressive, and less sympathetic than that to which the middle classes of the nineteenth century had been accustomed."[3] The new humor reached audiences regardless of their class and ethnicity while depicting the new immigrant classes, their cultural values, and their stories of becoming US citizens. It created a communal system of communication through laughter, combining comic sensibility with narratives drawn from their struggles with assimilating into the ever-fluctuating American culture of the Progressive era.

From the new humor's inception, critics and aesthetes attempted to discredit it, disdaining its "folk" and "peasant" humor. They and others feared that this new humor laughed at the audience and was trying to displace the sophisticated wit of the stage as inherited from the western European tradition. Comic vaudeville and the new humor came to be associated with the underclasses of new, southern and eastern European immigrants and their corrupting laughter. I argue that comic vaudevillians of the early twentieth century used the new humor to disrupt the dominant notions of Americanness and to resist attempts to Americanize them.

The new humorists successfully reached audiences from all social strata, particularly the working and middle classes. In 1910 it was reported that one-third of vaudeville audiences were working-class women and girls, while working-class men made up the rest. A Greenwich Village study noted that "some of the women" went "regularly every week all winter to Proctor's, Weber and Field's, or the Fourteenth Street Theatre, but rarely to an uptown theatre."[4] These "new women" were to become a driving force both on- and offstage as suffragists and union advocates, demanding autonomy from the roles of wives and mothers.

Vaudeville would come to dominate popular entertainments from the 1880s to the early 1920s. It became one of the most significant and ubiquitous stage forms, employing more than 25,000 performers across the country. Vaudeville's influence at the beginning of the twentieth century was universal and its impact was felt from the big time of Hammerstein's Victoria Theater and the Palace Theater of New York City all the way to far-flung stages in Ada, Oklahoma; Butte, Montana; and Youngstown, Ohio.[5]

Vaudeville acts by their diverse nature created a "something for everyone" bill, as promoted by entrepreneurs and showmen like Edward F. Albee and his partner Benjamin Franklin Keith. These producers meant to capture as large and varied an audience as possible by appealing to the new melting pot of immigrant spectators. Rather than reject the new immigrants and their new humor, producer teams like Albee and Keith and A. L. Erlanger and Marcus Klaw, along with Marcus Loew, were able to capitalize on these millions of new audience members, who showed where American society was moving. Vaudeville therefore came to reflect this integration of classes and cultures in its acts.

The new humor of vaudeville had several qualities that allowed it to reach a large audience, the most important being that anyone could perform it. In 1915, *Billboard* remarked on the acts at the Palace Theater, noting: "Here genius not birth your rank insures."[6] As playwright and performer Edwin Royle put it in 1899, "Whatever or whoever can interest an audience for 30 minutes or less and has passed quarantine is welcome."[7] The reference to quarantine pointedly alluded to the new immigrants. Acts did not move to the professional stage because of parentage or national origin. They were truly democratic: anyone who could "put an act over" had a shot at making it in vaudeville.

"Putting it over" became the way of describing how the new humor, being more direct and aggressive than conventional humor, was realized. "While this ability of 'putting it over' is universal among vaudeville artists," comic vaudevillian Will M. Cressy wrote in 1916, "no two use precisely the same method of accomplishing the same result. One can talk it over; another can sing it over; a third will act it over."[8] Cressy, a small-town New Hampshire farm boy who became a comic vaudeville performer from 1899 to the late 1920s, further defined this prime directive for the vaudeville performer: "Putting It Over: To speak a line, to sing a line, to do a piece of action in such a way as to cause an audience to see, understand, comprehend and appreciate the intention and meaning."[9] Cressy's then seventeen years of experience in vaudeville put in perspective the essential element of any vaudeville comedian's craft. "While this ability to 'put it over' is an important help on the legitimate stage," he wrote, "it is an absolute necessity in vaudeville."[10] Many vaudevillians talk about putting it over as the key to their success. Critics were also aware of this unique ability and its necessity. Caroline Caffin's 1914 book, *Vaudeville*, provides an exceptional resource on the importance of vaudeville during the Progressive era. In it, she wrote:

> There is another quality, however, of which we become conscious only by degrees. It is the feeling for rhythm—the sense which indicates the exact timing and phrasing and accent which are most expressive. The rhythms vary; some performers command a large range of them while some employ only a few. With some the rhythm is very marked. One can feel distinctly the phrasing in speech and action. The pause—the movement of the head or hand—the pacing across the stage—we can feel how they are timed and accented…For it is an essential of what is known as the ability to "get it over."[11]

Both performers and critics alike agreed that vaudevillians had a special quality that connected them with their audiences. This skill of putting it over was what made vaudeville uniquely accessible to all those who wished to try their luck on the popular stage. As long as they could "put it over," they had the potential for success.

Comic vaudevillians closely watched audiences' reactions to their acts. During a five-a-day[12] performance week, all it would take was one routine to "die" to send the act packing for good, since management had a lineup of many alternatives to take the failed act's place. The terms to "kill," to "draw blood," or create "a laugh riot" indicated the immediate necessity not only to entertain, but also to "knock 'em dead"—that is, entertain in a big, bold, and directly effective way, outdoing everyone else. These metaphors speak of an intensity tantamount to physical violence, one that arises without warning, hits its mark, ends quickly, and, if successful, inspires a massive response of cheers, clapping, and foot stomping.

Vaudeville required "accurately timed physical buffoonery," noted critic Mary Cass Canfield. "All art is exaggeration," she wrote. "But in the American exaggeration there is always self-criticism, an undertone of humor, which is an attempt at fire extinguishing that does not reduce but curiously discolors the flame."[13] This notion that vaudeville had deceptive "undertones" that could be subversive influenced many of the comments of Progressive-era reformers and critics. Freud also noted the subliminal nature of laughter in his 1905 study, stating: "The need for energetic redirection as the circumvention of internal prohibitions" unleashed a sense of humor that, as reformers feared, mocked and laughed at authority. According to Freud, joking through ethnic humor was used to make public statements about illicit subjects, providing "a purpose... whose satisfaction would otherwise not have taken place."[14] By putting it over, comic vaudevillians could confront issues of class, ethnicity, and gender, whereas other forms of entertainment could not.

The new humor's success in vaudeville was linked to the changing social conditions of the early twentieth century. The efforts of reformers, critics, and municipal authorities to Americanize the new immigrants came into conflict with vaudevillians and their new humor. As discussed in chapter 1, the new humor produced laughter so loud and offensive that it posed a threat to established Anglo-American cultural dominance.

Caroline Caffin wrote a trenchant evaluation of vaudeville's effect as a vital and attention-getting performance form, the kind that reformers and highbrow critics feared:

> If humor be the medium, not a single line must misfire. If it be vulgarity, it will be grosser than the audience, as individuals, would stand for. If it be skill, it must be proved as you watch it. You could never amuse an audience by displaying to it a specimen of skillful and minute engraving, the result of many years of toil... In every case the effect must be vivid, instantaneous, and unmistakable.[15]

Caffin exemplifies a Progressive-era critic who encouraged the extreme behavior that shocked and pleased with a "vulgarity" that would titillate and energize its spectators with its eccentricity. She saw this as a way for the audience to show its appreciation while being a vital part of the performance itself. The connection that audience and performer achieved through putting it over was something that reformers and authorities could not control.

The notion of putting it over proved to be what cultural conservatives like Edward Harrigan and Ellwood Cubberley had feared all along: a form in which the performer laughed at—not with—the audience. Echoing Harrigan's anxiety of being laughed at by the new humor, Caffin takes another view of putting it over. Advocating for the audience's active participation in vaudeville comedy, she noted that the vaudevillian "knows that, above all things, the audience is there to laugh. Give it an excuse for that, and it is his. It will seize any excuse to indulge in this, its favorite pastime, and, if it may not laugh with you, it will need very little to make it laugh at you."[16] The difference for Caffin is in the control that the audience feels it has over the relationship to the performers in vaudeville. Whereas the highbrow audience respected the distance between spectator and performer, the underclass audience appreciated a comedian who put it over and would not abide one that did not. The connection between audience and performer in either case was created through the shared experience of laughter.

Vaudeville was especially appealing to the underclasses because it discarded self-consciousness and the pretensions of separating the stage artists from audiences by breaking "the fourth wall" that divided them in the legitimate theater. Vaudevillians were encouraged to develop an original and surprising relationship with their audiences. The comic's natural inclination was to get laughs by directly communicating with spectators.

Whereas advocates of the vaudeville stage appreciated the bond of performer and spectator, certain reform committees, such as the Twentieth Century Club and the Committee of Fourteen, were hostile to such cavalier attitudes to the Victorian theater's rules of propriety. They worried that what had characterized the legitimate stage was now "evidently the beginning of a further breaking down of those barriers that separate the audience from the performer upon the stage," which could not "but make the spectator less able to enjoy genuine dramatic art."[17]

Progressive reformers' fears of unsophisticated audience reception to comedic vaudeville acts, although extreme, were not entirely unwarranted. Comic vaudevillians courted audience response by working very close to the edge of the stage—if not in the auditorium itself—for maximum contact with spectators. As Robert Lytell of the *New*

Republic noted in 1925: "They seize you and do pretty nearly anything they want with you and while it is going on, you sit with your mouth open and laugh and laugh again."[18] Complicity between comedian and spectator developed as performers addressed their audiences directly and made them feel as if they were in on the jokes. The vaudeville performers reached their audiences in a visceral, direct way; distinguishing themselves from their competition obligated them to push the boundaries of middlebrow propriety, sometimes encouraging youthful rebellion among their patrons. The rowdiness and call-and-response with the audience created an atmosphere that not only broke the rules of the legitimate stage but was feared it would permeate the rules of behavior in American society as well.

This points to an important distinction between the fear of the new humor that the Anglo middle-class audiences may have felt of being ridiculed by vaudevillian laughter, and the empowerment it imparted to an audience of new immigrants. Putting it over created collusion with the audience, which was feared would endanger the values of Americanness. It scorned those who were trying to improve and put in place a prescription for American respectability. Vaudeville laughter openly derided this desire to Americanize through moral codes of behavior.

The success of the vaudeville act also hinged on whether performers could put over the exaggerated types that marked the ethic immigrant and the native folk humor of the disenfranchised. Considered an affront to middle-class decency, the new humor was performed by comic entertainers who came from humble beginnings as outsiders from the underclasses. This lower class consisted primarily of the new immigrants and the indigenous, marginalized populations of the United States and its working poor.

Popular entertainment historian and theorist Henry Jenkins explains that an "elaborate system of typage developed: exaggerated costumes, facial characteristics, phrases, and accents were meant to reflect general personality traits viewed as emblematic of a particular class, region, ethnic group, or gender." Jenkins calls this the "vaudeville aesthetic."[19] Much of the vaudeville aesthetic was constructed from the sociocultural types that had been inherited from nineteenth-century performance forms such as minstrelsy, medicine shows, burlesque, and variety theater. Along with a newly revived fear of the lowbrow humor found in vaudeville's precursors, the newly forming Anglo-American middle classes were encouraged to be wary of, if not outright hostile to, this vaudeville aesthetic. This was especially noticed in the fear of the foreigner in the guise of the new immigrant, and the emerging liberation of women from the Victorian era's sexual and cultural strictures.

Vaudeville comedy's aesthetic evolved from various forms, including the entertainments at concert saloons, the variety theater, and burlesque comedy. One of the most important influences on vaudeville was the minstrel show.[20] Minstrelsy had emerged during the 1830s as a series of sentimental ballads, comic dialogue, and dance interludes based on white entertainers' image of southern "Negro life." It is said to have originated with white performer-playwright T. D. Rice, whose blackface imitation of an elderly southern "Negro" produced the overwhelmingly popular character known as Jim Crow.[21] Most of the original minstrel performers and composers were white northerners who had no firsthand knowledge of life in the South.

Structured as a semicircle of four or five, white male performers with black greasepaint or burnt cork painted on their faces, wearing absurdly oversize or ragged "Negro" costumes, sang and played a variety of instruments, including the banjo, fiddle, tambourine, and bone castanets. The show was divided into three parts: the first featured a random selection of songs interconnected with stereotyped "Negro" jokes and foolishness. In the second part, known as the "olio," performers who specialized in comedic dialogues would give malapropism-laden stump speeches or cross-dress and impersonate "wenches." The third part was a playlet, usually set in the South, comprising music, dancing "darkies," and burlesques of Shakespeare plays and melodramas.[22]

The show began when the all-male performers entered in a "walk-around" (the performers moving forward in a solo or group dance) until the Interlocutor, an aristocratic Anglo authority figure, usually dressed in a tuxedo with tails, announced, "Gentlemen! Be seated!" Energetic song and dance numbers as well as sentimental ballads would be interspersed with comic banter between the "endmen"—two white performers in blackface, playing the characters Mr. Tambo and Mr. Bones, named after the musical instruments they played, the tambourine and the "bones," a set of curved wood pieces (originally actual bones from animals) played against the knee or clapped together.[23]

The minstrel form is well archived in Buster Keaton's silent short film *The Playhouse* (1921), which re-creates a traditional minstrel show from the nineteenth century. With title cards substituting for the dialogue of a live performance, the film begins with Keaton as the Interlocutor announcing, "Gentlemen! Be seated." Then he addresses one of the blackfaced endmen, Mr. Bones, also played by Keaton: "Mr. Bones! I understand you had a cyclone in your town." Keaton, as Bones, replies, "Yes, sir! The wind blew so hard it blew a silver dollar into four quarters." "That's nothing," counters Tambo, also Keaton in blackface. "The wind blew so hard it blew a wart off a man's nose that broke a window two blocks away!!!" The film then cuts to an Anglo middle-class husband and wife (both portrayed by Keaton) who seem unimpressed as they look at the show's program listing Keaton in all the parts. The husband comments: "This fellow Keaton seems to be the whole show."

After cutting to other audience members, including a working-class mother and child (both Keaton) in the "galley gods" section, and an elderly aristocratic couple (both Keaton) who are being tormented by the young boy sitting above them, the film returns to the minstrels onstage. The Interlocutor has the line of eight men (four on either side of him) rise as Tambo and Bones, on either end of the lineup, do a ridiculous jig with their tambourine and bones as accompaniment (the walk-around). The minstrels then wave their hands in the air, imitating a "hallelujah" gesture.

Non-race–related humor was also a large part of minstrelsy in the mid-nineteenth century, including lampoons of aristocratic whites, such as politicians, doctors, and lawyers, through stump speeches (monologues that mocked political speeches or religious sermons) and satirical scenarios. Women's suffrage was also ridiculed during antebellum minstrelsy. A typical joke about women's voting rights has a blackface character named Mr. Johnson saying, "Jim, I tink de ladies oughter vote," and the Jim Crow character replies in malapropism-laden English, "No, Mr. Johnson, ladies 'am supposed to care berry little about polytick, and yet de majority ob 'em am strongly tached to parties."[24]

The first minstrels were all men, but among the "colored minstrels" who later emerged, there were many women performers.[25] As burlesque and vaudeville evolved, white minstrel shows began to include female performers, who were required to wear burnt cork masks, and, like singer-comedian May Irwin, became "coon shouters" singing "coon songs," which consisted of ragtime numbers whose lyrics reflected stereotypes of the rural southern Negro dialect.[26]

Comic minstrelsy thus focused on racial types and the denigration of the "Negro" character, relying on broad and often insulting blackface routines. The central white performer controlled the movements of his "darkies," making them tell foolish jokes and perform absurd song and dance numbers to entertain white audiences. It was calculated to mock the talents of black performers through the lens of a white man's interpretation of stereotyped "Negro" behaviors.

Blackface continued with female "coon shouters" as well as with male performers like Eddie Cantor and Al Jolson, and would be used onstage into the 1920s and in films well into the 1930s and 1940s.[27] With its tortured-English dialogues and racially charged songs and dances, minstrelsy had a profound effect on what would later become vaudeville, particularly in show formats such as the olio and burlesque playlets. Minstrelsy would also cross over and influence another form of popular entertainment, the "medicine show," in which charlatan showmen reminiscent of characters in minstrelsy wooed audiences with their charms and promises of miraculous cure-alls and moneymaking schemes.

The connection to minstrelsy and vaudeville can be seen especially clearly when female comedians, including Marie Dressler and Sophie Tucker, used blackface to suppress their womanliness (and supposed unattractiveness) during their coon shouting. Their character-driven songs were related to Irish, German, Italian, and Jewish numbers that also relied on stereotyped, accented lyrics and physical gestures that lasted in their popularity well into the 1920s.

A second influence on vaudeville was the concert saloon that exploded in popularity during the late nineteenth century. Concert saloons emerged in the 1850s and were in immense demand in the United States during the Civil War. Essentially these were drinking establishments with makeshift stages—tables and chairs facing a raised platform in the corner of the main room. In 1872, there were seventy-five to eighty concert saloons in New York City alone centered in the lower-class districts of the city, including the Bowery, Broadway, and lower Manhattan.[28] Concert saloons were showcases for a variety of acts before burlesque and vaudeville reached the status of big-time entertainments. Piano players, many of whom had moved from brothels, provided music and atmosphere, while "waitress girls" not only served drinks but also danced and showed their undergarments in an effort to encourage customers to buy more drinks. Some of these serving women were recruited for their performance skills and received "throw money" that landed near them. Although demeaning, this way of earning money was an alternative to working twelve-hour shifts six days a week in a mill or garment factory.

The concert saloons also featured ethnic acts that would come off the road from extensive touring doing blackface minstrelsy. "Dialect" acts were quite popular, as the first waves of primarily Irish and German immigrants during the middle to late nineteenth century provided easy targets for comic send-ups. When dialect comics got into staged quarrels with each other, they devolved into slapstick knockabout routines. The seeds for the Three Keatons' family act and the Marx Brothers' chaotic destruction of social institutions were in these early concert saloon favorites. Actual fighting was also featured with 30-round, bare-knuckle pugilists, a source for gambling.[29] As noted in the *New York Herald* in 1883, concert saloons featured even more eccentric acts that had "a wind up of some outrageously absurd farce, replete with patriotic soldiers and comic Negroes, and screeching devotion to the flag, closing with a grand transparency of General McClellan or of President Lincoln."[30]

Moralizing reformers and cultural critics rebuked concert saloons right from the beginning—and not without some justification—as sites of criminal activity, including prostitution, gambling, and public drunkenness. A report in the *New York World* called them "the most abominable nuisance and vilest disgrace of the metropolis."[31] In April 1862, the New York State legislature passed a law that required licenses for all places of entertainment and prohibited the sale of alcohol and the use of waitresses in concert saloons. This was thanks to a crusade by the Society for the Reformation of Juvenile Delinquents, which was funded by fees collected on all places of amusements in New York City, to reform theaters, concert saloons, and public amusements thought to be corrupting the city's youth.[32]

Nineteenth-century social historian Junius Henry Browne cast aspersions on the concert saloons' patrons, who he said included the "laborer and mechanic, the salesman and accountant, the bank-clerk and merchant," with a surprisingly large portion of middle-aged men from out of town. Browne feared that this combination of working- and middle-class audiences, coupled with the temptations of urban vice that was being bred in concert saloons, was harmful, even explosive, and that it might destroy American decency.[33] According to Browne, reformers and public authorities were concerned with concert saloons that promoted a "bawdy atmosphere" and denigrated the new middle class's principles of "self-control and self-improvement." The essentially male clientele of concert saloons kept decent family men away from their wives and children and poisoned the minds of younger men, who had yet to establish their own families, and thwarted the desire to establish and maintain a family in the first place.[34] Concert saloons continued into the 1880s and began to wane in the 1890s. They became virtually nonexistent with the advent of burlesque and vaudeville.

Vaudeville would eventually emerge from these concert saloons by taking the acts out of the barrooms and putting the performers into theaters with actual stages. It would also move the alcohol and put it in small bars in the theater lobbies and away from the entertainers and audiences. Further, the shows began attracting women and their children by offering matinees and family-friendly bills. The spirit of the concert saloon would remain in vaudeville, particularly in the evening shows when comedians, singers, and dancers would feature the "adult-oriented" fare of the saloons.[35] When the Volstead Act of 1919 went into effect and banned alcohol in both public and private enterprises, the concert saloons were resurrected as speakeasies, as comically depicted in the Marx Brothers' 1931 film *Horse Feathers*, complete with covert passwords and "bathtub gin."

"Variety theater" grew out of the concert saloon and referred to a bill of unrelated acts that happen with no particular agenda except for balancing a lineup. Every act had to be different from the one before or after it to ensure patrons' interest. During the 1840s, variety theater was often performed in urban areas, as well as in remote regions of the American frontier. Variety shows were almost exclusively performed for all-male audiences. Performers had to work against the noise of drunks, gambling, and the solicitation of "waiter girls." The programs were lewd, crude, and simplistic.[36] Variety theater became so notorious that after the Civil War and for the remainder of the nineteenth century, middle-class citizens, religious groups, and news organizations demanded that it be reformed. Unlike concert saloons, the variety show had wooden benches, rather than tables, to emulate a typical theater setup. "Variety" was a descriptor, unlike its next incarnation, vaudeville, which denoted an institutional business. From 1876 to 1893, variety was split into two branches consisting of burlesque for lowbrow, working-class male audiences and the more respectable and middle-class oriented vaudeville for family audiences.[37]

Variety acts eschewed narrative structures for the short, fast shock of the moment, discarding the rules of the legitimate theater. Its evolution into vaudeville comedy reflected that modernist ideas, as well as the rejection of conformity, was being brought to middle-class audiences. In 1913, the Italian avant-garde theorist F. T. Marinetti wrote a manifesto titled "The Variety Theater," which popularized the notion that late-nineteenth-century variety theater represented the future of art in relationship to popular entertainment, embracing the modernist age and the intensity of the industrialization of the Western world. "The Variety Theater," wrote Marinetti, "exalts action, heroism, the open-air life, skill, the authority of instinct and intuition. In opposition to psychology it offers what I call *body-madness*."[38] Body-madness—translated from the Italian *fisicofollia*—took the form of the physical gag found in variety theater comedy. Typical of the variety shows of the 1860s, these acts focused on former minstrel performers and chorines "after the decline of the leg show" featuring "broad comedy and exuberant dance," and their body-madness. This style of comic performance, also known as "honky tonk," would split into burlesque and vaudeville as the nineteenth century came to a close.[39]

Burlesque was a significant and often overlooked form of popular entertainment that informed vaudeville, especially with regard to its female performers. Burlesque in America was a product of the Victorian music hall beginning in the 1840s. It became popular when performer

Lydia Thompson and her "British Blondes" came to the United States from England in 1868, merging the Victorian stage tradition with an American sensibility that would be quite successful with audiences all over the country until the 1890s.

Beginning in the 1870s, New York burlesque shows drew from other American popular entertainments such as minstrel shows with their three-part structure, which included (1) songs and lewd comedy sketches; (2) olios and male acrobats, singers, and magicians; and (3) either parodies (burlesques) of politics (using the stump speech) or a current play. The "wow" finish was usually a male-oriented entertainment such as an erotic dancer or a boxing or wrestling match. As popular entertainment historian Robert C. Allen points out:

> The takeoffs on venerated objects of high culture and punning rhymed couplets spoken by cross-dressed women were gradually eliminated as burlesque increasingly became centered around feminine sexual display—in the cooch dance of the 1890s; in its jazzed-up successor, the shimmy, in the 1910s.[40]

The American form of burlesque flourished in the 1890s with an ever-increasing movement toward female nudity as the final act. For female burlesque comic dancers, like Lydia Thompson, the new trend toward displaying the female body began the separation of the voice (her comic commentary) from the body (her erotic dance that would become the "cooch" and the "shimmy"). Female burlesque performers who wanted to continue the success of their comic sketches and stump speeches, as well as the sexual innuendo of their songs and dances, would attempt to clean up their acts in order to move up to the more respectable vaudeville stage.

By the early twentieth century, burlesque would tour on two national circuits (known as "wheels") in competition with, but separate from, the vaudeville circuit. In New York, burlesque houses like Minsky's at the Winter Garden would become the place for a mostly male working-class audience to see the sensual, and sometimes fully nude, cooch and shimmy dancers. Vaudeville would be performed at upscale venues like the Palace and Victoria Hammerstein theaters, which catered to a lower- and middle-class clientele of men, women, and their children.

As vaudeville began to attract a more middle-class audience, burlesque began to change, especially with regard to representations of womanhood onstage. Allen notes that "between 1870 and 1940, burlesque troupes toured every part of the United States and its territories—from New York to Klondike mining camps."[41] However, the early success of burlesque threatened Anglo middle-class moral sensibilities, provoking a backlash that marginalized and condemned it. The first season of American burlesque in particular was disruptive and threatening because it represented a theatrical world without limits, where any male-dominated institution or authority was perceived as under attack. Ultimately, "the burlesque performer—showing herself, showing off, showing up the hapless male characters she took on in repartee—literally and figuratively embodied this world" where anything might happen.[42]

The more burlesque began to grow in popularity, particularly with middle-class New York theater audiences, the more it unsettled critics and reformers. There was "something new and troubling in [burlesque's] power to entrance the spectator with displays of women in revealing costumes who were dangerously impertinent in their mocking male impersonations, streetwise language, and nonsensical humor."[43] The mockery of middle-class American values in burlesque was to find its way into vaudeville comedy in the form of comic commentary on class, ethnic, and gender roles.

The popularity of burlesque in 1869 led critic Richard Grant White to comment: "The peculiar trait of burlesque is its defiance both of the natural and the conventional... the result is absurdity and monstrosity. Its system is a defiance of system. It is out of *all* keeping... Burlesque casts down all the gods from their pedestals."[44] Grant's assessment—of burlesque and its "defiance" of social systems through laughter and satire of male-dominated authority—as an affront to "the natural and the conventional" confirms the contention that burlesque humor posed a threat to the established order of Americanness.

The transition from the world of burlesque (and minstrelsy as well) to vaudeville comedy can be observed in the comic vaudeville actor, singer, and dancer Sophie Tucker. Born of Russian-Jewish parents, Tucker (née Kalish) immigrated to the United States in 1887 when she was only three months old. She began as an amateur in New York

City at the 125th Street Theatre in Harlem, where she performed for the first time in blackface, and was soon billed as the "World-Renowned Coon Shouter." One of her first professional appearances was at Tony Pastor's Fourteenth Street Theatre, and she was subsequently booked on the Manchester and Hills burlesque circuit.[45] In 1909, the *New York Dramatic Mirror* reviewed Tucker's act, noting her connection to burlesque: "Sophie Tucker is another recruit from the lower rungs of the vaudeville and amusement ladder, who is about to find her own. She certainly deserves it! Seldom is such a vivacious, intense, and entertaining personality found in one body."[46] What Tucker brought from the "lower rungs" of burlesque was a comic voice along with bawdy humor in her songs and dances—all "in one body." The *Dramatic Mirror* anticipated that Tucker would not remain a comic vaudevillian for long, and she would be wooed away from "the variety stage and we will no longer hear her sing 'The Cubanola Glide'... and 'The Wild Cherry Rag,'"[47] both popular numbers in her burlesque act as well.

Tucker brought into her numbers the excess of burlesque with its mocking portrayals of blacks, ethnic Jews, and Irish, as well as incorporating a sexualized vamp—she embraced the extremes of body and voice, as the appellation "coon shouter" promised.[48] Tucker recognized that her success in vaudeville owed a debt to her burlesque days, as she explained to the *New York Dramatic Mirror* in a 1919 interview. "When I was a coon shouter," she said, "I executed a Jazz and Shimmie rhythm with every song. As inventors of Jazz and Shimmie, these other birds are wonderful aviators—their imagination takes such long flights. But don't wake them up. Just let them dream."[49] Sophie Tucker took full credit for bringing blackface minstrelsy and jazz along with burlesque songs and dances to the middle-class, family-oriented vaudeville circuit. The burlesque influence on vaudeville offended the middle-class sensibilities of some critics and entertainment reformers. As Laurence Senelick notes, "The blatant double entendre in the dialogue between straight man and 'talking woman,' as well as runway interplay between strippers and audience, enraged moralists."[50] It was this notion of the "talking woman" in particular that disturbed them.

The talking woman consisted of three burlesqued female types, including the ingénue, the soubrette, and the prima donna. The ingénue was an over-the-top rendition of the naive girl and the principal talking woman in a show equal to the comic and straight man. The soubrettes were characterized as "semicoquette-semitomboy free spirits who whooped out blues and 'pep' songs, and twitted the men along the ramp about their baldness and virility," as comedy historian Rowland Barber observes.[51] The power of the soubrettes lay in the "older, wiser women who were sexual teases even more inaccessible than the ingénues," as performance theory scholar Jill Dolan writes.[52] The final talking woman was the prima donna and the principal singer of the show. She represented women of authority, often portraying the overbearing wife or wealthy society matron. This burlesque female character type is represented by Kathleen Howard in W. C. Fields' film *It's a Gift* (1934), as well as by Margaret Dumont in relationship to Groucho Marx in *Animal Crackers* (1928 Broadway; 1930 film). On the burlesque stage, the dominant authority is invariably the prima donna.[53]

The focus of burlesque as it moved further into the twentieth century shifted to the sexualized female body, and was consigned to the touring "wheels" that catered primarily to working-class men. The "talking women" of burlesque comedy were lost. For the Anglo-American middle classes, burlesque came to be associated with a distorted vision of female sexuality onstage. Its grotesque combination of age, race, and ethnicity, together with an excess of voice and body types, was distasteful compared with the demure actresses of the generation that screen idol Mary Pickford would come to represent in early silent films as "the girl next door" and "America's sweetheart." Sexually aggressive performances that burlesqued the white bourgeoisie—especially its patriarchal authorities—threatened respectable definitions of Americanness.[54]

As the new humor began to assert itself, cultural authorities feared that all this was leading to the collapse of categories and rules that Eurocentric artists and critics had worked so diligently to develop. Ultimately, this fear of the social order's disruption in art and culture led to a backlash of condemnation in the popular-entertainment industry. Benjamin Franklin Keith and his partner Edward F. Albee in vaudeville, Will Hays and the Production Code in early sound films, and the National Association of Broadcasters in radio attempted to make popular entertainment orderly and safe for consumers. To combat the influx of vaudeville comedy and its offenses, and to appeal to more patrons with disposable income for their newfound leisure time, the formidable entrepreneur B. F. Keith dominated the vaudeville circuit in 1898 with his pronouncement to a middle-class magazine audience: "The state show must be free from all vulgarisms and coarseness of any kind, so that the house and entertainment would directly appeal to support ladies and children—in fact that my playhouse must be as 'homelike' an amusement resort as it was possible to make."[55] Keith's battle to bring decency—and more audiences that included middle-class women and their children—to vaudeville often took issue with the acts he promoted, particularly the comedians.

Critical reception of vaudevillians noted the aesthetic divisions between low- and highbrow classes through popular entertainments. In 1910, *American Magazine* wrote that vaudeville—contrary to entrepreneurs like B. F. Keith and Marcus Loew, who claimed they were providing a "Sunday School Circuit" of entertainments—trafficked in uncouth material just as the late-nineteenth-century variety theater had. "In the days before vaudeville had developed its present money-making capacities [it] was both wholesome and cheap," he proclaimed. "Those days are passed. Nowadays it is anything to get a laugh or a shock."[56] And two years later, the *Dramatic Mirror* admonished vaudevillians and their acts "where the impropriety and obscenity were no whit less offensive than they are at a so-called burlesque show."[57] *American Magazine* saw the effects of popular entertainments as detrimental to Americans' mental and physical health, noting that vaudeville had "done more to corrupt, vitiate and degrade public tastes in matters relating to the stage than all other influences put together."[58]As a result of these attitudes, vaudeville shows were often labeled dialect, eccentric, and nut acts by cultural critics of the period.[59]

These acts can be analyzed as contrasting studies in the evolution of the new humor in vaudeville. Vaudeville comedians' relationships to the cultural conflicts of the Progressive era varied, and the multiplicity of vaudeville acts cannot be emphasized enough. To lump them all together would ignore their diversity and importance to American culture during the modernist period. What made vaudeville unique in the early twentieth century was its variation of acts, the skill required to execute them, and how they were structured within any given theater manager's bill. These qualities are registered in a magazine article on popular entertainment by Frances Peck Smith in 1912:

> In vaudeville there are six different types. There are the people from the "legitimate": musical comedy people who have been trained by competent managers; the old-time variety actors; young boys who have procured most of their training on the streets, learned a song and dance from some source or other and graduated on the stage as "Musical Comedy Fours," etc.; rathskeller stars, who after a number of years of café singing came out as vaudeville artists; and the specialty people, among whom may be included acrobats, divers, prize fighters, and animal trainers.... And practically all nationalities are represented.[60]

These multiple "nationalities" consisted largely of new immigrants converging with turn-of-the-twentieth-century audiences to create an American cultural phenomenon.

The structure of episodic acts in vaudeville differed significantly from earlier forms of popular entertainments. In 1916, George A. Gottlieb, booking agent for the Palace Theatre in New York, described the coordination and arrangement of a standard vaudeville program, emphasizing the unique function within the whole of each act.[61] Since ensemble numbers and short playlets were no longer part of the bill, a consequence of this restructuring made the comic vaudevillian a "specialized agent within an industry."[62] In the modernist era of industrial production, vaudevillians were hired specifically for their ability to specialize in an act with machine-like precision, upwards of three times a day, six days a week, for as many weeks of the year as they were booked on the vaudeville circuit. The pressure to make an act stand out ensured that comic vaudevillians created acts that avoided the decency and conventional middle-class morality that was expected of the "cleaned up" vaudeville that producers like Keith and Albee had promised.

Vaudeville comedy would be structured on comic routines and scenarios performed in short bursts of between five and fifteen minutes in what would become colloquially known as gags. Gags were the bread and butter of vaudeville comedians. These simple physical responses would give way to the virtuosity of the gags that had no necessary bearing on the stage action and became the primary reason audiences would come to see certain vaudeville comics. Their gags defined and distinguished the comedians from one another. In fact, straightforward storytelling, with its logic and plot structure, was eschewed for the enjoyment of the gags in and of themselves.

The plotless accumulation of gags, sketch comedy, and pratfalls created a humor that had an immediate emotional impact on audiences. The popular theater was concerned with leaving an impression first and foremost, so that people would come back for more. The lack of narrative structure reflected a world in flux with unexpected turns of events that either aided in upward mobility or left families struggling for survival. The chaos of daily life for vaudeville audiences, as well as the burgeoning new middle class of Americans, was therefore mirrored on the vaudeville stage.

Making nonsense out of authority was the primary function of the vaudeville gag. Employees defied their employers, children openly disrespected and disobeyed their parents, and the underclasses consciously undermined the upper classes, as societal power structures began to be questioned and distressed. This upending of established hierarchies through gags and slapstick physicality found its way onto the vaudeville stage and into silent film comedy of the 1900s and 1910s. Many comic vaudeville performers were able to defy the strictures and economics of the lower classes they were born into and have lucrative careers in these popular entertainments. Vaudeville performers like Weber and Fields, the Marx Brothers, May Irwin, and Eva Tanguay—all of whom came from humble beginnings—were now making anywhere from $1,000 to $4,000 a week at the height of their popularity. The more money they made, the louder and more ubiquitous their voices became. The mockery of institutions and class rankings and the irreverence to these authorities through comedy threatened the dominance of the established Anglo-American classes.

The work of Buster Keaton, one of vaudeville's most successful and still relevant comedians, demonstrates not only how vaudeville acts were performed but also how they innovated and worked from the changing social conditions and upheavals of the early twentieth century. An undisputed expert of onstage routines and gags, Keaton later became one of the acknowledged masters of silent-film comedy. What is less known is that he began his comedy apprenticeship on the vaudeville stage with his parents in an act called the Three Keatons.[63] By focusing on Keaton's stagecraft rather than his film work, I examine the influence of nineteenth-century popular entertainments on vaudeville comedy, showing that Keaton is a superlative example of how minstrelsy, variety, and burlesque comedy merged in vaudeville during the first two decades of the twentieth century.

How Keaton became a "Buster" is a vaudeville legend. Keaton himself claimed that the famous escape artist Harry Houdini named him after watching the young Keaton go crashing offstage, then return to the boards unscathed. "My, what a buster!"[64] Houdini exclaimed, according to Keaton in his autobiography, *My Wonder World of Slapstick*.[65] The image of a five-year-old boy being thrown across and offstage by his father, and audiences of adults and children alike laughing as the boy bounces back onstage, thwarting his father's efforts to control him, provides a window on the many aspects of nineteenth-century popular entertainments that survived into early-twentieth-century American vaudeville acts. Though many of the Three Keatons' routines had a simple format, Buster's father, Joe, encouraged them to switch it up nightly and trained Buster to improvise right from the beginning of his apprenticeship. Keaton observed, "We never bothered to do the same routines twice in a row. We found it much more fun to surprise one another by pulling any crazy, wild stunt that came into our heads."[66] This kind of shock-and-awe surprise was the stock-in-trade of the Three Keatons—father (Joe), son (Buster), and mother (Myra)—and at the heart of vaudeville comedy.

Using the available stock scenery depicting a picturesque and tranquil lake scene, Keaton describes an act in his autobiography that encompasses the dynamics of the father and son as a two-man traveling act.

> [Joe sauntered] to the footlights and, pretending it was the brass foot rail of a saloon, put his foot on the curved metal guard over the footlights. I did the same thing. As we stood there, each resting an elbow on a knee, he would ask:
>
> JOE: What will you have, scotch?
> BUSTER: [Shakes his head, "no."]
> JOE: Rye?
> BUSTER: No.

JOE: Gin?
BUSTER: No!
JOE: What do you want then?
BUSTER: Water!

> Grabbing me by the back of the neck he would turn me around and walk me toward the curtain, meanwhile grumbling, "So it is *water* you want?" Then he would hurl me into the painted water scene. As I hit the curtain, it would give quite a bit. While sliding to the floor, the drop's wooden strip would flap up, and I would be trapped in it. The stagehands then would pull up the curtain a few inches to help me free myself.[67]

All the while, mother Myra would accompany these father-and-son battles improvising on the saxophone. The patter between performers, also improvised, did not necessarily have to make sense or drive a storyline forward. In fact, the mere fact of a young boy of five being chastised for not ordering a proper drink in a bar (by his own father, no less), then being thrown into the scenery (or offstage or into the audience, depending on the moment in question) as a way of reinforcing discipline, was surreal in its logic, and this nonsensical cause and effect would follow Keaton into his later one-man acts and silent films.

Comic vaudevillians would use whatever was at hand while on the road to create improvised physical gags in which their acrobatic skills would be exploited for laughs. The scenarios involved reversals of power and authority, as in the Three Keatons' case, in which a father tries to discipline his son, only to have the son come right back and undermine his authority, physical strength, and paternal dominance. The significance of the struggles between fathers and sons, between the powerful and the powerless, and between masters and servants is key to the comedy of Buster Keaton in vaudeville. It shows Keaton to be a descendent of touring performance forms like minstrelsy and medicine shows.

Keaton's white-faced deadpan with "slap-shoes" (oversize shoes that slap the ground when walking) and a crushed hat lying flat on his head was created during his apprenticeship while playing small-time vaudeville houses. Keaton's stage career from a young age was informed by the legacy of slapstick, a word derived from the name of a prop from *commedia dell'arte* (the Italian sixteenth-century improvised comedy form) that consisted of two pieces of wood slapped together to create loud, sharp sounds as if hitting someone and knocking them down. Keaton worked from improvised scenarios that did not rely on plot or character development, and his improvisations were created with his fellow performers using props, sets, and costumes as a basis for in-the-moment inspiration. These ensemble gags were held together with a tenuous plot, with young Buster almost always being disciplined and chased by his father. The endings concern Buster getting away unscathed from his father after a series of physically dangerous and near-death experiences.

This examination of the comic vaudeville stage, as represented by Keaton, reinforces the notion that it was not the theater that was necessarily changing but the social demands of the new audience of Anglo-Americans that was in flux. A set of new rules to control lewd and libidinous impulses—particularly those of the lower classes of ethnic immigrants—needed to be put in place according to reformers, cultural critics, and moral authorities, so that these vulgar notions of culture would not infiltrate the new middle-classes and their efforts at Americanization.

The family act of the Three Keatons represented the conflicts that were presented by the modernist era. Early-twentieth-century comedy was influenced by the paradoxical relationship of the new machine age's excitement and intensity, on the one hand, and an impulse for the "looking backward" of aesthetic theorist Edward Bellamy to the nineteenth-century folk culture and performance traditions of eastern and southern European immigrants, the comic Yiddish theater, as well as to American popular entertainments such as minstrel shows, concert saloons, and burlesque comedy.[68] This comedic legacy created a theatricality and tension between past and present that characterized vaudeville comedy during this period. The return to ensemble playing and improvisation showed the modern-era man as a protean mix of possibilities of slipping into roles that would not be possible to enact in the strict class and social structures of nineteenth-century Europe and the United States.

Servants rebelling against their masters, children against their parents, workers against their bosses, lower classes against the upper classes, and the call for labor unions and women's suffrage in the United States during the first decades of the twentieth century became fodder for comic vaudevillians, as will be considered in subsequent chapters. The social and aesthetic paradigm shifts are symptomatic of the advent of the new immigrants and the new women. Reaching back to the massive ethnic migration to the United States in the early twentieth century, sociocultural upheavals can be seen as reflected in the new humor. How these clashes between comic vaudevillians and their new humor and campaigns for Americanization played out can be witnessed in the next chapter through an examination of ethnic acts and family acts.

3. The New Humor: Ethnic Acts and Family Acts

Standard vaudeville acts of the late nineteenth and early twentieth centuries comprised a series of specialty turns; two of the most popular were ethnic acts and family acts. These acts included a wide range of comic routines, such as the straight and the Jew; the single, double, or triple "Dutch," "Irish" or "Wop" act; the Five Columbians; the Happy McNultys; and the Three Dolce Sisters.[1] According to vaudevillian turned historian Joe Laurie Jr., the acts popular in the early 1900s "followed a pattern of our immigration." These ethnic immigrant acts combined Irish, Italian, German, and Jewish character types derived from popular stage entertainments of the middle to late nineteenth century, as discussed in chapter 2. Ethnic humor was not necessarily thought of as offensive in and of itself, and if we can believe Laurie's account, the performers were aware of the stereotypes that they were perpetuating and commenting on:

> And let me tell you right now that in early variety and vaude nobody took exception to the billings of the different character acts, like "The Sport and the Jew," "Irish by Name but Coons by Birth," "The Mick and the Policeman," "The Merry Wop," "Two Funny Sauerkrauts." It was taken in good humor by the audience, because that is what everyone called each other in everyday life.[2]

The most successful vaudeville entertainments spoke to the independent spirits of the new immigrant American audiences. They encouraged imaginative thinking and knowing laughter, and a vision of a more enjoyable world giving temporary relief to the difficulties of life in the modern age. Commercial entertainments like comedic vaudeville were popular for the solidarity and collective joy that audiences could share and appreciate, giving them a sense that they were not alone in the chaos of urban existence. They could smile knowingly that even if the odds in the new world were stacked against them, they were not alone and perhaps there was a way to tip the scales in their favor as well. Popular entertainments gave place to the dreams and fantasies that had driven ethnic immigrants to seek a better life in America, and not to corrupt and denigrate them as the "bogeys" had feared.

Certain reformers felt that American family life was coming under attack through popular entertainments and began to agitate in support of Americanization through moral, educational, and civic-minded diversions. The social divisions that Progressive-era reformers sought to exploit to promote an Anglo-American agenda and the targeting of new immigrants for supposedly sullying the aesthetics and culture of the American middle class can be seen in evaluations of the ethnic and family acts of Weber and Fields, the Three Keatons, the Marx Brothers, and the Elinore Sisters. These acts demonstrate that the new humor intentionally disrupted Anglo-American values through satire, broad physical behavior, and the mocking of middle-class propriety. Sociocultural advocates and critics' responses to the new humor on the vaudeville stage bring us nearer to an understanding of the significance of comedy to American familial values during the Progressive era.

The importance of vaudeville can be witnessed as early as 1895, when the *New York Dramatic Mirror* created a new department to add to its already extensive theater coverage: "The Vaudeville Stage." The periodical saw that the popularity of vaudeville was on the rise and "steadily coming into nearer relations with the regular stage." Editors cautioned, "It is evident that the leading newspaper of theatre should lift this class of intelligence to the dignity of a carefully maintained and occasionally illustrated department."[3] Senior editor Harrison Grey Fiske embraced this stance but made sure that the new and "carefully maintained" vaudeville section was hidden in the back pages of the newspaper.[4] In an attempt to acknowledge the growing commercial vaudeville market, the paper warned of this popular amusement's ethnic influence in its legitimate theater pages and made clear that these two stage forms were distinct—the legitimate theater and vaudeville. Fiske and reviewers were also a part of the Anglo-American upper classes, which were determined to reinforce their dominance as critics and arbiters of cultural values and taste.

Reform groups would corroborate the notion that the new immigrants were corrupting the stage. Associations like the Twentieth Century Club of Boston felt that vaudeville "was lowering public standards of morality and decreasing the average efficiency of the individual citizen by attracting audiences from the ethnic underclasses."[5] The new humor triggered fear among the Anglo-American middle class, including both critics and reform organizations, for its perceived refutation of social structures and institutions. By rebuking these reformers and critics, who promoted a more Americanized culture in the theater, vaudeville comedians challenged their authority and the conformity they promulgated.

The reformers especially condemned vaudeville comedy for corrupting young people. Citing its vulgarity and denigration of Anglo-American morals, leading youth to drink, have sex, and gamble, they warned of a life of irreversible criminal behaviors of all kinds. In 1907 reformer Josiah Strong wrote about the ills to be found on the vaudeville stage: "the vaudeville or variety show which abounds and is largely patronized is generally poor and often vile. Coarse theatricals, promiscuous public dances, and drinking saloons prepare the way for easy ruin."[6] The social roles and strictures that came under scrutiny in the ethnic and family acts encouraged audiences to question the authority of localized institutions like churches, public schools, family enclaves, and political interest groups from the left and the right. Popular performing arts like vaudeville were thought to challenge the segregation and quarantine of the Progressive movement's vision of the social order.

The changing of social masks was a significant part of the vaudeville aesthetic. The control that comic performers had over the mutable masks of ethnicity and nationality were perceived as a threat to the class stability of Americanness. The ethnic act's success depended on whether the performer could put over the exaggerated types that marked the new immigrant and the native folk humor of the disenfranchised. However, no vaudevillian, whether in blackface, yellow face, or any of the myriad ethnic disguises ever entirely disappeared behind these masks, making it clear that ethnicity was performed and not to be taken literally.

The new immigrants were foreign to native Anglo-Americans in every way. The bulk of them were not Protestants and spoke odd new languages that most Americans had never come into contact with before, such as Polish, Yiddish, Lithuanian, Czech, and Greek.[7] In daily life the immigrants seemed suspect, and their seemingly impenetrable and inscrutable appearances and accents raised questions about their willingness or ability to assimilate.

Many comic ethnic acts in vaudeville began their careers in the Yiddish theater. The significance of the comic Yiddish theater of New York's Lower East Side and American vaudeville can be seen in the phenomenal success of new humorists such as Fanny Brice, Eddie Cantor, Danny Kaye, and Sophie Tucker, and double acts such as Joe Weber and Lew Fields. By 1900 the comic actors of the Yiddish theater were becoming as popular as their more mainstream rivals in the American vaudeville form of comedy, and in 1905, scholars of the settlement-house movement commented that saloons and dance halls were being converted at an alarming rate, as "every important street on the Lower East Side has its glaring electric sign which announces 'Jewish Vaudeville House' or 'Music Hall.'"[8] Sixty percent of the vaudeville audience in 1910 was working class, according to a settlement-house survey, with only 36 percent comprising the "clerical class." Yiddish vaudeville was more often than not located in the commercial entertainment areas, either within or at least bordering working-class neighborhoods. Theaters in Manhattan alone were founded in large numbers in such impoverished locations as 14th Street, 125th Street, Eighth Avenue, Grand Street, and the Bowery.[9]

The Yiddish comic theater would come under scrutiny as early as 1905. Ethnic performances were thought to be coded through foreign languages and stage traditions that encouraged the immigrant-friendly audiences to question their assimilation to the American middle class. Responding to the Yiddish music hall performers, one settlement worker observed, "The songs are suggestive of everything but what is proper, the choruses are full of double meanings, and the jokes have broad and unmistakable hints of things indecent."[10] One of the many stage techniques that the Yiddish comic theater used that authorities perceived as suspect, yet that would become a successful tool on the vaudeville stage, was dialogue. The development from Yiddish theater and the language of the Eastern European *shtetl* and its Anglo-American confrontation proved useful for the new humor. Language itself was a place to differentiate class and culture distinctions. As sociologist John Murray Cuddihy writes with regard to Jewish versus gentile representations in American society in the early immigrant days of the twentieth century: "The 'serious and restrained' words of your liberal-Reform Jews will 'pass,' but the mocking impudence of your *schlemiels*...will not pass."[11]

To raise the question of how and where this concern with Americanness began to influence comic vaudevillians, we must consider that ethnic humor had a long life in vaudeville. This longevity resulted not only from the overly simplistic mockery of the lower social orders, but also from vaudeville's having engaged with conflicts that went far beyond aesthetic issues. The new humor and its reliance on ethnic immigrant types, interclass strife, and social mobility made ethnic acts staples of vaudeville comedy in the late nineteenth and early twentieth centuries. These foreign masks were identifiable markers of oversimplified foreign stereotypes and were easily exaggerated onstage. The subversion of the new humor was that any role could be portrayed by any and all comic performers, and vaudevillians adopted these stage stereotypes to destabilize and contradict—as well as capitalize on—these crude defamations of ethnic immigrants.

One did not have to be Irish to perform a "Mick" act or Italian to go onstage as a "Wop," as could be witnessed by performers turned vaudeville producers Weber and Fields. Joe Weber (born in New York City, 1867) and Lew Fields (born in New York City, 1867, as Moses Schoenfeld) were a comedy act that began in burlesque and brought their act to vaudeville, starting out in the 1870s in New York's variety houses and touring successfully for many years, becoming one of vaudeville's most popular and profitable acts. In 1896, they became producers of their own Broadway house—the Weber and Fields Music Hall, where they produced very successful burlesques of popular Broadway shows. These burlesque shows were mainly about laughing at contemporary vogues or socially fashionable trends of middle-class Broadway audiences. A typical show was arranged in the tradition of a burlesque revue of songs, chorus girls, and tangentially connected satirical sketches. Casts featured popular performers and comedians of the American stage, including Lillian Russell, Fay Templeton, and DeWolf Hopper. The titles of some of their shows indicate their devil-may-care brand of humor: *Hurly Burly, Whirl-i-Gig, Fiddle-Dee-Dee, Hoity-Toity, Twirly Whirly*, and *Whoop-De-Doo.*[12] The team separated acrimoniously in 1904 as Weber took over sole operation of the Music Hall. Fields went on to produce many musicals that toured the United States, one of which featured soon-to-be vaudeville and film star Marie Dressler.

Weber and Fields had a two-man "Dutch" (a corruption of the German *Deutsch*) act in which the duo portrayed recent German immigrants; this "dialect act" was a staple of ethnic acts (see figure 3.1). The performers mangled the English language with their mispronunciations and malapropisms as they attempted to sound and behave "American." Their act featured two characters, Mike and Meyer, who, through ethnically stereotyped costuming and physical behaviors, attempted to assimilate. Many of their sketches featured crafty schemes of "making it big" in America or simple survival scenarios of urban life. Their routines, according to vaudeville critic and historian Douglas Gilbert, were based on being raised on New York's Lower East Side ghetto, "born in an Essex Street house that harbored a saloon," and were an exaggerated send-up of their real-life experiences as Eastern European Jews on the streets of New York City.[13]

Weber and Fields's touring show of 1888 depicts the Double Dutch in action. Here we see Mike, the overweight and perpetually angry little man in a grotesquely padded fat suit of clashing colors and patterns with a ridiculously long watch chain that looks like a parade sash, complete with a goatee that looks more goat than human, trembling with fury as he confronts Meyer. "Vhat kindt ov logick iss dot? Idt dondt make no sense, Meyer," he says. The tall, thin, and ever-obsequious Meyer keeps his partner at arm's length with his long fingers pressing into the overstuffed cotton batting of Mike's costume. Mike, leaning into Meyer's long fingers, balances himself against the lanky comic in a tense standoff. Meyer responds, "Py gollies, idt's as clear as der nose on your face," and to make his point, he viciously twists Mike's nose. Mike retaliates with flailing arms in an attempt to strike, but alas his arms

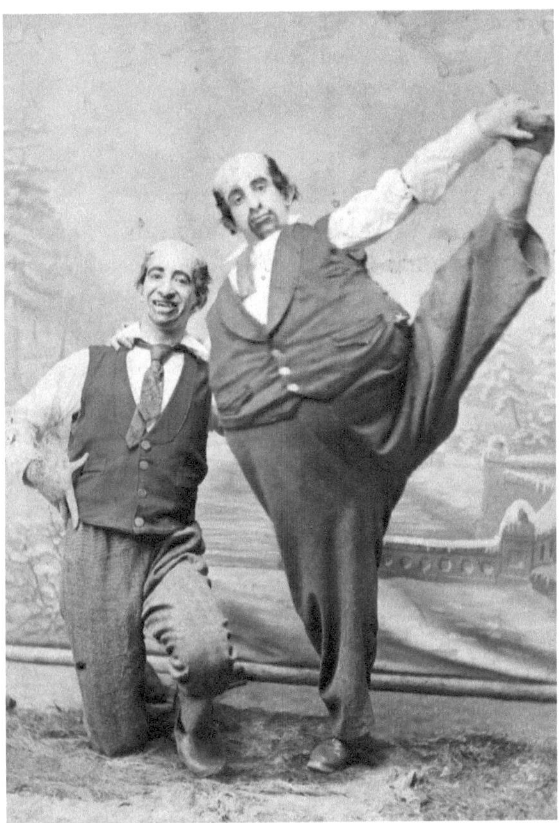

Figure 3.1 Weber and Fields in the "Double Dutch Act," 1914; Billy Rose Theatre Division, New York Public Library for the Performing Arts, Astor, Lenox, and Tilden Foundations.

are too short to reach Meyer, as he shouts, "Idt dondt make no sense. You aindt no politickaler. Der ain't no vay dot you could know idt dot Harrizon vould beadt Clevelandt in der elecgshion for prezident!" The two-man act continues with the following exchange:

MEYER: Vhat no vay? Ass ve came acrossdt der coundtry, I kebpt dtelling you dot Harrizon vould vin. Evveryvhere ve schtopped, der vere der panners zaying Harrizon, Harrizon, Harrizon. Efferyvehere der panners—Harrizon.

MIKE: Yah, der vere panners for Harrizon, Meyer; panners vere efferyvhere for him. Budt, panners dondt vote.

MEYER: Shure, panners dondt vote. Budt, dey shure do show vhich vay der windt is plowing.

Meyer ends this Double Dutch act, shoving Mike offstage with all his towering might, as Mike protests in vain, "Don't poosh me, Meyer!" This was their standard ending for every confrontation, and it brought the house down.[14] Of note in this act is the political, if morbid, new humor with reference to President William Henry Harrison, who died after serving only one month in office from complications due to pneumonia, which he had contracted standing in the severe cold "windt" during his swearing-in ceremony—and the importance of ethnic immigrants in the awareness of and participation in the democratic process.

Reformers and cultural critics took exception to acts like Weber and Fields. In 1916, Randolph Bourne's essay "Trans-National America" advocated progressive reforms in ethnic-oriented popular entertainments. "We may thrill with dread at the aggressive hyphenate" who performs his native culture on the streets of urban centers, and the exaggeration of this same "aggressive hyphenate" on popular city stages, Bourne wrote, but "just so surely as we tend to disintegrate these nuclei of nationalistic culture do we tend to create hordes of men and women without a spiritual country, cultural outlaws, without taste, without standards but those of the mob." Bourne assumed that ethnic immigrant performers defamed and denigrated their native character and culture.[15] While Bourne called for ethnic singularity and difference to be preserved, he inadvertently reinforced Progressive reformers' notions that when popular entertainments portrayed ethnic immigrants it denigrated and debased the attempts to improve the cultural and aesthetic landscape of Americans.

Corroborating Bourne's notion that acts like Weber and Fields were dumbing down the national discourse, critic and humorist Robert Benchley wrote in a mock review of a revival of Weber and Fields' act in 1926, from the perspective of its origin in the 1890s: "Here we have the new philosophy of the subconscious, the stirrings of a new American humor which derives from the modern German school of

Merkwurdigkeit, or *Es-giebt-also-es-it*. In the American mind is being born, through the medium of the music hall, a consciousness of national social satire which bids fair to revolutionize thought on this side of the Atlantic." Benchley provides his readership with an instance of their "dialectic," noting, "Could a better example be found than in the following dialogue between these two superclowns in their latest show?":

> MIKE, *referring to offstage noises*: A soldier has been shot.
> MEYER: Vere vos he shot?
> MIKE: In de eggcitement!

"Here, in these words, lies America," Benchley taunted in his typical ironic tone. He continued: "The America of today, with its flaring gas lights, its thundering cable cars, the clatter of its hansoms, and the deafening whistle of its peanut stands. The young, vibrant spirit of America, locked in the message of two clowns! And, with the coming of jazz, twenty years from now, we shall see the full expression of the young nation's strivings toward the Greater Smooch."[16] Benchley, who performed in vaudeville and later comedy films himself, was ambivalent at best when it came to the importance of ethnic acts like Weber and Fields. Suffice it to say, he spent a lot of ink on these reviews, perhaps protesting too much.

Literary and cultural critic H. L. Mencken, in an essay titled "A Plea for Comedy," attempted to move the conversation in another direction by embracing ethnic acts like Weber's and Fields as significant to the cultural zeitgeist. Mencken saw the necessity of the comic vaudeville stage as an antidote to the self-serious rules and moral codes of Progressive-era reformers and their sympathetic audiences. In 1910, realizing the necessity of the new humor, Mencken wrote, "I have no desire to weep, to think or even to sleep when I go to a vaudeville show, but only a strong, animal yearning to guffaw."[17]

It is worth quoting Mencken at length here as he hits on key elements for explaining the necessity of the new humor's offensiveness in early-twentieth-century America. He discussed in great detail an act that was developed by Weber and Fields, whom he praised, noting that their use of "the device of fighting a duel with billiard cues, now so common on the burlesque stage, is another of their delightful inventions." Why, asks Mencken, "do we laugh so heartily when the slapstick comes down upon the assistant comedian's skull?" It was certainly not that the comedy was lowbrow and just for underclass audiences. Mencken claimed to have attended burlesque houses where "genuine vaudeville" was "still nourished and acclaimed." These audiences were "certainly not made up of newsboys and criminals" but had "plenty of both classes, true enough, upstairs," and on the first floor, "fully half" of the audience was "of the eminently respectable type." Mencken declared to have been part of audiences that comprised a diverse mixture of "doctors, lawyers, and business men, including not a few members of the Merchants and Manufacturers' Association."[18] The class division of audiences was clearly demarcated by their location either into "upstairs" and "downstairs," but the enjoyment of vaudeville's new humor and the innate desire for such rowdy, raucous, and offensive laughter bridged all social and economic boundaries.

In the 1910s, the Marx Brothers gave a unique spin to the vaudevillian ethnic act. They amalgamated several different ethnic types in varied, random, and capricious performances by donning the disguises of ethnicity and then contradicting the behaviors associated with these ethnic masks. Indeed, the Marx Brothers' highly successful career was due in no small measure to their formula of having each brother play an ethnic immigrant characterization. As early as 1910, Groucho performed a German-accented martinet of a teacher in *Fun in Hi Skule*, and although he dropped the accent after World War I and all things associated with Germany, he performed this character for almost fifteen years. Harpo began by playing a version of the Irish type known as Patsy Brannigan, an Irish peasant immigrant with a thick brogue (he was speaking at the time) and a red fright wig. Although he went silent during the tour of their vaudeville revue *Home Again*, Harpo would keep the red wig and the scrappy working-class bully character for the rest of his career. Chico began his character with the poor, fast-talking, piano-playing Italian immigrant. Chico retained this characterization for his entire career as well. Milton (Gummo), who retired from the act after only a few years to enlist during World War I, played the "Hebrew" stereotype of the Yiddish-accented Old World Jewish prototype. Even Herbert (Zeppo), playing the straight-man role, was a version of the Anglo-American pretty boy, fulfilling the stereotype as the young rake who gets all the girls with his sweet-faced and ballad-singing ingénue type.

The Marx Brothers submerged their Jewish personas and names to create a distance between their real selves as sons of Eastern Europe. Therefore Julius, Arthur, Leonard, Milton, and Herbert became Groucho, Harpo, Chico, Gummo, and Zeppo. Their caricatures of fellow eastern and southern European immigrants of German, Irish, Italian, Jewish, and Anglo heritage were donned, as they effectively disguised their ethnicity with clearly stereotyped and not very convincing immigrant masks. Their personas became iconic, and the Marx Brothers never wavered from them over their extensive and internationally successful years on the stage and screen. Even their mother, Minnie Marx, changed her name to Minnie Palmer to sound more American, and get more respect and presumably more work for her boys.

A 1919 review of *'N Everything* (a reworking of *Home Again*) emphasizes the ethnic act as played by the Marx Brothers referring to them not by name or character but by type:

> The merriest item of a good bill at the Palace Theater is provided by the Four Marx Brothers in their time-tried sketch, "['N] Everything," altered in lines here and there to keep up with the calendar. The old frame [from *Home Again*] is still used—the landing of the voyagers, the dock controversy between the Redhead, the Italian and the policeman and the Hudson house party in celebration of the arrival. The dialogue is slight, but bright, most of the merriment coming from the eccentric doings of the host [Groucho] and his guests [Harpo and Chico].[19]

The "Redhead" (Harpo) and the "Italian" (Chico) as working-class "toughs" are referred to only by their ethnic types, and their confrontation with the "policeman" is typical of the treatment of ethnic immigrants by law enforcement (even though many police officers were children of immigrants themselves). The "eccentric doings of the host" refers to Groucho in the character of the retired "German" teacher, now called Henry Hammer in this revised version of the show. The reliance on ethnic stereotypes identified by accent, hair color, and their "foreign" behavior was typical enough of ethnic acts, but the difference is the "eccentricity" and illogic—especially with physical gags—that set the Marx Brothers apart from other acts of the period.

The Marx Brothers' "nonsense" new humor of strange and nonlinear behavior onstage would be preserved famously on film—especially in *Animal Crackers*, *Monkey Business*, *Horse Feathers*, and *Duck Soup*. The comic aesthetic of these films was created in vaudeville through these early ethnic immigrant acts. *Animal Crackers*, for instance, opened on Broadway at the original 44th Street Theatre on October 23, 1928, and ran for 191 performances. It then had a yearlong national tour before its Paramount film version appeared in 1930.[20] It features a scene that describes the importance of the ethnic act as it survives in the post-vaudeville work of the Marx Brothers.

How Groucho converges with Chico and Harpo with their ethnic ambivalence can be observed in *Animal Crackers*, when they expose a character who has a part in the authoritarian structure of society and who was once from their old neighborhood. As portrayed by Louis Sorin, Abe Mandelbaum, or Abie the Fish-Peddler as they call him, is trying to pass himself off as Roscoe W. Chandler (note the ethnic, as well as social, name change). Chico confronts Chandler as "Abie the Fishman from Czechoslovakia." Chandler, when his birthmark is revealed (the mark of the social outsider), must admit that indeed he "*was* Abie the Peddler." Chico then threatens to expose Abie the Fishman by singing this lowbrow title in public while Harpo accompanies him by whistling the taunt.[21] Chandler/Abie is so afraid of being found out that he (unsuccessfully) attempts to bribe both Chico and Harpo. The scene ends in complete chaos, with Harpo stealing the symbols of Chandler's status: his pocket handkerchief, silk tie, and garters. As Chandler walks off calling Chico and Harpo "nothing but thieves," he exposes his own identity theft in the process. Harpo has the ultimate last laugh by "stealing" the evidence of Chandler's former persona in the birthmark that he has appropriated through theatrical magic onto his own arm.

Chico and Harpo have effectively exposed Chandler as someone who formerly had no part in high society and who has now been returned to his former status, thanks to the brothers' deconstructing the definitions of authority. Chico and Harpo are not so much concerned with destroying Chandler's new identity as much as with confronting the outward appearances of class and privilege as a deception that is easily uncovered by outsiders. Throughout the rest of *Animal Crackers*, we see Chandler as Abie the Fish-Peddler; however, Chico, Harpo, and Groucho know that they are playing both sides of the outsider–insider binary through their contrived roles.

Groucho adds the third part to this scene. After Chandler has been manhandled by Chico and Harpo, he is intercepted by Groucho (playing the character of Captain Spaulding), who sits him down and dismantles Chandler in a verbal tirade that strips him of any last pretentions he may have had of being an art collector and an insider. Groucho recites a monologue that brings his nonsense logic to a crescendo:

> But after all, we must remember that art is art. Still, on the other hand, water is water, isn't it? And East is East and West is West. And if you take cranberries and stew them like applesauce, they taste much more like prunes than rhubarb does. Now you tell me what you know.[22]

Chandler cannot respond at this point and indeed "forgets" his own name when he calls Groucho "Captain Chandler," to which Groucho (as Captain Spaulding) responds by finishing his sentence: "You're Chandler and I'm Spaulding. [*To audience.*] Could I see a program a minute? It might be intermission for all he knows."[23] This vaudeville-inspired two-man scene features Groucho breaking the binaries of rich and poor, high- and lowbrow, ethnic and Anglo-American. It echoed the ethnic acts that the Marx Brothers began their careers with and continued to develop into their later film, radio, and television work.

Family acts were also instrumental in defying expectations of Americanness in vaudeville. To ensure an American assimilation of sociocultural values, Progressive reformers, under the aegis of legislative and legal authorities, especially with regard to public education and leisure-time activities and entertainments, began to call for controls and reformations around the burgeoning city populations at the turn of the century into the first two decades of the twentieth century. The new working- and middle-class relationship to culture, and popular comic entertainment in particular, became a defining element in becoming an American. Self-appointed reform groups, like the Committee of Fourteen, the New York Society for the Prevention of the Cruelty to Children, and the League for Social Service, began campaigns to negotiate and develop social structures and laws that would adhere to the newly forming standards of middle-class Anglo-Americans.

Vaudeville's myriad performers and acts represented a larger sociocultural shift that symbolized the ever-changing demographics of America at the turn of the twentieth century. Multiple generations of comic performers began to spread across the United States under the auspices of the vaudeville circuit. "In early acts," according to Joe Laurie,

> the material consisted of what [I] call "knick-knacks"—song and dance, cross-fire talk of unconnected gags, playing musical instruments, and acrobatics. They put everything they knew into their acts. Ninety-five per cent of them were Irish; later the Germans, Hebrews, and Italians came along; and still later the children of all of them, Americans, took over.[24]

The direct link to the eastern and southern European tradition from "ninety-five percent" of immigrants can be attributed to the acts that Laurie followed in his youth.

Vaudeville's fusion of American performance traditions like minstrel shows, concert saloons, variety shows, and burlesque combined with the eastern and southern European forms of comic entertainment found in the *commedia dell'arte*, the Yiddish theater, and the circus. The new humor exposed the immigrant influx of cultures and ethnicities that was in the process of redefining the notion of being American and, more significantly, the American family. For many Americans, this was their first contact with unfamiliar customs, languages, and ethics of people now living all around them. Vaudeville relied on the family as many performers started very young, like Buster Keaton, the Marx Brothers, and the Elinore Sisters, and for many comedians in family acts, this continued the traveling and migration that led them to America. The family act presented a comic look at ethnicity and class within the domestic dynamic from the confusions and trials of being an outsider in a new country to generational and marital strife.

How vaudeville comedians chose to undermine the strictures that were being forced on them by Progressive reformers and critics can be witnessed in the family act. Laurie describes the family act in his vaudeville history, writing that "the kids got tired waiting in the wings, and eventually Pop and Mom would take them out for a bow." According to Laurie, the children would develop an itch to be part of their parents' act. "It was a short step from just taking a bow to letting the kid do a bit," he writes. By being backstage and on the road for so many years, children began to know all the acts they came into contact with. Laurie goes on to say that they "could imitate anybody, so when they did something real good, the parents were kinda proud, and instead of standing 'em up in a parlor to recite to the company, they would stick 'em on the stage to do it in front of an audience, and if it was good, they'd keep it in the act (where there were no laws against it)."[25] Another reason for featuring kids in the act was the profit motive, pure and simple. As Laurie puts it, "Some of 'em made more dough at the age of eight than most bank presidents."[26] The family act called into question the values of the middle-class family and its Anglo-American restraint and civility, in comparison with the outspoken Jewish families of the Lower East Side of New York City, the boisterous Irish clans of the Five Points, and the Italian *famiglias* of Little Italy.

A family act that confirmed the importance of the new humor featured Buster Keaton in the Three Keatons. Keaton was to become famous as a child and young adult star of vaudeville beginning with his first entrance on the vaudeville stage at the age of six months. He was soon to be a staple of the family act of father, mother, and son at the age of three, and from then on he became the star attraction. Keaton was ultimately catapulted into the world of silent film comedy, which he dominated along with Roscoe "Fatty" Arbuckle during the 1910s and early 1920s. As Keaton's career began overshadowing his parents', his mother retired and his father would stay with him performing secondary roles in his films. Buster's two siblings, Harry and Louise, also took to the stage as child performers, but they soon chose lives outside the entertainment world, while Buster would become an international sensation.[27]

In this family act, Joe Keaton would don the garb of a stereotypical drunken Irish "Mick" from the old country who gets intoxicated and flies off the handle, ready to beat his disobedient son. Joe Keaton is quoted in his son's memoir, saying, "One day I got the idea of dressing [Buster] up like myself as a stage Irishman with a fright wig, slugger whiskers, fancy vest, and over-size pants. Soon [Buster] was imitating everything I did, and getting laughs."[28] This bizarre doppelgänger, the Irish costume, and drunken violence brought a stereotyped image of the ethnic immigrant family to the comic vaudeville stage. As one reviewer noted in 1903:

> Keaton *père* comes on the stage in the full glory of red galways, a comic makeup, consisting of face white-plastered to the cheekbones, where a rosy flush forms a sharp angle, coming to a point just beneath the eyes. He wears loose, baggy trousers, no coat, and white spats. Baby Buster is made up and dressed exactly like his father, but his diminutive face and figure increase the ludicrous effect in his case.[29]

Buster Keaton and father Joe, as mirror images, parodied the Irish immigrant of the lower classes. Father and son as comic "foreigners" traded on the hunger for the new humor of ethnicity in America.

For those Anglo-Americans who did not comprehend the social satire, the lowbrow types and their simplistic surface pleasures provided amusement. The clashes of class and ethnicity, both onstage and in the audience, reflected not only the difficulty of assimilation but also the rejection by some comic vaudevillians of being easily mocked as ignorant and crude stereotypes. The hierarchy of authority between parents and children was also derided, as well as notions of class and ethnicity. The success of the new humor was reinforced as acts like the Three Keatons "killed" audiences from all backgrounds across the United States wherever they toured. In 1909, the *New York Dramatic Mirror* would reflect what many critics and audiences felt about this trio of comedians, and Buster in particular:

> [The Three Keatons] came on third, opening with the comedy tumbling done by Joe and the now quite manly Buster, who attained his sixteenth year on October fourth. The throws, falls and tumbles done by him are on a par with the best work of this sort that has been seen on any stage, and the laughter caused by the comedy business, facial [Irish] make-up, eccentric costumes and the clever clowning of both father and son, was incessant during the entire act.[30]

The Three Keatons serve as a distinctive example of the effectiveness of the new humor in ethnic immigrant family acts, and how performers could put it over in vaudeville.

Ethnic humor–based comedians appeared to be well aware of the absurd aspiration to the American myth of success that was built on keeping immigrants and the native-born lower classes from achieving the status of "real" Americans. The new immigrant's need to assimilate to the prescribed Americanness was reflected in the satire of rejecting one's ethnic origins, which appeared to comic vaudevillians as a foolish attempt to seek upward mobility.

The danger that the Anglo-American middle classes perceived was the rise in popularity of these lowbrow comic entertainers who laughed at their desire to achieve the status of middlebrow respectability. In mocking the triumph of this fantasy image of Americanness over the socioeconomic realities of urban life, as well as using conflict between classes to produce satirical laughter, the family act reflected the new wave of comedy that would begin to dominate not only the American stage, but migrate to silent and early sound comedy films well into the 1930s, thanks to the success of vaudevillians like the Three Keatons.

Another means of Progressive reform would threaten the well-being of the family act. Associations like the Committee of Fourteen and the New York Society for the Prevention of Cruelty to Children, which barred child actors from the stage, would, over the next ten years, attempt to shut down the Three Keatons and jail Buster's parents for the supposed abuses they were enacting onstage with their underage son. However, the popularity of the act ultimately overruled the reformers' objections. A typical review, when Buster was only eight years old, from the *New York Clipper* reads, "The tiny comedian is perfectly at ease in his work, natural, finished and artistic, and his specialties have proved a fetching addition to the favorite act of the Keatons, that is known all over the land by its title, 'The Man with the Table.'"[31] This act began when Buster was five years old and included his parents and one prop: a battered kitchen table. As Buster describes it in his autobiography, the act "went on with our rage mounting until we were fighting wildly, blasting, kicking, punching, and throwing one another across the table and all over the stage...with the audience shrieking, Mom placidly continued playing her saxophone."[32] This family act with the child Buster being chased and thrown around by his real-life father can be viewed as a form of comic satire on the son who baits his father and rejects patriarchal authority. The father in turn becomes a violent despot determined to make his son behave by his rules, while the mother appears oblivious to this domestic violence. The kitchen table, which

Buster uses as a playground and a refuge to elude capture and hide from his abusive father, symbolizes the domestic world that has spun out of control.

The table chase was re-created in *The Taming of the Snood* (1940), a short sound comedy.[33] The athleticism and stage violence that left Buster, as child and adult, unscathed is a testimony to his skill. Keaton described the early act in a pleasurable and proud way:

> Even in my early days our turn established a reputation for being the roughest in vaudeville... He began these by carrying me out on the stage and dropping me on the floor. Next he started wiping up the floor with me. When I gave no sign of minding this he began throwing me through the scenery, out into the wings, and dropping me down on the bass drum in the orchestra pit.[34]

The irony of audiences embracing the Three Keatons, while reformers tried to shut down these "harmful" performances, was evident when audiences clamored for more and critics praised their skills. In 1914, the *Syracuse Herald* recognized the early stage genius of Buster Keaton:

> For The Three Keatons, I feel an almost family interest... How the Keatons ever managed to raise that boy I am sure I don't know. Beating a boy up and slinging him around the way Joe Keaton does twice daily would not be my method of raising, unless I wanted to plant the boy and raise him like a string bean. But Buster enjoys it and gets his share back at "the old man," and the unique knockabout fun of the Keaton family is just as funny as ever.[35]

As Keaton's career would attest, for the child Buster, one way out of the poverty of the working classes was through the vaudeville circuit. Progressive reformers would continue to haunt the Three Keatons until Buster's coming-of-age in 1912.

Meanwhile, the critique and satire of American society was given a unique spin by the Elinore Sisters, a comedy duo who merged the ethnic act with the family act. Will M. Cressy, in "Putting It Over," cites only one female comic performer as having mastered this aspect of vaudeville, writing that not only did Kate Elinore put it over, she "*blows* them over."[36] Kate and May Elinore worked as a comic vaudeville duo from 1894 to 1909. Kate portrayed the wild and masculine Irish, immigrant, working-class servant to May's Anglo-American feminine authority figure. Kate, born in 1876 and raised in Brooklyn, New York, made her first appearance with May in an "eccentric act" in Atlantic City, on July 30, 1894. According to the *Who's Who in Music and Drama* from 1914, the Elinore Sisters were "reputed to be the first act of the kind to be shown."[37] In 1896, the Elinore Sisters joined Tony Pastor's Company in New York and later joined Harry William's Own Company and Hopkins' Trans-Atlantics. Kate and May's last recorded performance as a sister act was at the Fifth Avenue Theater, New York, June 1909.[38] Kate Elinore went on to star as a musical comedy actress, most notably in the 1910 Victor Herbert comic opera *Naughty Marietta*. She married Sam Williams, a musical composer, working together in vaudeville from 1909 to 1924. Kate Elinore worked right up until her death in 1924, playing the Palace Theater in New York and the Los Angeles Orpheum Theater that same year.[39]

The Elinore Sisters' acts critiqued and satirized the conflict between servants and their masters in the American class system, particularly the Irish immigrant in conflict with her Anglo-American superior. Kate Elinore mocked and exaggerated traits associated with the Irish underclass, while also commenting on the ethnic immigrant's ability to outwit and undermine the supposedly more civilized Anglo-American women of authority, as portrayed by May. Kate and May portrayed contrasting American characters: women divided by culture, class, and ethnic identity. The many misunderstandings between Kate's rude, tough, and rebellious immigrant characters and May's refined, American-born, middle- and upper-class ladies made them one of the early female family acts to perform ethnic acts.

A 1906 interview with Elinore noted that she had "determined to carve out a new pathway for herself, one which women had never before trodden. 'I'm going to do something different, something grotesque,' she said."[40] This notion of the grotesque is recalled again in 1909, when one reviewer was shocked but pleasantly pleased by Kate's lowbrow and "masculine" comedy. "She is one of those marvels Heaven seldom sends us—a truly funny woman," he explained. She "is a low comedienne who does not mind making herself look ugly or ridiculous in order to make her audience laugh."[41] In her 1914 history of vaudeville, Caroline Caffin writes about Elinore's onstage persona, saying, "Never was a woman less troubled with self-consciousness. Her face is one broad, expansive smile which seems to radiate from the top of her little nob of hair . . . and from every angle of her square built frame."[42] Describing Kate Elinore in a sketch from *The Adventures of Bridget McGuire*, one critic wrote, "No woman ever made such a persistent attempt to look ugly,"[43] and still another reviewer noted, "Her make-up is a nightmare of milliner's art. Her voice makes a fog horn sound like an echo."[44] As Kate Elinore discussed in one interview, "It's quite a common thing with us to have the daily papers insist that I am a man for reasons all their own, and many is the letter received asking us to settle a dispute or wager."[45] Kate's supposed grotesque masculinity and that of her various stage characters was formed from traditions associated with two immigrant types: the Irish domestic and the "old maid."

Kate is a prime instance of the female slapstick clown who ran counter to male-driven ethnic comedy in vaudeville. One of the reformers and theatrical producers' principal objections to female comic vaudevillians was not only their lowbrow new humor but also their usurpation of the ethnic immigrant act, considered the sole purview of male comedians. Elinore was an early anomaly, a female performer who could portray characters and use language usually reserved for men onstage. In 1908, theater reviewer Robert Speare objected to the new woman on the comic stage, describing Kate and May as an "absolutely novel woman act . . . The idea is that of the straight comedian and the rough comedian, only instead of its being two men now it is two women."[46] However, not all theater producers rejected the notion of female comic vaudevillians, and some even found them a welcome relief and a lucrative asset to old and exhausted acts. Vaudeville theater manager Charles Lovenberg, referring to Kate Elinore during another 1908 sketch with a male partner, writes:

> This act was a great surprise for in it was found a woman who is actually funny almost as much so as the comedienne of the Elinore sisters. She makes up as an eccentric country girl and has a very funny line of talk, and the novelty of the woman doing the comedy and the man, the straight work, is very acceptable.[47]

The reversal of the female/male double act was to play a significant part in the Elinore Sisters' success. As early as 1897, Kate began playing tough soubrettes, as in *The Irish 400*, in which she portrayed Mrs. Murphy, who torments and embarrasses her daughter, played by sister May. In defiance, Mrs. Murphy's daughter is overwhelmed by her mother's crudeness, her over-indulgent and nostalgic reverence for Ireland, and her lack of femininity. As recorded in the Elinore Sister's vaudeville archives, in one scene, "May admonishes her mother for spitting on the floor of the streetcar. Mrs. Murphy then spits into the conductor's pocket, and they are kicked out of the car."[48] In another part of the act, May is visibly upset when her mother interrupts a concert by a famous Polish pianist, Ignacy Paderewski, to ask her during a very quiet moment, "Phwat county in Ireland did Paddy Roosky come from?"[49] Not only is Kate portraying a loud and abrasive Irish immigrant mother, she plays it with a masculine crudeness that had been associated exclusively with male character comedians up until this time.

The Elinore Sisters appeared in a series of maid–employer sketches titled *The Adventures of Bridget McGuire*. Featuring the relationship between an Anglo-American employer and her Irish immigrant housekeeper, the sketches toured on the Keith circuit in 1902. Bridget McGuire, played by Kate Elinore, has large appetites for both food and alcohol that upset her employer, Mrs. Rapps, portrayed by May. A typical sketch involves Mrs. Rapps discovering Bridget as she reaches for a decanter of whiskey, and Bridget braying at her, saying, "That's not the first time whiskey has been the downfall of Ireland."[50]

The subsequent scenes highlight Bridget's brazen forthrightness and Mrs. Rapp's upper-class pretensions and aspirations. When Mrs. Rapps mistakes Bridget for her wealthy, eccentric aunt and flatters her in hopes of winning an inheritance, she offers Bridget some "refreshment," which Bridget initially declines, assuming the manner of what she believes to be a wealthy dowager, saying, "No thank you, I never drink anything." However, Bridget "grabs a glass" from her "hostess" and then begins to drink straight from the decanter, explaining, "If you insist—I don't mind if I take a little drop."[51] Bridget continues drinking throughout the sketch, and this allows her to openly defy and insult her employer. Mrs. Rapps professes a belief in the fashionable "spiritualism" of the time, cagily asking, "Are you afraid of spirits, Auntie?" to which Bridget responds, "Not when I can get them by the neck," as she holds up a bottle of whiskey.[52] Ultimately, this simple mistaken identity scenario reinforces Bridget's immigrant toughness and crudeness, as she raises her status over that of her employer by exposing her posturing.[53]

The gender transgressors portrayed by Kate in sketches like *The Adventures of Bridget McGuire* depicted various defiant female characters placed in direct opposition to society ladies, portrayed by her sister, for whom she was in service. As performed by Kate, the Irish maid—with her fighting spirit, insults, sexual curiosity, and outrageous bluntness—challenged and mocked the definition of the female so central to the reformers' notion of appropriate women's social behaviors, while exposing the hypocrisy and snobbery of the middle and upper-middle classes with respect to May's characters. The resistance of working-class women characters in positions of submission exhibited a rejection of upward mobility on Anglo-American, middle-class terms. Comic performers like Kate Elinore refused the notion that the working poor, and in particular the women of the working class, should stay in their place in terms of both their prescribed class and gender roles.

Caroline Caffin remarked that Kate was "the most familiar of friends with her audience, not only as a whole but individually and separately."[54] Elinore's influence over the audience was witnessed when she used "a gesture," wrote Caffin, "to mark when she thinks her points have hit the mark." This gesture between Kate and her audience acknowledged a collusion between performer and spectator when she pointed "her finger, as though it were a pistol, at some individual in the audience," screwed "up one eye as though to sight," and clicked "with her mouth to make the sound of a shot."[55] Her control over her audience and her attitude that she shared a personal relationship with her fans broke the aesthetic distance that highbrow stage shows encouraged, as if to say, "We are the same, you and I, and like friends we share a special coded language of solidarity." As Caffin concluded, "Her audience is speedily engulfed in laughter like a rock at high tide. And how she responds to and gloats over their mirth, and reabsorbs it to radiate it on them again."[56] The audience was acknowledged by her performances as fellow outsiders, laughing together at the ethnic and class divisions suffered on both sides of the footlights. By undermining the power and authority of established Americans by ethnic immigrants who were meant to be their inferiors, performers like the Elinore

Sisters exposed the sociocultural divisions embraced by middle-class Progressive reformers and critics.

The new humor of the American underclasses revealed how vaudeville comedy capitalized on a fragmented, gag-driven humor reflecting a world in social turmoil and its restructuring of values with significant emphasis on the new, the unique, and the protean. The pressures from Progressive reformers forced the comic vaudevillians to either go underground or work around the parameters of their restrictions with the new humor. Progressives exploited class divisions in their attempts to Americanize citizens. Lower-class ethnic immigrants were targeted for bringing their lowbrow values and culture from eastern and southern Europe, as well as from Ireland and Germany, to infiltrate, denigrate, and laugh at the American middle classes from the vaudeville stage. The fear of America's underclasses' sociocultural values, which opposed those of the genteel middle classes, provided Progressive reformers with the initiative to censure popular entertainments. The popular comic stage came to represent the continuous struggle against the "culture of the power-bloc,"[57] which in the late nineteenth century was represented by the Anglo-American middle and upper classes. The new humor, through ethnic acts and family acts, questioned these values and began to blur the boundaries of American culture and morality. The "Double Dutch" act of Joe Weber and Lew Fields, along with the ethnic and family acts of the Three Keatons, the Marx Brothers, and the Elinore Sisters, illustrate how the new humor presented challenges to Americanization, even as Progressive reformers, critics, and authorities attempted to curb and shield these acts from middle-class Anglo-American audiences.

4. The Marx Brothers Go to School

The conflict between progressive education reformers and comic vaudevillians can be observed with the Marx Brothers and their school act. The Marx Brothers, from their beginnings in the third-tier vaudeville circuit where they formed the core comedic trio of Chico, Harpo, and Groucho, will be explored through an evaluation of the ethnic, class, and comic social commentary in their various school acts. I bookend the vaudeville performances of the Marx Brothers beginning in 1910 with *Fun In Hi Skule* and ending with the 1932 film *Horse Feathers* (their final incarnation of the school act), examining the three central Marx Brothers, Chico, Harpo, and Groucho, collectively and individually, in order to trace the development of their unique interpretation of this vaudeville routine.[1]

In order to examine the school act it is first necessary to look at the state of education reform during the Progressive era. In the early 1900s, Progressive reformers, such as Jane Addams, John Dewey, Elbridge Thomas Gerry, and Edgar Gardner Murphy, had taken on the transformation of public education and child labor and welfare. One instance was seen under the auspices of the New York Society for the Prevention of Cruelty to Children (the Gerry Society) that insisted minors on the vaudeville stage were required to be sixteen years or older before they could perform legally. Although this law was meant to keep children out of the sweatshops and factories and in schools, it would have adverse effects on the working-poor classes that depended on a daily income in order to survive. Buster Keaton's father, Joe, noted the hypocrisy of the Gerry Society that ended up contradicting its benevolent ideals by ignoring the real issues of child welfare. Joe Keaton pointed out that there were thousands of homeless, hungry, and abandoned children roving the streets of New York, "selling newspapers, shining shoes, playing the fiddle on the Hudson River ferryboats, and thousands of other small children working with their parents in the tenement sweatshops on the Lower East Side." Joe Keaton could not understand "why the S.P.C.C.[2] people didn't devote all of their time, energy, and money to helping them."[3]

As the twentieth century began, reformers were trying to promote a way of life that allowed new immigrants to adapt in order to become model American citizens from an early age. In 1903, southern child labor reformer Edgar Gardner Murphy created a platform in order to reach the youth population as soon as possible in order to get them on the road to Americanization before they had a chance of being corrupted by sociocultural changes. Murphy thought schools should teach four key "disciplines": "punctuality, order, and silence," and most importantly, "association."[4] Association referred to the company a young person kept and interacted with. It dictated which collective he or she was to become part of, and ultimately how that association would reflect on them in the greater social setting. Institutions known as "Associations" would become popular tools for reformers to spread their message including Lodges, Social Groups, Boys' and Girls' Clubs, and Guilds.[5]

In 1909, Professor Ellwood Cubberley put forward a strategy for education reform writing, "Our task is to break up [new immigrant] groups or settlements, to assimilate and amalgamate these people as part of our American race and to implant in their children, so far as it can be done, the Anglo-Saxon conception of law and order and popular government."[6] The assimilation of the underclasses into the "American race" was to begin in public schools. The extent to which education reform was to be used to Americanize students was extolled by former Princeton University professor and US President Woodrow Wilson who, in 1916, praised the "self-examination, a process of purification, a process of rededication to the things which America represents and is proud to represent," through school reforms.[7]

In addition to Murphy and Cubberley, education reformers such as Jane Addams, John Dewey, and E. A. Ross would champion public schooling as a path to Americanness. The Americanizing of public school students was important in influencing and reinforcing an Anglo-American, middle-class heritage, morality, and nationalism. By instituting the "Pledge of Allegiance" to ensure loyalty to America, silencing native languages, and erasing cultural markers in order not to appear or sound foreign, early childhood education emphasized and insisted upon an American ethos beginning at the earliest possible age.

"A far-sighted policy, such as the training of the young is," as early-twentieth-century American sociologist E. A. Ross remarked, "preferable to the summary regulation of the adult."[8] Social molding and control of children was to begin in public school education in order to combat the individualism of the new immigrant who could not yet fully comprehend nor appreciate the values of Anglo-Americans. Concerns arose about such individualism being permitted and perhaps encouraged by parents of children newly arrived to the United States. In 1904, Colorado education reformer Anna Garlin Spencer speculated whether immigrant mothers and fathers allowed their children too much freedom writing, "We have removed from the single pair and their children all the props and discipline of the patriarchal family, and now we are rapidly democratizing the family. We are even afraid of controlling effectively our own children lest we check their growth toward self-government."[9] The solution, according to Progressive-reform historian Joseph F. Kett, was public schooling, as it was "the period of childhood when character is plastic and can be moulded for good or evil as clay in the potter's hands."[10] Ross referred to this process as "breaking in the colt to the harness."[11] In an effort to "break" the willful and unruly habits of the ethnic immigrant child, reformers advocated for the increased centralization of control over the upbringing of American youth through teachers and school administrators. Reformers assumed a cultural illiteracy simply because immigrant students spoke in accented English and were from working-poor backgrounds. It was implicit that these children were ignorant and had to be trained and tamed like unbroken wild animals in order to transform them into loyal and dutiful Americans.[12]

Education reformer and philosopher John Dewey, who ran an experimental "Laboratory" School at the University of Chicago, and was the author of such books as *School and Society* and *The Child and the Curriculum*, helped launch what would become known as Progressive education. Dewey, although advocating the learning of "individuality" by the respective child, did not think that students should develop arbitrarily as the spirit moved them, but had to be shepherded. He warned that "the danger of the 'new education' [is] that it regards the child's present powers and interests as something finally significant in themselves."[13] Therefore, while at the same time advocating for the education of students as individuals and opposing generic group learning, Dewey pressed for a middle-class Anglo-American version of culture and literacy. Education reform was meant to encourage the development of students by moving them away from their eastern and southern European immigrant cultural values and heritage. The Americanization of new immigrant children was often rejected by their parents, who looked to private schools for educational needs or simply had their children go to work in family-run shops and labor-intensive jobs, providing an apprenticeship for them alongside adults with similar backgrounds, languages, and ethics.

Progressive reformers had a profound impact on education reform. According to sociologist Hal S. Barron, "from 1900 to 1909, the enrollment rate for children aged 5 to 19 in all types of schools rose from 50 per 100 to 59; public secondary-school enrollments grew from 519,000 to 841,000; expenditures per pupil in public schools increased from $14 to $24; and the average public school term lengthened from 144 days in 1900 to 155 days in 1909."[14] The shift in higher enrollment was primarily due to reformers and the pressure they put on parents and school administrators alike. Ultimately, the reformers supported the child's individuality because it served their interests in regulating, if not outright eradicating, the behavior of other classes—especially the working underclasses. When they encouraged "the young creature's assertion that he is unlike any other human being," they were really hoping that the child would reject their parents' way of life, and embrace an Americanness born of the Anglo-middle classes.[15]

Popular entertainments became a battleground for reformers, critics, and authorities in the efforts to Americanize immigrant children. Vaudeville would come under attack particularly with regard to ethnic comedy acts that featured children and young people. Reformers and critics alike saw a need to combat immigrant popular entertainments by diverting the attentions of the younger generation with leisure time that produced more edifying pleasures and wholesome divertissements that could be strictly monitored by adults who shared their same Progressive values. In the early 1900s, reformers like Jane Addams noted what she called "the insatiable desire for play."[16] She felt the need to deter young people from dance halls, saloons, and vaudeville, which she thought inevitably led to criminal and sexual experimentation. "To fail to provide for the recreation of youth," according to Addams, "is not only to deprive all of them of their natural form of expression, but is certain to subject some of them to the overwhelming temptation of illicit and soul-destroying pleasures."[17] Children were meant not only to play in carefully monitored environments, they were to be separated by gender in the effort to Americanize them. This would lead to the promotion of "girls work" and "boys work" from 1900 to 1910. For instance, social critics like Marion Lawrence, an upper-class Boston "concerned citizen," touted the North Bennet Street Boys' Club for the "underprivileged"—mainly Irish and Italian adolescent boys—that would ensure that immigrant boys adhere to the club rules and that they "mustn't get excited, chew gum, spit, swear, cheat or talk Italian."[18] These clubs were meant to reinforce American values and gender roles, according to Lawrence and other members of her social circle who saw these young immigrants as an affront to Americanness. The playground and club movements were encouraged by reformers and authorities who wanted professional supervisors to schedule and regulate children's leisure activities. Addams and her fellow reformers felt that the influence of stage performers would encourage these same young people to explore immoral behaviors in addition to encouraging the rejection of authority of familial, religious, and political leaders, as modeled from comedic vaudeville acts. One of the acts that would directly confront and satirize the education reformers' agenda was the school act.

The Marx Brothers are a case in point of a family act comprising children of new immigrants who derided the American public school education system onstage (see figure 4.1). Born of eastern European Jewish immigrant parents and growing up in New York City's then Upper East Side ghetto at the end of the nineteenth century, the Marx Brothers—Leonard (born 1887), Arthur (born Adolph, 1888), Julius (born 1890), Milton (born 1892), and Herbert (born 1901)—spent nearly twenty-five years in vaudeville before their international success in Hollywood films. Their formative years on the vaudeville stage took many forms and multiple variations of individual acts, until they

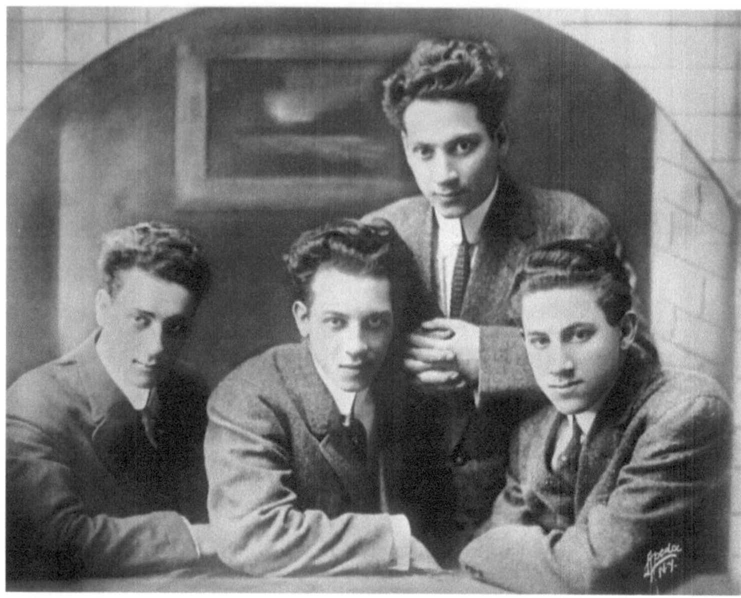

Figure 4.1 The Marx Brothers—Groucho (age 26), Chico (age 29), Harpo (age 28), and Gummo (age 23)—December 1916; Billy Rose Theatre Division, New York Public Library for the Performing Arts, Astor, Lenox, and Tilden Foundations.

formed the now ubiquitous characterizations known as Chico, Harpo, Groucho, Gummo, and Zeppo.[19]

Before the brothers became a family vaudeville act, the youngest of the three, Groucho (but long before he was called by his stage name) set them on the road to stardom. Groucho was the first Marx brother to work in vaudeville beginning his career in 1905 at the age of fifteen when he joined an act called the Leroy Trio.[20] According to Groucho's autobiography, *Groucho and Me*, he discovered an ad in the *New York Morning World* stating: "Boy singer wanted for star vaudeville act. Room and board and four dollars a week."[21] Robin Leroy, a middle-aged singer/dancer, and self-proclaimed vaudeville star, hired the fifteen-year-old Groucho as a singer, along with a teenaged male dancer named Johnny Morris to complete the trio. Groucho observes his youthful exuberance for his newfound profession in his autobiography: "I was in show business, even if it was only two weeks…I felt for the first time in my life I wasn't a nonentity. I was part of the Larong [sic] Trio. I was an actor. My dream had come true."[22]

To give a taste of what the quality of this small-time act was like, Groucho describes the end of his first vaudeville tour in Grand Rapids, Michigan, where, "Larong [sic] closed the act dressed as the Statue of Liberty and holding a torch in his hand. Morton and I were decked out as Continental soldiers, guarding Miss Liberty from her unseen enemies. The unseen enemies turned out to be the audience, and only the fact that the theatre was almost empty by this time saved us from being stoned."[23] The reality of show business became clear to Groucho when they played their final engagement in Cripple Creek, Colorado, and found that Leroy had skipped town with the act and Groucho's pay. "I don't know where dire straits is," reflects Groucho, "but I certainly was now in that neighborhood. No money, no job, a minimum of talent and far, far from home. It was no use writing my mother and father for money. They didn't have any, either."[24]

Soon after his ignominious return from the road, Groucho's development as a vaudevillian would become closely aligned with his early collaboration with his brothers and their act put together by his mother, Minnie, in 1907. Of the three brothers, only Julius spent more than two years in grammar school—he attended until he was twelve years old. Chico spent two years in school and Harpo only for a year and a half.[25] Minnie Marx, seeing no prospects for her public school dropout sons, and witnessing the success of Groucho's vaudevillian uncle, Al Shean (who would become partners in a successful double act with Edward Gallagher), decided that a show business career was a way out of poverty for her family. Minnie created the act out of a conventional group of singers and dancers first known as the Three Nightingales. This trio consisted of Groucho, his brother Milton (Gummo), and a young female singer named Mabel O'Donnell.[26] As the act progressed, it would become the Four Nightingales, adding Arthur (Harpo) as a fourth nightingale. Eventually Minnie's marketing plan for the act would include her adding more performers and renaming the act the Six Mascots—regardless of how many actual performers there were in the act at any given time. Faced with stages that often were not stages at all, but unstable benches at one end of an open hall, dressing rooms that were really backyards, and pay that they more often than not never received, the Nightingales and/or Mascots ultimately became the Four Marx Brothers by adding Herbert (Zeppo) in 1917—when Gummo left the act to enlist in the army during World War I. The Marx Brothers ultimately distanced themselves from their Jewish immigrant roots by renaming themselves: Leonard became Chico; Adolph (aka Arthur) became Harpo; Julius became Groucho; Milton became Gummo; Herbert became Zeppo.

The pressure of pleasing audiences through improvisational and nonsensical comedy only improved the Marx Brothers' craft of disruptive humor. According to Groucho, the intensity of a diverse vaudeville-touring schedule was the key to their success: "We played three days in Burlington, Iowa, caught the train overnight and played the following four days in Waterloo. This was very hard work: four-a-day[27] for five days equals twenty shows; five-a-day for two days equals ten more shows, for a total of thirty shows per week."[28] A review from this period comments on the importance of their far-reaching appeal: "the Marx Brothers introduce a variety of amusements, indeed it is hard to find a theatrical accomplishment they do not excel in that is not incorporated in their performance."[29]

The brothers' first successful vaudeville routine was a school act titled *Fun In Hi Skule* (1910)—the intentional misspelling of the title confirmed how poorly public school had educated them. The failure of the public schools for these children, in addition to the Marx Brothers' resistance to the American formal education system, paved the way for their school act. *Fun In Hi Skule* and its later incarnations with *Mr. Green's Reception* (1912), *Home Again* (1914), and the film *Horse Feathers* (1932) demonstrate how the new humor satirized and critiqued Progressive-era education reform at the beginning of the twentieth century.

The focus of education reformers was on reinforcing the insider status of Anglo-Americans by making sure that the outsider position of ethnic immigrants and their children would remain in place if they did not assimilate and embrace Anglo authority. The Marx Brothers in the school act represented the insider/outsider conflict of class and ethnicity. Harpo relates a childhood anecdote in his autobiography that shows how the public school system treated the underclasses: "my formal schooling ended halfway through my second crack at the second grade." Harpo attributes this unceremonious ending to his formal schooling with "two causes," one being "a big Irish kid, and the other was a bigger Irish kid," and "I was the only Jewish boy in the room."[30] In addition to the anti-Semitic bullying, Harpo's second grade teacher, Miss Flatto, "had pretty much given up on teaching me anything. Miss Flatto liked to predict, in front of the class, that I would come to no good end." He was constantly harassed by his "Irisher" classmates who "would pick me up and throw me out the window and into the street" from an eight-foot drop. Miss Flatto, who scolded him for leaving the room without permission, saying, "'Some day you will *realize*, young man, you will *realize*!' I didn't know what she meant, but I never forgot her words." After months of this treatment, "one sunny day when Miss Flatto left the room and I was promptly heaved into the street, I picked myself up, turned my back on P.S. 86 and walked straight home, and that was the end of my formal education."[31] This childhood incident would be recreated in the school act, with Groucho as Herr Teacher, berating Harpo with "can't you get *noddings* [sic] through your thick head?" Harpo, portraying Patsy Brannigan, the ignorant, trouble-making "Irisher," proved Herr Teacher right, becoming a street tough who survived by being a thief, a gambler, a liar, and a fighter. He reappears in *Mr. Green's Reception* after twenty years as a garbage man who has amounted to no good, because of the poor schooling he received at the hands of Herr Teacher.

The school act was not unique to the Marx Brothers as it was a vaudeville routine with many incarnations. As described by former vaudevillian Joe Laurie, Jr., the standard school act featured a teacher ("a Dutchman with chin piece" or faux goatee) and a cast of students representing ethnic and physical types ("Tony—Italian; Abey Maloney Goldstein—Jewish Boy; and Jesse James—Tough").[32] In the school act, an authoritarian primary school teacher led a class of ethnically stereotyped students. The perceived ignorance of the typically European immigrant students, and the overbearing teacher's frustration with them, were the sources of the comedy. The focus of the act was the frustration of the teacher with the stereotypical ignorance of the students. The institution of school was represented by a teacher who demanded that the students correctly answer his relentless and arbitrary questions. Ultimately the teacher sought a rote answer that his students should have parroted back to him. A series of "wrong" answers would come from the uncomprehending students. Some students deliberately misunderstood while others simply did not know the required answers. Each time a student gave a wrong answer, he was hit "on the head with an umbrella," among other objects readily at hand.[33] Henry Jenkins states: "Perhaps why 'school acts' were so popular with audiences had to do with the nature of comedy and its relationship to the defiance of authority."[34] The "defiance of authority" came naturally to the Marx Brothers.

By the first decade of the twentieth century, vaudeville featured many popular school acts, including Gus Edwards, Herman Timberg, and the Marx Brothers. In 1908 Herman Timberg was the star of Gus Edwards's *School Days* that played at the Circle Theater. Edwards had developed an act featuring vaudeville comedian Timberg, creating a success with what would become the popular school act. According to the Brooklyn-based newspaper *The Citizen*:

> One of vaudeville's keenest comedy noses, [and] not a bad looking one at that, arrives with the person of Herman Timberg, music hall impresario, at the E. F. Albee Theatre this week. Herman and his brother Sammy, two of the smartest young Jewish boys from New York's East Side has produced, which is saying something, are offering a sportive and diverting concoction which they have named, appropriately enough, "The Laugh Factory."[35]

Timberg and his "Laugh Factory" had established an excellent reputation by producing one of the most accomplished school acts in vaudeville at the turn of the twentieth century. As Timberg himself told *The Citizen*, "it was his dependable sleuthing that unearthed the Four Marx Brothers, who lately starred in: *The Cocoanuts* [written with Herman Timberg] and supplied them with much of the comedy material which brought them recognition, first in a Timberg production in vaudeville [known as *School Days*]."[36]

The Broadway version of a school act called *School Days* opened at the Circle Theatre in New York City on September 14, 1908. With lyrics by Will Cobb and music by Gus Edwards, the song "School Days" was the featured number of the show and by 1910 vaudeville was full of imitations of this successful act. The then-unknown comedy team of the Marx Brothers followed the trend of the school act that had assured fellow comedians of financial and artistic rewards and led them to create their own adaptation of *School Days—Fun In Hi Skule.* The success of this Marx Brothers' school act lasted two years, beginning in the summer of 1910, and ending in September of 1912 when they switched to a sequel to this show entitled *Mr. Green's Reception. Fun In Hi Skule* was the Marx Brothers' first show in which comedy was the featured attraction and not the songs or dances. Their first variation of the school act became the Marx Brothers first real success with the idiosyncratic characters that made them famous and wealthy stage, film, and television performers.

The Marx Brothers created their own variation of this act that would guide their unique anarchic comedy. The school act featured Chico, bringing with him what would become his signature character of the "eye-talian-accented" peasant immigrant, known by many pseudonyms including Signor Ravelli, Baravelli-the-Iceman, Fiorello, and Chicolini; Harpo and his fighting Irish character of "Patsy Brannigan"; Groucho as the German-dialect "Herr Teacher'; Gummo as the Jewish "Yid" stereotype named "Izzy"; and Zeppo as the straightman juvenile. Eventually the school act established the Marx Brothers in the personae that singled them out as unique, eccentric, and one of the most popular family acts in vaudeville. Their school act characters were new immigrant comedic types that Edward Harrigan had warned would spread the "new humor" by "laughing *at* and not *with*" Anglo-American audiences at the beginning of the twentieth century.[37]

With the advent of Herr Teacher in *Fun In Hi Skule*, to *Mr. Green's Reception* and *Home Again*, to the film *Horse Feathers*, Groucho became famous for his "eccentric" comedy in the role of a teacher. The school act was an early example of what the Marx Brothers did best: destabilizing rigid institutional settings. Groucho's authoritarian perpetually wheedles his way into positions of power only to undermine his own authority through his intentional ineptitude and indulgence in his abuses of power. Groucho countered the democratic explosions of Chico and Harpo by institutionalizing and fusing the role of outsider with that of the insider. The Marx Brothers would bring their own unique take on this school act in recognition of their own failed attempts at being educated through the New York City public schools.

An early review of the brothers reinforces how they were moving away from the standard fare of shows like *School Days*. *Variety* found the tour of *Fun In Hi Skule*[38] to be unique and singular, featuring:

> [Harpo] a natural comedian. Also he is a harpist, and a good one...he scored an unusually large success, deservedly so, too. The teacher [Groucho] does well as a "Dutchman," and makes quite something out of [his role] as worked by him...will be liked on almost any bill, playing differently from the usual run. It is the best "school act" seen...since Herman Timberg well known for his school act.[39]

The Marx Brothers had scored a victory over the popular school act of vaudevillian Herman Timberg by "playing differently." The highly respected and commercially successful Timberg was so impressed by the Marx Brothers that he offered to co-write their vaudeville show *On the Mezzanine* (1921) and their second Broadway hit *The Cocoanuts* (1925), with George S. Kaufman.[40]

The success of the Marx Brothers in the school act and its quality and distinctiveness was observed directly by *Variety* in 1912:

> When Gus Edwards' "School Boys and Girls" recently appeared at Hammerstein's, it was mentioned in a criticism in this paper that there were "school acts" on the "small time" much better than Mr. Edwards' played out turn. The act arrived sooner than expected. It is the Marx Brothers, from the west, with seven people [in *Fun In Hi Skule*]. They make the Edwards number look foolish.[41]

The differences in the Marx Brothers' school act were exemplified by the construct of their vaudeville performances, calculated to reach a wide-ranging audience, and the unique interplay between their three diverse comic skills.[42] In an interview for the *Utah Democrat*, the Marx Brothers revealed their performance strategy to an unidentified reporter, who wrote:

> Since some people like one style of comedy and don't care for another, it behooved the Marx boys, if they wanted to stick to their agreement, to offer every style of comedy known to the stage; if one of the brothers did not please, one of the other three would be sure to; and thus the four brothers, individually and collectively, would be credited with being a

> "hit." Accordingly, they divided up the field of comedy among themselves thus: Julius [Groucho] took up eccentric comedy; [...] Arthur [Harpo], nut comedy; and Leonard [Chico], boob comedy.[43]

How these three forms of comedy came to create a distinctive style when fused together can be seen in the following scene from *Fun In Hi Skule*. In his autobiography, Harpo describes how Groucho as Herr Teacher tried to show off his classical singing voice during a music class lesson with his tenor's aria, and how he and Chico built an act around this set piece. Groucho suddenly stopped singing and turned to Chico who was providing the piano accompaniment, "I don't like your key, Giuseppe." Chico responded with, "How about this key, boss?" and transposed the key to C-minor. "Worse," Groucho criticized. Then according to Harpo:

> I ran onstage and bumped Chico off the stool and began to play "The Holy City," the quickstep-march variation. Groucho knocked me off. Chico knocked Groucho off. I knocked Chico off. Through the whole wacky round-robin the piano kept being played and Groucho kept singing "*La donna e mobile*"[44]—in double-talk Italian.

The now-frenzied opera turn devolved into "a six-hand, three-key version of 'Waltz Me Around Again, Willie.'" This popular Tin Pan Alley song was played with, "Chico on the stool, me sitting on Chico's shoulders, and Groucho behind us, reaching his arms around Chico like tentacles, and all of us singing." The number ended with the brothers collapsing into a heap onstage, then they sprung back into action, and "grabbed [...] mandolins, and sailed into 'Pease Weasie.'"[45] The willful destruction of highbrow opera that became a popular vaudeville song, and then erupted into a chaotic and surreal manic physical comedy sketch made the Marx Brothers' school act a singular experience. The escalating violence and surreal accretion of absurdity and chaos in the classroom showed a disregard for public education with its insistence on exposing high art to students, while depicting the inability of school reforms to serve the children from the ethnic underclasses. The school act was significant in establishing the Marx Brothers as singular vaudeville performers. As Groucho states in his autobiography, *Fun In Hi Skule* would mark "the first time in our career we realized that we could succeed as an act without any outside help...we were now a unit. We were the Marx Brothers."[46]

This scene also shows how the Marx Brothers mocked Americanization simply through deconstructing the regimented music lessons of the public school classroom. The singing of pro-America songs was thought to aide in the socialization of immigrant children through public schooling. How this was achieved can be observed in a letter dated 1911, from a young immigrant to his mother:

> [T]he really impressive sight was the presentation and oath of allegiance to the American flag which takes place at 9 o'clock every morning. First they sang a number of American songs and some of the children recited and then came this ceremony to an end, every child stretching out its hand towards the flag. It really made one feel that America was a land of freedom."[47]

The Marx Brothers destabilized the authority of the classroom, aesthetic hierarchies, and loyalty to American nationalism through their version of the school act.

Fun In Hi Skule was constantly being reinvented, as the show responded to a variety of audiences during the brothers' tour of the United States. The school concert that was featured in the second act took the form of a reunion twenty years later, titled *Mr. Green's Reception*. Initially the two acts played as a double bill but by September 1912, *Mr. Green's Reception* was being performed on its own. *Mr. Green's Reception* was another version of the school act that was a major success for the Marx Brothers. It toured for two years until September 1914, when this most recent version of the school act was reinvented yet again with new sketches and songs as *Home Again*.

The setting of *Mr. Green's Reception* was a garden party reception given by the old "Dear Teacher" (an Anglo-German wordplay on "der Teacher"). "Mr. Green was the new name we gave to the Teacher," wrote Harpo:

> On the anniversary of his retirement, he invites his old pupils to a reception at his vine-covered cottage in the country. Patsy, Giuseppe, Izzy and Mama's Boy are grown men now. They have become, it so happens, singers of songs, players of the piano, pluckers of the mandolin, and fun-loving comedians. They give their old teacher a gala entertainment.[48]

Mr. Green's Reception was a larger-scale, extravagant piece with an onstage crew of twenty-one: four Marx Brothers,[49] Paul Yale, George Lee, and fifteen female chorus members, enthusiastically advertised as "[girls] with short skirts, yaller hair and pink stockings,"[50] including Vera Bright, Dot Davidson, and Saba Shephard, who toured with the show for many years including its sequel, *Home Again*.

This new version of the school act, which highlighted the students from *Fun In Hi Skule* twenty years later, began straight off by featuring Harpo as the mute Patsy Brannigan, as Groucho was later to recount: "[We] had a bowl on the stage with lemonade, and Harpo would stick his whole head in the bowl. Harpo liked lemonade."[51] Harpo delivers the class conflict right away by disrupting this fashionable garden party overlooking the Hudson River Valley with his crass behavior. *Mr. Green's Reception* was a commentary on the result of public schooling advocated so vociferously by reformers, as none of the students appeared to have any education to speak of twenty years on. Harpo as Patsy still had the same ratty red wig—although with two decades of wear—turtleneck sweater, and now blacked-out teeth. He arrives at the party carrying a trashcan, and Mr. Green having no recognition of this rag picker asks:

> MR. GREEN (GROUCHO): And who might you be, my good fellow?
> PATSY (HARPO): Why, Patsy Brannigan, the Garbage Man.
> MR. GREEN: Sorry, but we don't need any.

Herr Teacher's lack of recognition of his own student that has come to honor him, coupled with Patsy's lack of propriety and any kind of socialization, reveals the futility and resistance of ethnic immigrant students—like Patsy Brannigan—with public school education. School reform from the point of view of this school act had clearly failed. The irony was that the Marx Brothers, by refusing the education offered by the public school system, were on their way to becoming one of the most successful, wealthy, and well-known comedy teams of the twentieth century. A 1913 review observes:

> *Mr. Green's Reception* is in three acts and is described as a "modern mixture of mirth, melody and motion." In it are an unusually large number of tuneful melodies...Among the special features introduced are the lazy levee

> slide, the spectacular ship scene, the big cabaret entertainment and fun in a country school, each of which is a winner as a pleasing musical comedy contribution.[52]

The nod to the modernist era and the new humor, in this review, and the spirit of speed and perpetual motion into the future shows how in tune the Marx Brothers were to the changes in American life in the early twentieth century, and a tribute to the success of their school acts. In 1914, the Marx Brothers would capitalize once again on this act in its final incarnation for the vaudeville stage.

Fun In Hi Skule and *Mr. Green's Reception* had one more stage variation two years later with *Home Again*. Once the Marx Brothers returned from honing this show on the road, they presented it in "big time" New York City vaudeville houses like the Royal and the Palace. *Home Again*, co-authored by their vaudevillian uncle Al, of the comedy team Gallagher and Shean, opened in September of 1914 and would run in New York and on tour for the next four years. A 1919 review of the Marx Brothers in the "New Acts" section of *Variety* reveals some interesting clues as to the development of the Marx Brothers' school acts that made them unique from other vaudeville acts of the time, and which would ensure their future Broadway and Hollywood successes:

> Julius (Groucho) Marx is developing into an actor... His asides are more funny than the set lines. He is a confirmed ad-libber and claims he has a right to interpolate, he having written the material for the act. Arthur Marx, known as "Harpo," because of his adeptness with the harp, is the sole survivor on the American vaudeville stage of the school of pantomime. Without saying a word he draws most of the laughs of the act, and that not by virtue of mere mugging, but by the utility of props, gestures, and psychological situations. Leonard (Chico) in the character of the "wop," backed by his nifty piano playing and ingenious "fingering."[53]

Home Again, a reworking of *Mr. Green's Reception*, featured Groucho still playing the now-retired Herr Teacher—now called Mr. Hammer—who is visited by his former pupils. Among those students are Chico and Harpo who portray petty criminals who work along the docks. They are antisocial characters who as outsiders are a product of Mr. Hammer's teaching. Chico and Harpo had begun a series of petty criminal characters in the guise of working-class roles that would appear in their later stage and film work. Harpo had also begun in earnest his "mute" characterization with the character of Patsy, since Shean had written only a few lines for him, and as a result, he decided to go silent. Not only is Harpo a poor Irish immigrant with no education and no prospects, but he is rendered completely inarticulate (save for the honking of a horn), and is only understood by his partner/brother Chico through gestures and facial expressions. *Home Again* marks Harpo's life-long career as a mute comedian who communicates perfectly in the world of those who are outsiders, and renders authoritarian insiders helpless by playing the part of a harmless and bumbling clown, who can operate under their radar. Chico (as the small-time gambler that he really was offstage as well) and Harpo, as they invariably did, portrayed marginalized working-class roles. These background characters were on the outside of any given narrative, and came to the foreground with their subversion of those in authority as represented by Groucho.

The success of their work in third-tier vaudeville circuits in front of audiences in far-flung and remote regions of the United States is reflected in their *Variety* reviews, which concluded that *Home Again* was "the best tab[loid] New York has ever seen ... an act big time could depend upon for a future."[54] *Home Again* was the show that linked the previous Marx Brothers' school acts together. Although no surviving scripts have been located, a structure in three parts can be pieced together from the memoirs of Groucho, Harpo, one of the Marx Brothers' script collaborators, S. J. Perelman—who saw the show in 1916 as a twelve-year-old—and newspaper reviews. *Home Again* would run in various guises from 1914 to 1920, as *The Four Marx Brothers Revue* opening on February 7, 1919, and was quickly renamed *N'Everything*, and ran for another year. After four years of playing *Home Again*, in October 1918 the Marx Brothers wanted to change to another show to further their careers, but when the new vehicle *Street Cinderella* flopped, they revived *Home Again* and played it until December 1920.

The first part of *Home Again* takes place on the docks and piers—suggested by four battered satchels and a grim backdrop representing the gangway—of the Cunard Line in New York. As a group of diverse ethnic immigrants get off the *Britannic*, Groucho in the guise of Mr. Hammer,[55] with swallowtail coat, spectacles, and an unlit cigar, is accompanied by his wife sporting a feather boa, on their return from a European voyage. The festive air filled with streamers and confetti was immediately disrupted with Groucho's complaints about seasickness: "Well friends, next time I cross the ocean, I'll take a train. I'm certainly glad to set my feet on terra firma. Now I know that when I eat something, I won't see it again."[56]

In *Home Again* the Marx Brothers were still honing their ethnic immigrant characterizations. Groucho in his "Dutch" accent—which he would drop during the 1917–18 season when the United States entered World War I—declares, "This must be the Far Rockaway boat." His wife asks, "How do you know?" Groucho sniffs the air and bluntly notes, "I can smell the herring." The stereotypical ethnic joke refers to Far Rockaway and its large Jewish population, and their diet of cheap herring. While on the dock, Gummo—replaced by Zeppo when he entered the army in 1917—heckled Groucho, who responded with an aside to the audience, "Nowadays you don't know how much you know until your children grow up and tell you how much you don't know."[57] This antagonistic relationship between a teacher/father and his student/son is featured in the film *Horse Feathers* almost fifteen years later. Harpo and Chico are hucksters and gamblers who roam the docks and happen to be Mr. Hammer's former students. A policeman comes on and explains that some of the ship's silverware is missing. Harpo notes: "Being a full-time pantomimist now, I worked hard thinking up stage business that didn't require spoken lines."[58] Harpo is discovered with over thirty pieces of silverware that are hidden in his expansive sleeve, and is summarily arrested. "I swiped a bulb-type horn off a taxicab and stuck it under my belt before going on in *Home Again*," writes Harpo, "When Chico and I started our fight and the cop clomped on and yanked me off Chico, the horn went whonk! and we got a hell of a big new laugh." The horn honking would become Harpo's new form of communication for the rest of his career that only Chico could interpret. This secret language between Harpo and Chico distinguishes them as outsiders, who develop an underground code to undermine the authorities like Groucho's Herr Teacher.

The second part of *Home Again* takes place a few weeks later. The setting is now a painted backdrop of the lawn at Groucho's (presumably he has married rich) villa overlooking the Hudson River. Groucho now sports a plaid-trimmed smoking jacket. Much of the second act consists of musical performances in honor of their former teacher, Mr. Hammer. This becomes a vaudeville show in and of itself, with its various unconnected acts featuring singers, dancers, and musicians. Harpo is introduced at the party by the "garbage man-joke" from *Mr. Green's Reception*, and begins guzzling the water out of the goldfish bowl and then swallows the goldfish. Another theft provided Harpo with an excuse to search two of the girls. Eventually Groucho gets tired of being annoyed by these two rambunctious guests, and when they start chasing a girl around the room, he gives up and joins them. The third and last part of the show has the former students all get into a papier-mâché boat mounted on wheels. They move off the stage with a rousing chorus. All the lights except on deck go out while the boat is seen going down the river in the distance. Harpo usually added a gag in the end, like tugging on a rope and sending the passengers tumbling, or some other improvised business of missing the boat and pretending to swim after it while spewing water. Harpo had once again missed the boat.

Home Again and its various scenes found its way into the brothers' Broadway shows (*The Cocoanuts* and *Animal Crackers*) and Hollywood films (*Monkey Business*, *Horse Feathers*, and *Duck Soup*), defying and destabilizing Progressive reformers' attempts at implementing an Anglo-American, middle-class agenda with ethnic, working-class immigrants, through public schooling. By using the vaudevillian school act, the Marx Brothers were able to satirize the futility and bigotry in this process of forced Americanization. The Marx Brothers point to the fact that as sons of underclass immigrants they were able to mock the stereotypes of the culturally deficient, ignorant, and indigent working-poor Jews. They were able to become an American success story themselves in spite of their refusal to assimilate to Progressive-era school reforms. The Marx Brothers, as ethnic-American Jewish outsiders, became iconic American stars and cultural touchstones that still have contemporary relevance with their ubiquitous personas of Chico, Harpo, and Groucho—or simply The Marx Brothers.

So far the examination of the Marx Brothers has been as a collective, however looking at them as individuals reveals the internal mechanics of this famous family act. As autonomous performers the three central brothers—Chico, Harpo, and Groucho—can be seen to represent various forms of comic dissention in relationship to the school act.

The fear of social delinquency was a "bogey" that permeated the Progressive era. A 1925 sociology textbook, using a social survey of Cleveland residents in 1920, came to the conclusion that juvenile delinquents and offenders spend most of their free time in "empty leisure and desultory activities" including "loafing on the streets, in pool halls, and bowling alleys," in contrast to the leisure activities of "wholesome" citizens who engaged in "a widely extended and richly diversified range of activities." By following "the guidance of parents, teachers, relatives, and friends," young people avoided the "inevitable" connection between popular entertainments and juvenile delinquency. According to the director of the Chicago Crime Commission, "the young delinquent has, in the majority of instances, grown up in the atmosphere of the saloon, the poolroom and similar hang-outs."[59] All three of the Marx Brothers, both onscreen and off, were to be found in any of these pleasure-seeking venues from early childhood onward. Chico and Harpo portrayed these characters on the vaudeville stage, and reformers were concerned that this would influence the underclasses to indulge in similar "degenerate" behavior. The glorification of the socially resistant outsider seen on the popular stage was to be curbed at all costs according to reformers like Jane Addams in her book *The Spirit of Youth and the City Streets* (1909), and in sociologist's evaluations of the 1910s and 1920s reform issues, with Arthur Evans Wood in *Community Problems* (1928), and Maurice R. Davie in *Problems of City Life* (1932). How the Marx Brothers combined to create sociocultural "problems" can be seen through the lens of their "boob," "nut," and "eccentric" versions of the new humor.

> CHICO: Who are you going to believe? Me? Or your own eyes?
> (*Duck Soup*, 1933)[60]

Chico was a master of disruption through his "boob" comedy. He played the Italian-accented immigrant who pretends to misunderstand, using puns and malapropisms in order to obfuscate his true intent: hustling his mark. There was never a card game, a chance to cheat someone out of a bit of money, or an attempt to get a "chick"[61] into bed that he would avoid. Chico performed the charming but seemingly doltish immigrant peasant, who plays the fool in order to get what he wants from those in authority. He created his brand of comedy by taking advantage of insiders who had the power he could not access to save through his outsider's deception.

Chico employed the most basic trope of ethnic humor—the accented immigrant. This "type" appeared on the US vaudeville stage as early as the 1880s.[62] According to S. J. Perelman, Chico appeared in *Home Again* as "Leo the Wop" although most sources name him "Toni Saroni." This can be compared with his persona in the stage version of *The Cocoanuts*, "Willie the Wop." Moving away from simply making a joke out of the malapropisms and ignorance of the uneducated immigrant, Chico embodied the persona of a street-smart gambler who could take advantage of any situation in his run-ins with authority. Chico simply pretended not to understand the more "sophisticated" authoritarian figure. In the case of *Fun In Hi Skule*, Chico rejected the notion of classroom education through his deliberate misunderstanding. Chico is seen in one of two modes during the school act—in the first part of *Home Again* he enters and starts climbing over couches to sit in women's laps. In the second part of the show, Chico begins another scene by stealing lingerie from the female passengers. Both routines involve antisocial behavior and the pursuit of women. Chico—as a petty thief and gambler—was often assisted by Harpo, but Chico was always the instigator and the one with the plan to rob the upper classes or seduce women. Harpo was along for the thrill of the adventure and the joy of the sheer anarchy he was causing. Chico enjoys disrupting bourgeois society and its conventions, in the spirit of the poor immigrant who in order to survive uses all means available to him, whether legal or not, necessary to get food, money, and sex, in a world where his outsider status denies him these essentials that middle-class Americans can readily acquire with little effort.

Chico made his first entrance to this school act by coming through the orchestra pit to stop the action onstage. He therefore began his stage career by being neither offstage nor onstage. When Chico first joined the cast of *Mr. Green's Reception*, he is said to have unexpectedly entered from the band as the pianist instigating a comic battle with his brothers.[63] Harpo claimed that he was taken by surprise when:

> I happened to look into the orchestra pit. I couldn't believe my eyes. Instead of giving the orange to Teacher, I let out a whoop, wound up like a baseball pitcher and heaved the orange at the piano player in the pit. The piano player caught it and threw it back. When Groucho and Gummo saw what was going on they started whooping too. We heaved everything we could get our hand on into the orchestra pit—hats, books, chalk, erasers, stilettos. The piano player surrendered. He climbed up onto the stage, sat at one of the school desks, and joined the act. It was Chico. I don't remember much about the rest of the performance that night, except that Chico adlibbed a hilarious part as an Italian boy.[64]

Chico's surprise entrance from the orchestra was such a success with audiences that it was kept as part of the act, and has been recreated in various forms in their films. As this scenario suggests, Chico appears as the fast-talking "Italian" who improvises both physically and verbally as a way of taking the other performers by surprise while at the same time resisting stage conventions. Chico played in that bridged space between audience and performer, which he would occupy both literally and metaphorically throughout the rest of his career. Always on the outside of the main narrative of the act, he plays the mysterious foreigner who is loyal to no one unless it serves his own interests. In reality, Chico loved the solitude of the gambler and the pianist who live in their own worlds, where he can lose himself in the task at hand.

> HERR TEACHER: What is the shape of the earth?
> HARPO: Square on weekdays and round on weekends!
> (*Fun In Hi Skule*, 1910)

Turning to Harpo, he represents the outsider in the guise of a silent satyr who disrupts scenes and defies authority through his use of props, sounds, and the surreal transposition of what is seen and how it can be reinterpreted. Harpo capitalized on the perception that he is "nuts" and confounds authority through his inscrutable silence. Harpo creates disruption as Patsy in *Fun In Hi Skule* through the traditional role of the ignorant/fighting Irishman as class clown. Harpo discovered that the use of silent gestures and props will distinguish him from the highly verbal Chico and Groucho. Harpo also uses his skills as a musician as noted in a 1913 review:

> [The] comedy harp playing by Arthur Marx is a winning card. He is not only a really good performer on this instrument, but he can make it do some laughable stunts, too. It's worth hearing and seeing, especially the way he hypnotizes the members of the company to do all sorts of freak movements to his accompaniment.[65]

One of Harpo's skills as noted in this review was to get the other performers to embrace his "nutty" and surreal physical humor. In order to disarm the insiders of authority like Groucho's Herr Teacher, as Patsy, and later in almost all his stage and film performances, he hooked his leg in the crook of the arm of an unsuspecting performer, as a bizarre form of handshake. Simultaneously playful and aggressive, Harpo is able to disarm and confuse characters who are attempting to bully or berate him. This defense of using disarming humor was a way of surviving on the streets of New York City as a child. Being "the patsy" or the victim who takes the rap for others, Harpo could not physically fight back but he could use humor and strange physical actions to throw off his tormenter long enough to get away.[66]

Before Harpo's silence, he still engaged in dialogues with Groucho as standard examples of the inability for the poor immigrant to learn in the public school classroom. A typical sequence from *Fun In Hi Skule* involved a geography lesson as taught by Herr Teacher to Patsy Brannigan, as remembered in an interview with Groucho:

> I'd ask Harpo, "What is the shape of the earth?" And he'd say he didn't know so I'd try to help him. I pointed to my cufflinks and said, "What shape are these?" He'd say "Square." And I'd say, "No, not these. The ones I wear on Sundays." He'd say, "Round." "Now, then," I'd say, "what is the shape of the earth?" And he'd answer, "Square on weekdays and round on weekends!"[67]

However, when Harpo went silent in *Home Again*, he was able to respond to any kind of questioning, with a sweet childlike smile, and then "leg hook" an authority figure like Groucho, which would defuse the tension and defer any kind of schooling, interrogation, or fight with this simple act. It became so popular it would follow him throughout his career, and become a trademark of Harpo's former street defenses against insiders who wanted to abuse this wily and crafty outsider.

Harpo's unique transition into a "pantomime act" is described in the "Silencing of Patsy Brannigan" chapter of his memoir, *Harpo Speaks!*, and with it a telling name change. Harpo, although still playing the character of Patsy Brannigan, was soon to be billed as "The Nondescript," dressed in striped shirt, torn raincoat, battered hat, and red fright wig, a costume that would also remain with him for the rest of his career. The description of an Irish working-class product of public schooling being called "The Nondescript" adds a further class and ethnic dimension to the social commentary of the school act. The attempt by reformers to eradicate ethnicity by creating a uniform Anglo-American pupil is mocked by Harpo's character, who is anything but nondescript. His horn-honking and clown's costume combined with his silent rejection of conformity—as witnessed with the "leg hook"—created an iconoclastic character that remains internationally well known.

Harpo added a new dimension to his stage persona when he went silent as a result of a bad review that denigrated his verbal acuity and praised his pantomime skills. Harpo's silence became a nonverbal resistance to authority. Harpo points out that as early as 1914 he created for the first time his "silverware drop from the coat sleeve" during the tour of *Home Again*:

> He [A hotel detective] turns to me and says, "You've got an honest face. You don't want to be a crook, do you?" I nod my head yes. "You just stay away from these other two guys [Groucho and Chico]," he says. "They'll only get you into trouble." I make a contrite face, stick out my lower lip, and shake my head. Impressed by sparing me from a life of crime, the detective shakes my hand. A knife falls out of my sleeve and bounces on the floor. The detective shakes harder. Three more knives fall out. Intrigued, he shakes my other hand. Half a dozen knives clatter to the stage. He shakes both hands, and still more silver comes spilling out.[68]

Harpo developed the bit over time and "eventually worked up to dropping three hundred knives, with a silver coffeepot," for the big finish.[69] This gag disrupts the logic of the narrative; how can three hundred knives and a coffeepot possibly come from a coat sleeve? The gag also disturbs the authority of the detective who believes in Harpo's "honest face" and is betrayed by his own misreading of logic and honesty. The "silverware drop" and the ownership of its meaning, and who has the capacity to understand the joke, sets up the outsider as a disruptive force that destabilizes the authority of the insiders.

Harpo, a grade-school dropout—after a little over two years of New York City public schooling—had to develop a new language to survive on the streets of working-class New York City. He ended up creating his comedy through verbal communication and its accepted meanings by developing a silent language that only he and his brothers could understand. In other words, only those on the outside can infiltrate those on the inside by creating their own capacity to know, comprehend, and interpret the outsider communication of Harpo's silence.

> GROUCHO: We three would make a beautiful couple!
> (*Animal Crackers*, 1928)[70]

Groucho Marx came into his own in vaudeville by playing figures of authority. On the surface Groucho was an insider confounded by Chico and Harpo. However, Groucho was neither insider nor outsider, but a free agent that could not be defined, as he had no allegiance to being on either side. Whereas Chico and Harpo were clearly outsiders thwarting authority, Groucho occupied an ever-shifting position of being both insider and outsider simultaneously. His seemingly irrational and illogical monologues and adlibbed dialogue were meant to keep both performers and spectators in a state of constant confusion as to his meaning and place in the act. Groucho exemplified the independence of the outlaw as someone who stood outside of the law while pretending to be its ultimate representative.

As Herr Teacher, Groucho lives between the two worlds of outsider and insider. He appears to be the ultimate insider with the authority that goes along with his role. However, even in the scenes between the teacher/Groucho and students/Chico and Harpo, we see that the parts of insider and outsider are connected when Groucho breaks the character of Herr Teacher to comment on the act itself. Groucho, as teacher, joins the fray in the battle of wits by engaging with Chico and Harpo as equals. A running gag from *Fun In Hi Skule* provides an example of their collusion. Groucho repeatedly told Harpo to take his hat off, only for Harpo to offer a token gesture of tipping it from behind, allowing the hat to fall back in place. Groucho says that he "hollered at Harpo about his hat. [Harpo] usually had an orange under it and when he finally took it off the orange would roll onto the floor and all the students would dive for the orange. That was considered a pretty classy piece of comedy."[71] Harpo adds: "We got a big laugh one night when the Teacher made me take my hat off and an orange fell out. I gave the orange to the Teacher, and he told me to put my hat back on because he'd like another one for later."[72] When Groucho acknowledged that he was in on the joke, in this case by asking Harpo to save him the orange for later, and joined Chico and Harpo in their gags, he crossed the line from authority to outlaw. Running gags like "the orange under the hat" afforded a chance for Groucho to step outside of the authoritarian character. They allowed him to comment on his position of power and align himself momentarily with his unruly students. Groucho's joining in on the anarchy of his disrupted classroom allows us to see him toggling back and forth in the role, as he is consistently inconsistent.

In *Home Again*, Groucho would perpetuate the character of Herr Teacher in a variation of *Fun In Hi Skule* and *Mr. Green's Reception*.[73] Groucho plays the now-retired Herr Teacher in the guise of Mr. Hammer, who is visited by his former pupils. Among those students are Chico and Harpo, who portray petty criminals working along the docks. The students have clearly learned nothing from their school days as they are now professional cheats, gamblers, and spies. Groucho's Herr Teacher has in fact taught them how to be better at undermining institutional authority.

Groucho's teaching methods were clearly incompetent and his ever-increasing frustration with his students was self-inflicted. A typical spelling lesson from *Fun In Hi Skule* shows Groucho and Harpo in confrontation. Groucho begins each lesson by "whacking his slapstick" made of "a pair of barrel staves," then announcing in a pronounced German accent, "Patsy Brannigan, no more shenanigans! You will stand up and give the alphabet." Harpo, as Pasty, clearly needs help and asks for a hint. Groucho "glares at Harpo," and comes "nose-to-nose" with him. Groucho berates Harpo, saying, "All right, dumkopf, I'll give you a start. Ah—ah—ah," Harpo repeats back to the teacher, "Ah!... That's the alphabet," and heads back to his seat. Groucho tells him to stop and go to the next letter but Harpo needs another hint. As Groucho and Harpo repeat "Buh," and "Buh?" back and forth, "they have sunk, nose-to-nose, nearly to the floor." Then Groucho calls him "Dumkopf!" again. Harpo finally understands that the next letter is "Bee! That's the alphabet—A, B," and "heads for his seat" once more. Groucho asks Harpo to continue again:

> HARPO: There's more? Gimme a hint what comes after B.
> GROUCHO: What's the first thing you do when you wake up in the morning? Sssssssss—
> *[Harpo gives Groucho a shocked, pop-eyed look.]*
> GROUCHO: "C," dumkopf! The first thing you do in the morning when you wake up is "see."
> HARPO: That's not the first thing I *do* in the morning.

Groucho "ends the hopeless lesson with a crack of the slapstick."[74] The futility of a new immigrant boy being schooled in English by another ethnic immigrant that results in threats of corporal punishment was a result of the Marx Brothers' public school experiences of the oppression of the poor outsider by an ineffectual and abusive insider authoritarian.

The new humor is used here to laugh at the representatives of Anglo-American assimilation. Reformers did not take into consideration that this process of Americanizing children could not be achieved by the dictates of good intentions. Groucho portrayed the failed representative of school reform in the guise of Herr Teacher. By joining forces with Chico and Harpo, he steps out of his assigned part as authoritarian, and now as the three Marx Brothers, they collectively break through the boundaries of outsiders and insiders. Through this destabilization of institutional authority, the Marx Brothers were able to transcend ethnic and class constructs.

The school act comes full circle for the Marx Brothers in the second to last of their Paramount era films, and arguably the pinnacle of their careers, with *Monkey Business* (1931), *Horse Feathers* (1932), and *Duck Soup* (1933). *Horse Feathers* brings the school act to Hollywood, and embraces the vaudeville aesthetic—including musical numbers and satirical sketches of teachers and criminals both in the school administration and in the underworld of organized crime—as a series of loosely related vaudevillian acts that eschew logical linear narrative for an accretion of comic gags.

Horse Feathers was released by Paramount Pictures on August 10, 1932. Directed by Norman Z. McLeod, hired because of his previous success with the Marx Brothers on *Monkey Business* (1931), and co-written by Bert Kalmar (*Animal Crackers*, *Duck Soup*) and Harry Ruby (*Animal Crackers*, *Duck Soup*) with additional material by S. J. Perelman (*Monkey Business*) and Will B. Johnstone (*Monkey Business*), *Horse Feathers* was another smash success for the Marx Brothers, landing them on the cover of *Time* magazine (August 15, 1932).[75] The loose narrative structure revolved around Groucho as the new president of Huxley College, Quincy Adams Wagstaff, and Zeppo as the perpetual college student and Wagstaff's son, Frank. Chico is cast as another faux-Italian, this time an "Iceman" (who doubles as a bootlegger) named Baravelli, and Harpo, as Chico's partner and part-time dog-catcher named Pinky. Baravelli and Pinky are mistaken for football "ringers" and recruited as college students and football players to help Huxley College win the "big game" against rival college Darwin. Huxley College is named after Thomas Henry Huxley, a fervent defender of Darwin's theory of evolution, and Darwin College named after the famous proponent of natural selection, Charles Darwin. The cast is rounded out with Thelma Todd, as the "College Widow," Connie Bailey, a woman who has remained at the college in order to find a husband long after her graduation, and is courted by all four Marx Brothers throughout the film. *Horse Feathers* ends in a bizarre marriage between all the brothers and the college widow.

Educational institutions, like Huxley College in *Horse Feathers*, are invariably led by characters portrayed by Groucho. Groucho's authority figure perpetually wheedles his way into positions of power and undermines his own authority through his intentional ineptitude and indulgence of his abuses of that power. Here, Groucho has melded the role of insider with that of outsider through his role of "Herr Teacher/ Professor Wagstaff."

Groucho reinforces the authority figure as someone who takes no sides but whose ambivalent acts are purely self-serving. As Professor Wagstaff sings in *Horse Feathers*, "Whatever it is... I'm against it."[76] By crossing the line of insider and outsider, he shows how the president of Huxley College is openly in collusion with the underworld through a series of cons including gambling fixes, check kiting, and consorting with bootleggers. A typical vaudevillian scene from *Horse Feathers* shows Groucho, after entering the speakeasy by saying the password "swordfish," presenting himself to Chico, whom he assumes to be a professional football player but is actually a rumrunner. A series of illegal transactions occur seconds apart from each other. Before Groucho has even attempted to "buy" football players for the college, he is drinking at an illegal bar that has to be entered with a secret password. He then confronts Chico assuming him to be a professional football "ringer." Groucho denigrates his position and insider status as the top official of a university, which is of little significance to the outsiders as played by Chico and Harpo, whom he engages to break the law. As Groucho introduces himself to Chico in a speakeasy, he presents him with a "business card" by holding out his empty clenched fingers as if there is something there, stating:

> GROUCHO (*Offering the "invisible" business card*): I am Professor Wagstaff of Huxley
> College.
> CHICO: That means nothing to me.
> GROUCHO: Well, it doesn't mean anything to me either.[77]

Groucho bribes Chico into pretending to register illegally as a college student, so he and his partner, played by Harpo, can play in the big game. Then Groucho "pays" for the contraband drinks by tricking the bartender into cashing a nonexistent check, and as the bartender gives Groucho the money, he promises that "as soon as I get a check for $15.22, I'll send it to you. Swordfish!" as he and Chico run for the door, making their illicit escape. In just a few moments, Groucho has broken several laws and has tricked Chico, Harpo, a bartender, and, ultimately, himself, since Chico is not really a football player at all but a con artist just like Groucho. The conman has been conned with his own con game. This two-man act, influenced by the Marx Brothers' school act routines almost twenty-five years earlier, puts over an act that brings together insiders and outsiders.

Groucho uses his insider status to subvert authority by collaborating with these outsiders. The ethical and social boundaries that Groucho crosses creates chaos out of sociocultural systems meant to promote integrity, fairness, and respect for knowledge and the law. Groucho is a character that is able to be all things to all people without changing his persona possessing the protean ability to be a doctor, lawyer, professor, or policeman, as required. Those on the inside who take Groucho at face value as a qualified president of a college are seeing a business card that is not there.

The defiance of authority and the blurring of boundaries can also be seen when Groucho, giving a lecture on anatomy after he has literally thrown the professor of the class out on his ear, ends up in a childish fight with his students. Chico and Harpo, in order to interrupt Groucho's pompous pontification on a subject he clearly knows nothing about, surreptitiously shoot peas at him while he is lecturing. Groucho, having been hit in the neck three times by the peashooters, suddenly pulls out his own and fights back. The scene ends in a chaotic conflict, with Groucho tapping Morse code signals on his desk, mock dying, and moaning, "They got me!"[78] The classroom has been rendered a battlefield through the professor's complicity with his defiant students.

The climax of the school act for the Marx Brothers comes in a scene that was considered by Paramount Pictures to be too risky and pessimistic for a middle-class comedy audience. The ending originally was shot and scripted for *Horse Feathers* dated February 11, 1932.[79] The original conclusion was to come after the football victory of Huxley over Darwin College, and a subsequent bonfire celebration was to ensue. However, Harpo, echoing the book-burning he performed in a brief earlier interlude, instead of starting the campus bonfire, ignites a campus building.[80] Rather than the brief comic wedding, *Horse Feathers* was tentatively scripted to end with the complete destruction by fire of Huxley College. According to the press book for the film, the Huxley students, in riot mode, tear apart the town to fuel the fire. It also includes a still from this finale depicting the Marx Brothers complacently playing cards while the chaos of an apocalyptic fire that they have created rages around them. A cross-like burning of two beams in the photograph's background suggests that the burning down of Huxley College was a willful destruction of culture and learning that would anticipate and lead to the horrors of the Ku Klux Klan and the Nazi Party. Another scene excised from the tentative script was to feature Groucho entering a burning building seemingly to save Jennings, the leader of the rival Darwin College. Instead, Groucho exits with a diploma and hands it to his son, played by Zeppo,[81] perhaps an allusion to Groucho's embrace of the Darwinian approach of survival of the fittest against the villain that has been plotting his destruction throughout the film. Groucho's final line mocks the death by fire of his nemesis, "I'll bet that'll burn Jennings up," as he plants his ubiquitous cigar in his mouth.[82] Book burning, cross burning, and the intentional death by incineration of Groucho's enemy were considered too grim for the studio to agree to release such a nihilistic conclusion to a comic film.

The Marx Brothers were to reach their apotheosis in 1933 with the film *Duck Soup*. By this point they were rich, famous, and internationally renowned for their comic satire that has continued to be a part of American culture since their recognition in vaudeville and on Broadway beginning in the early twentieth century. Chico, Harpo, and Groucho were able to achieve their success through the new humor and the vaudeville aesthetic. Literally going from rags to riches, outsiders to insiders, the Marx Brothers were able to satirize and critique Anglo-American hegemony, while becoming one of its most famous examples of the American success story. As sons of Jewish immigrants that became stars by creating stage names and personas that essentially erased their former status of having no authority, the Marx Brothers moved from Leonard, Arthur, and Julius to Chico, Harpo, and Groucho.

In the final scene of the stage and film versions of *Animal Crackers*,[83] Groucho and his brothers come on singing "My Old Kentucky Home" as a barbershop quartet. When they finish, Groucho remarks in the style of a radio commentator, "This program is coming to you from the House of David."[84] Four Jewish sons of immigrants singing a southern Christian homesick homage to Kentucky creates the perfect irony of language that breaks the easy identification of ethnicity brought to the audience courtesy of these descendants of the House of David. This vaudevillian Marx Brothers' moment uses the language of obfuscation of identity through the conflation of Jewish and Christian, as well as northern and southern, for their satire. The Marx Brothers' House of David is the point of origin for these infamous social assassins; for Groucho and Chico their main weapon was spoken language, and for Harpo it was body language.

The ethnic component is key to the misunderstandings that are perpetuated in the comic language derived from the *shtetl.* Not understanding, and even willfully misunderstanding, words and meanings that are communicated both verbally and physically, is the key to this form of humor derived from the vaudeville gag. The gag therefore becomes the site of confrontation between three characters who present various sides of perceived stereotypes and who use those types as subterfuge to comment on the behavior and understanding of ethnic types in order to get laughs and comment on Americanization.

The new humor of the Marx Brothers captures their "whatever it is, I'm against it" philosophy. Beginning with their school act in 1910, the Marx Brothers spent the next twenty-five years being against anything that goes along with an authoritarian, Anglo-American consensus. The resistance to the "can't you get *noddings* [sic] through your thick head?" exhortation of the public school teacher in *Fun In Hi Skule* had found its way into the student's adult consciousness—not only am I not able to get anything through my head, I simply do not want to.

These children of new immigrants deployed a comic derailing of narrative, first of America as the land of opportunity, and the paradoxical, Anglo-American notion of embracing individuality through Americanization. As sociocultural historian Patricia Bradley writes, "there was something subversive about vaudeville—too much flesh, too many immigrants, and a bit too much freedom."[85] The new immigrant and their ethnic roots of eastern and southern Europe, as seen in the new humor of the vaudeville-inspired films of the Marx Brothers, reinforced the fears of Progressive reformers and critics that the freedom and subversive nature of the new humor was a threat and a danger to Anglo-American dominance and authority.

Comic vaudevillians like the Marx Brothers exposed the myth of American success and assimilation for the many while paradoxically creating it for a select few. Through its lasting notoriety and enjoyment, the new humor debunked the concept that it could only appeal to the prurient and vulgar working classes by continuing to entertain and enlighten audiences of all ethnicities, classes, and political convictions.

As we will see in chapter 5, the new women at the turn of the twentieth century, including May Irwin, Eva Tanguay, and Marie Dressler, would also use ethnic acts, family acts, and burlesque acts in order to challenge Americanization during the Progressive era.

5. The New Woman and the Female Comedian as Social Insurgent

In 1913 the periodical *Current Opinion* stated that "'Sex O' Clock' had struck in America."[1] Twenty-two years earlier, a warning that "sex o' clock" was about to strike appeared in the periodical *Nineteenth Century*, titled "The Wild Woman as Social Insurgent."[2] The article characterizes the reaction of the diminishing authority of nineteenth-century Victorian values to the so-called offensive behavior of women in the early twentieth century. The notion of a social insurgency signaled a cultural conflict that led to the advent of the new woman.

The new woman suffered two exclusions from mainstream Americanness—being an immigrant and being a woman. These exclusions were confronted on the comic vaudeville stage. The threat of popular entertainment and the rise of the new woman as new humorist was summed up in 1902 by a theater critic who declared that "the day of the comic actress has dawned. She is now the essential thing." This author labeled these newcomers as "'comedian' girls" who had "jump[ed]" to the front" and created "a New Sphere for Stage Women."[3] The demand for these female comic acts, and the wealth that was generated by their performances, was so great that reformers and critics feared an insurgency that would adversely affect their attempts to Americanize underclass women.

Working from the concept of "the wild woman as social insurgent," I argue that the new humor in relationship to the new woman was a form of sociocultural mutiny. Female comedians began to remove the emphasis from their sexuality and perceived promiscuity by refocusing attention to their comedic skills and social commentary through the new humor. How women in comedy challenged not only the notion of purity and the moral codes left over from the nineteenth century, but also the imprimatur of being "tough girls" by becoming socially independent and culturally significant performing artists will be evaluated through the work of three successful female new humorists of the vaudeville stage.

In addition to Kate Elinore, as discussed in chapter 3, examples of female comic performers considered here include May Irwin whose popularity as "the Funniest Stage Woman in America" pioneered the female comic vaudevillian; Eva Tanguay, whose comically wild and unruly sexualized singing and dancing made her the "Queen of Vaudeville";[4] and Marie Dressler whose unconventional body image and attractiveness with her "Big Girl" portrayals led to her being described as an "Amazon" comedian.[5] These performers shared an affinity because of their chosen profession, which challenged class-biased notions of womanhood, especially as related to ethnicity, immigration, and sexual permissiveness.

All three comedians had a common Canadian immigrant heritage born of working-poor backgrounds. In the late nineteenth century, many Canadians—particularly French Canadians like Eva Tanguay—arrived in New England and New York State from Québec, Ontario, and New Brunswick to work in the textile mill cities of New England. During that same period, Canadians soon became a majority of the workers in the saw mill and logging camps in the Adirondack Mountain region of upstate New York, while others sought opportunities for farming and blacksmithing. Canadian women like Irwin, Tanguay, and Dressler saw New England and New York State as a place where they could reject the stifling and impoverished family farms they grew up in to create economic alternatives for themselves. The turn of the twentieth century witnessed Canadian immigration to the United States as a rite of passage during a time of autonomy for women away from their social and religious upbringings. Already in defiance of their working-class backgrounds and the repression of provincial life, they were eager to establish new lives away from their families as independent and self-reliant individuals. The northeastern United States allowed them a place to do just that during this time of social change.[6] Fortunately for performers like May Irwin, Eva Tanguay, and Marie Dressler, the vaudeville stage was a place that accepted and encouraged their unique talents as new humorists.

These comic insurgents began in the era of vaudeville's popularity, spanning from the 1890s at the height of burlesque entertainments to the mid-1920s. Female new humorists were linked by their humble beginnings that led them to address class conflicts and gender roles in their vaudeville acts. The fact that these performers all had very successful careers and spent as many as twenty years on the stage is a tribute to their resiliency and success as social commentators and funny women.

Female comedians used the new humor to challenge standard Anglo-American middle-class notions of womanhood. As a consequence, the new women as comic performers often found themselves at odds with middle-class reformers and critics during the Progressive era. Progressive reformers who advocated for the equality and civil rights of women soon objected to images of the new women that did not conform to their image of the Anglo-American middle-class woman whose cultural and aesthetic appreciation was to be promoted against the underclass, immigrant, "wild women." Women who did not adhere to the reformers' image of the new woman were labeled social insurgents out to defy and undermine the expected morality and behaviors of the new era.

The new women of vaudeville comedy, whose roots were planted in nineteenth-century performance forms such as minstrelsy, variety theater, and especially burlesque, came into their own at the turn of the twentieth century in the United States. The excorporation of the female comic vaudevillian from the burlesque shows of the late nineteenth century was thought to move the new women away from middle-class culture and reform the representation of American feminine behavior. Burlesque, associated with its three-part structure of the minstrel shows of the 1870s, and its satires of the personages and values of highbrow culture, "increasingly became centered around feminine sexual display—in the cooch dance of the 1890s; in its jazzed-up successor, the shimmy, in the 1910s; and the striptease of the late 1920s and 1930s."[7] The new women of the vaudeville stage were still associated with the burlesque world of the 1880s–90s, and were attacked for bringing the degenerate aesthetics of this popular entertainment with them into the supposedly more respectable form of vaudeville. These new female performers were seen as insurgents who infiltrated the family-oriented vaudeville stage that Keith and Albee had worked so hard to cleanup. The new humorists presented both a challenge and a warning to the anxieties of nonconformance with middle-class gender roles. The new humor was able to capitalize on these pejoratively described "rank ladies" and "unruly women."[8] Female performers were perceived as making their fortunes from openly sexual innuendos and suggestive dancing, and more importantly a disregard for social conventions and gender roles.

The ascendancy of the new woman as female comedian also raised questions concerning what constituted a woman's sense of humor. The debate over women and comic appreciation in the early twentieth century confronted the idea that the enjoyment of the new humor in vaudeville contradicted women's supposed natural proclivity toward dignified behavior. A 1901 column for *Harper's Bazaar* quoted French comic performer Constant Coquelin's article titled "Have Women a Sense of Humor?" who commented that "the lighter, the more fantastic, the daintier the humorous fancy, the quicker it appeals to a woman."[9] In a similar *Harper's* article one year later, Robert Burdette an American humorist and clergyman reaffirmed Coquelin's pronouncement regarding women's sense of humor, writing that "the sense in her is delicate, sympathetic, refined to the highest culture. True humor delights her, while buffoonery, if it be brutal, shocks her."[10] Women's humor was meant to be defined as witty, light, and sensitive. The new women, by emulating the lowbrow male comedians found in concert saloons and variety theaters of the Bowery and the Lower East Side, were thought to have lacked an ethical and moral center. These perceptions of the new women provide an indication of the judgment and condemnation of female comic vaudevillians that came from journalists, cultural watchdogs, politicians, and fellow performers alike. The fear of the uncontrollable new woman onstage was palpable.

One of the first female social insurgents to appear on the comic vaudeville stage was May Irwin (see figure 5.1). In 1910, former vaudeville

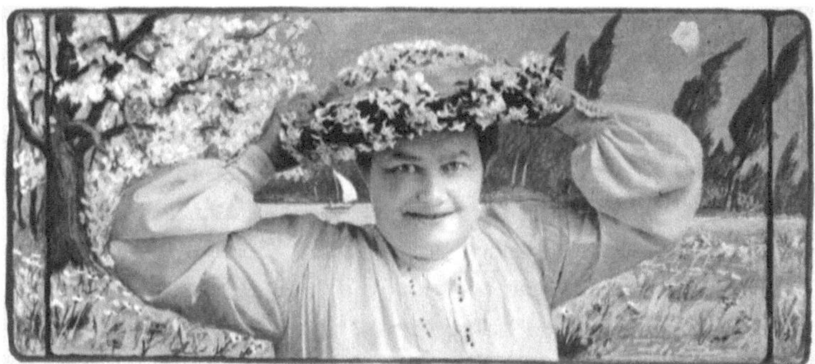

Figure 5.1 May Irwin, 1904; Billy Rose Theatre Division, New York Public Library for the Performing Arts, Astor, Lenox, and Tilden Foundations.

booking agent and popular entertainment chronicler Robert Grau wrote of her incredible success:

> May Irwin is accounted in the millionaire class, and though a great portion of her career was spent in musical and farce comedy, it is as a vaudevillian that she will be remembered. While in this field, where once she was accorded about $150 a week, recently she received $2,500 weekly for a long season for singing a few "coon" songs.[11]

As this assessment indicates, Irwin, born in a remote province of Canada in 1862, was one of the first female stars to make it big in comic vaudeville. Her success as a woman in comedy during the late nineteenth century was unprecedented. Cautiously praising her, a critic wrote, "although there are some . . . who say no woman can possess it, [she has] a very keen sense of humor."[12] Another noted that Irwin did what other women could not on the comic stage as "it is not easy for a woman to be funny and retain the sympathy and respect of her audiences."[13]

Although she spent over fifty years on the stage, the height of her popularity was between the late 1890s and World War I. Irwin appeared in over a dozen plays, mostly slight but enormously successful comedies under her own management. They were principally vehicles for her comic performances. Irwin's vaudeville tours gave her the reputation as "The Funniest Stage Woman in America." She was also known as

"The Dean of Comediennes," and was so popular that she attracted the attention of Woodrow Wilson who jokingly wanted to create a special cabinet position of "Secretary of Laughter" just for her.[14]

From humble beginnings singing in a church choir, Irwin moved to Buffalo's Adelphi Variety Theatre, and from there toured the Midwest as a "coon shouter." The "coon song" was a stereotypical white reflection of "Negro" exuberance with lyrics in a pseudo-Southern dialect not unlike the character numbers in Irish, German, and Jewish variety shows that relied on exaggerated character types with hyperbolic accents and behaviors meant to denigrate ethnicity and race for laughs.[15] Typically, one of Irwin's controversial hit numbers from 1896 was titled, "All Coons Look Alike to Me." Irwin put over her coon songs with absurd gesticulations, but distinguished herself from other female performers of these songs as she did not use blackface. Part of a sister act with Flo Irwin, May was discovered by vaudeville impresario Tony Pastor, who brought them to New York to perform at the Metropolitan Theatre in 1877. The sisters went their separate ways in 1883 when the well-known writer and producer of American melodramas Augustin Daly offered May a place in his company. In 1896, The Edison Company filmed Irwin in a famous early short movie of the first screen kiss, simply titled *The Kiss*. It is the only film record of her work, and was to seal her fate as the harbinger of female immorality at the turn of the twentieth century.[16] In 1895, she was cast in the lead role of a musical comedy, *The Widow Jones*, which featured "The Bully Song." This coon song by Charles Trevathan was soon incorporated into her vaudeville act, and was the showstopper from a national tour during the 1907–08 season. Typical of Irwin's coon numbers were "When You Ain't Got No Money" (1896) and the "Frog Song" (1896), whose lyrics reflect the "Negro" dialect used in coon songs: "A' runnin' into trouble jus' to pass de time / An' de devil's allus loafin' round heah jus' to grab de kind / Dat nevah hasn't nothin' else to do."[17] Laziness, ignorance, and superstition are features of these songs, presumably from the perspective of a black male persona (here characterized as a "bullfrog"). As sung by a white woman these coon songs give some idea of the layers of complexity that accompanied race and gender with the new humor.

May Irwin's new humor derived, as a 1895 *New York Times* review points out, from the juxtaposition of a female comic as "round, as blonde, as innocent looking—when her mood is not reckless—as pink and white and as blue-eyed as ever" whose "fund of personal humor is prodigious."[18] The cautionary admonition that when "her mood is not reckless" is quite telling in that it points to the portrayal of intentional innocence combined with the potential out of control undercurrents that made Irwin a star of vaudeville comedy.

May Irwin was one of the first women to utilize the new humor and pushed the boundaries of taste and propriety at the turn of the twentieth century. Chicago critic Amy Leslie, writing in 1899, recognized her as a "brighter, wittier, and noisier entertainer" who "could hardly be asked by even longshoremen, politicians, and schoolboys" for a more notorious rendition of "darky music and rough colloquial comedy."[19] Aligning Irwin with the rough, rude, and boisterous company of men and boys known for their dirty jokes and crude vocabulary and manners is indicative of the boundaries that she crossed between female propriety of the demure woman and the "wild" new woman of burlesque comedy.

Leslie notes that May Irwin put her act over with "conversational entertainment." She describes Irwin's act in detail writing, "[She] comes out and takes her audience into her confidence, tips a daring wink to the knowing, and 'plays horse' [makes fun of] with the ingenuous... She has reduced the art of intimacy with an audience to so exact a science."[20] Irwin exploited the interplay of performer and audience that was the hallmark of putting it over. She balanced the danger of the perceived collusion of the working-class immigrant foreigner and her audience of likeminded conspirators with a joyful exuberance that exacerbated Anglo-American anxieties.

May Irwin was so popular with her coon shouting that white female singers in imitation of her black "wench walk" created an "entire army of song-and-dance women" who performed, "limping bowlegged about the stage in something bordering on locomotor ataxia, producing the effect of an epidemic hip disease."[21] Irwin's "body-madness" was combined with her sizable frame, thus presenting an outlandish and carnivalesque physical performance.[22]

Irwin presented such a travesty of traditional womanhood onstage that even she derided the notion that she could be taken seriously as an actress in legitimate theater. For instance, she laughed at the idea of playing Camille saying, "Imagine me, the wan-faced, delicate little flowerlike Cammy, with a hectic flush and springlike cough." In mock-tragic concern, she asked, "Where could I sing my coon songs?"[23] Her size and her rowdy stage behavior was characterized in an 1897 review describing Irwin's "gladiator shoulders…tread of a goliath and…nervous energy of a locomotive."[24] Irwin also made use of the "cakewalk" in her act. This routine was based on the plantation dance that was originated by enslaved blacks in the southern United States. The cakewalk was a mocking pseudo-elegant send-up of white plantation owners and their families who participated in promenades and grand marches at parties and social events.[25] According to one reviewer, May Irwin's cakewalk "never fails to secure a laugh when she ambles down [to] the footlights,"[26] while another critic dubbed it a "funny, bulky substitute for a dance."[27]

Her more subtle physical comedy was reflected in 1906 when May performed the vaudeville sketch "Mrs. Peckham's Carouse," written especially for her by celebrated humorist and playwright George Ade. Ade's playlet was a satire on social moral codes and outward displays of respectability. May portrayed the upper-class lady who proceeds to get progressively drunk as the scenario develops, all the while simply sitting in a chair. Presaging the work of Kate Elinore and Charlie Chaplin, Irwin was a tour-de-force that left her audiences standing and cheering for her comedic skill. The sketch was so popular that Irwin included it as a set piece for her vaudeville act and interpolated it into several musical comedies as well.[28]

May Irwin's deliberate burlesque of femininity represented the new woman in comedy who used the new humor—previously a male domain—making it her own. Strong, passionate, and boldly exuberant, she was a comedian in the truest sense of the word. May was not afraid to make fun of herself in the process of making others laugh. Irwin would pass the torch to Eva Tanguay and Marie Dressler whose eccentric and highly physical comedy created further tensions between the new humor and the new woman.

Progressive reformers in the first decades of the new century began as advocates for the new women and their rights to education and political participation in the voting booth. They set out to curb the moral decay that they perceived as leading Americans, particularly of the lower and working classes, to social and ethical ruin. However, reformers, in addition to their positive commitment to women's suffrage, soon began to advocate for the regulation of the sociocultural behaviors of the underclasses of new women. Progressive reformers objected to women being openly sexual, bawdy, crude, and unsophisticated. Restraint of "unfeminine" behaviors of the lower classes and the excesses of women from the upper classes created a false binary that projected middle-class American women as the moral center of respectability and decency. Female Progressive reformers—most of whom came from the educated middle-classes—became spokespersons of American womanhood who curtailed the excesses of the new women.

The image of women as mothers, wives, and caretakers of their families had begun to fragment during the 1880s and 1890s. As the industrial revolution created a new middle class of managers, clerks, and secretaries, women left the confines of their homes for the workplace. At the dawn of the twentieth century, the new women soon became characterized by their refusal to be constrained by the sociosexual principles of a repressive nineteenth-century moral authority.

The role of women was being redefined particularly for middle-class women looking to combine family and household care with work and pleasure outside the home. According to sociocultural historian Kathy Peiss, "the roles of bourgeois women had extended far beyond the home, to include philanthropy and reform, political activity, and professional work. This 'New Woman' questioned the 'natural' division of women and men's lives into separate spheres of social activity."[29] However, nineteenth-century Victorian values still informed many of the attitudes toward women. The virtues of chastity and proper social behavior, and the importance of marriage and motherhood, still informed the dominant view of a woman's position in the first decades of the twentieth century. Progressive-era reformers, troubled by the sexual freedom, particularly of working-class youth whom they deemed as being influenced and exploited by the commercially popular entertainment industry, advocated for the regulation and creation of alternative amusements. Class conflicts between working- and middle-class women, as well as interclass tensions, arose as the appropriateness of leisure time activities were being contested. One of the principal sites of social divisions between Progressive-era reformers and the new women was the comic vaudeville stage.

Reformer Jane Addams, in an attempt to save lower-class single women from their supposed vulnerability to lurid pleasure, argued:

> Apparently the modern city sees in these girls only two possibilities, both of them commercial: first, a chance to utilize by day their new and tender labor power in its factories and shops, and then another chance in the evening to extract from them their petty wages by pandering to their love of pleasure.[30]

In 1905 reform groups began to put pressure on city governments to deal with women whose behavior, styles of dress, and attendance at popular entertainments marked them as "loose" women. In tandem with reformers, city officials set up vice commissions to create censorship laws for police to enforce rules and regulations in entertainment venues like dance halls and vaudeville theaters. Of particular interest for reformers were the comedy acts performed by women that they believed encouraged imitation for its female audience members.

During the mid-to-late 1910s, multiple regulations at the state and municipal levels took aim at New York's inexpensive popular entertainments. Progressive reformers and authorities enforced regulations, guidelines, and strict policies that encouraged suitable divertissements for the working classes. Vaudeville with its improvisational nature was especially difficult to regulate, as it relied on audience interaction and participation that changed with every performance. However, by 1918 the moral reformers had achieved a partial victory in closing down "combination houses" that featured inexpensive small-time vaudevillians with short silent motion pictures. Since films could be more easily censored—not being live or improvisational in nature—the reformers paid particular attention to cheap amusements that ensnared spectators with their promise of surprise, shock, potential immorality, and especially "dirty" comedians.[31]

The advent of the new immigrant and the new woman created a perceived need for censorship by reform organizations like the Committee of Fourteen. As a result of the manipulations of business and politics by this committee, these organizations were sanctioned in cities all over the United States by politicians and law enforcement alike dedicated to changing the moral character of urban centers in the United States. Reformers had a powerful influence over popular entertainments. For instance, many concert saloons in the late nineteenth century that had been rowdy gathering places where prostitutes openly solicited sex and proprietors frequently ignored the one o'clock closing time were, by contrast in 1919, on the eve of national prohibition, forcibly concentrated in commercial districts, as prostitution went underground. Many drinking establishments stopped admitting women entirely to curb the sexual solicitation and corruption that saloons were perceived as encouraging. The places that did admit women only allowed them to stay without a male escort until nine or ten o'clock. All of this was a direct result of the efforts of reformers like the Committee of Fourteen.[32]

Barrooms and concert saloons that had been home to burlesque performers in the last decades of the nineteenth century produced female performers like May Irwin, Eva Tanguay, and Marie Dressler. These new humorists were now under attack for promoting sexual promiscuity and solicitation from the vaudeville stage. Also, women who were in attendance at these lowbrow entertainments were categorized in the same fashion and condemned for lewdness in part because they were not under the supervision of men. Progressive reformers, regardless of gender, attributed the moral decay of New York City in particular to women who resisted the middle-class values of family life by attending popular entertainments.

Female comedians on the vaudeville stage were rebuked by reformers and critics for burlesquing the image of respectable women. Women as comic vaudevillians were singled out for their sinful and lust-filled ways. They presumably flaunted them through innuendo and crude jokes about sex that enticed single and married men with their "naughty" performances. These acts were assumed to give female audiences similar encouragement toward unscrupulous behavior and open sexual display.

Vaudeville ethnic and family acts that were thought to be offensive and destructive by reformers and cultural critics were even more suspect when performed by female comedians. The 1900s had ushered in a new era in comedy as performed by women, as one theater critic put it, where "the girl shows are more so than ever, but to the singing girls, the dancing girls, the posing girls, the revealing girls, the alluring girls, there has been added the comedian girls."[33] Vaudeville was considered a home for the new humor in popular entertainment as well as the new vision of women as seen from the comic stage.

Progressive reformers who embraced women's suffrage and the unionization of workers could not reconcile the independence of the new women as new humorists. Female stage comedians were seen as a threat to the advancement of women's ideas and achievements being taken seriously by the American public at large. The new women as comic performers were judged at one and the same time as culturally advancing the position of women and their self-reliance in American society, but also insulting the image of the respectable and cultured middle-class women that reformers wished to promote.

Progressives rarely regarded middle-class Anglo-Americans as the source of social problems. Rather the issues being raised were emblematic of the "wealthy, workers, and farmers" from other classes.[34] The concern over the poles of upper and lower classes and their unruly behaviors is reflected in reformer Josiah Strong's comment: "[I]n the city, the home is disappearing at both social extremes."[35] Early-twentieth-century sociologist Albion Small confirmed this perspective, noting, "the American family is out of gear in two strata, in both of which pretty much everything else is out of gear."[36] The concern over the home, with its nuclear family of husband, wife, and children, represented the American ideal of a middle class that focused primarily on the home and the morals instilled in their children. For Small, protecting middle-class youth from social extremes of "the stratum of the over-wealthed [sic], over-leisured, over-stimulated, under-worked, under-controlled," in comparison with "the stratum of the over-worked, under-fed, under-housed, under-clothed, under-hygiened [sic], physically and morally, under-leisured, under-stimulated except by the elemental desires," was the goal of sociocultural Progressive reforms.[37] The wealthy upper classes and the working underclasses were considered by Progressives to share a common ground in that both were potentially corrupt and fed off each other: one because they had too much, and the other because they had too little.

Middle-class propriety meant adhering increasingly to the ideal of the married female running a household with two or more children in which the wife would not have to work because of the success of her husband and father of her children. A wife who did not have to work, and could devote her time to the raising of her young, became the ideal that marked one's movement from the lower classes to the middle classes for men and women alike. Even a woman's right to vote served different purposes among these two classes. The middle classes needed a woman's right to vote in order to secure the values of "decent" married women who represented the American ideal of marriage and motherhood. She would become a role model for other women of her class and vote accordingly to support her husband's middle-class values as well.

However, for single working-class women, suffrage became a way to exercise freedom from the bonds of marriage and motherhood and assert their own needs, desires, and opinions. The working woman's need to have access to her own rights without being married was reflected in what she could do with her leisure time. Her free time was earned by entering the work force and having a disposable income not tied to family, but for her own disposal and pleasure. Therefore, popular entertainments became a destination for single working-class women who began to enjoy dance halls, amusement parks, and vaudeville. The attendance at these "cheap amusements,"[38] either in groups of likeminded women or on dates with various men and groups of friends both male and female, posed a threat to the conventions and pursuit of family life. These working-class amusements led to perceived decadent behaviors of public drunkenness (therefore the need for another reform crusade of prohibition), carousing with the opposite sex, and worst of all engaging in promiscuous sex before settling down to marriage, if they married at all. In short, it was feared that the stage performances of the so-called wild women would lead to an epidemic of the devaluation of the Anglo-American way of life.

Jane Addams for instance condemned popular entertainments that focused on "vaudeville shows" and "the five-cent theaters . . . full of the most blatant and vulgar songs."[39] Addams took it upon herself to advocate for an art theater movement in the United States, by refocusing the Hull House Theatre in 1907 to present plays by Ibsen, Galsworthy, Shaw, Synge, and many other well-established Western European playwrights.[40] Progressive reformers like Addams wished to reinforce highbrow entertainment as a way to civilize and educate the working classes. She remarked on the enthusiasm of working-class children for Shakespeare and Molière plays put on for their benefit writing, "every settlement in which dramatics have been systematically fostered can also testify to a surprisingly quick response to this form of art on the part of young people...children whose tastes have supposedly been debased by constant vaudeville, are pathetically eager to come again and again."[41] Addams' praise of Shakespeare and Molière ignores the fact that their theater was the popular entertainment of its time—much like vaudeville was for the early twentieth century. In 1917, Thomas H. Dickinson's book *The Insurgent Theatre* would also extol the virtues of the moral and aesthetic uplift of plays that would improve the standards of middle-class audiences and enlighten and educate the underclasses: "[T]he encouragement and support of an American drama, the giving voice and tongue to a neighborhood, the production of great masterpieces of the world, the elevation of taste of the community" became the goals of stage reforms.[42] The highbrow designation of the literary theater as profound and lowbrow characterization of "constant vaudeville" as debasing the sensibilities of young Americans became an aesthetic judgment of edifying art versus corrupting popular entertainment that would lead to the censorship of live performances well into the 1930s.

The upending of social well-being was the ultimate fear as female comedians began to incorporate ethnic immigrant sketches, slapstick gags, and eccentric songs and dances into their acts. The performance of desire through "racy" and innuendo-based humor appealed to patrons who wanted to appear "sophisticated" enough to appreciate the jokes being put over. The appropriateness of women in comic vaudeville routines revealed a concern that the tastes of the lower classes that populated the cheap seats of the gallery were setting the tone and creating a demand even among audiences in the higher-priced seats. The increasing awareness of class divisions in the audience and between reformers and producers of vaudeville were being played out onstage by comic acts.

Whatever obstacles working-class or immigrant men faced, women confronted all of these plus sex discrimination. However, in vaudeville, women could potentially begin an independent career and be paid wages that were often unattainable to them in other professions.[43] A case in point was the singer/dancer/comedian Eva Tanguay, born in 1878 and raised in rural poverty in the province of Québec (see figure 5.2). By

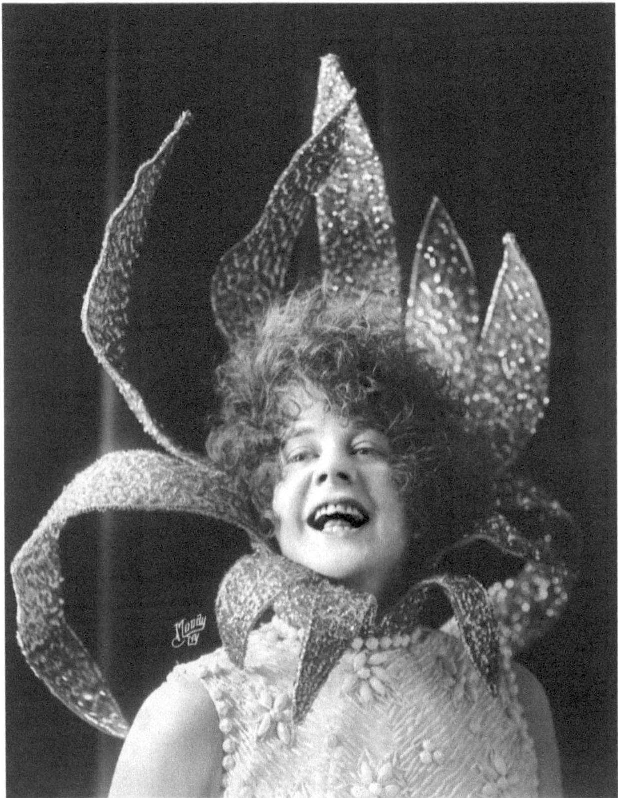

Figure 5.2 Eva Tanguay in her Flower Petal Costume, 1919; Billy Rose Theatre Division, New York Public Library for the Performing Arts, Astor, Lenox, and Tilden Foundations.

1884, Tanguay's family immigrated to the United States to the industrial factory township of Holyoke, Massachusetts. It was there that she was introduced to the popular stage, winning first prize during an amateur night at the age of eight. Tanguay's mother was unable to afford a proper dress for her performance and made one out of the fabric of an old umbrella.[44] Two years later she was cast in a touring production of *Little Lord Fauntleroy* performing the leading role. In 1901, Tanguay landed a minor role in the musical *My Lady*, and her next featured role in *The Chaperon* in 1904 would mark the beginning of her stage success in New York City.[45] Her solo vaudeville act appeared in 1905, and by 1910 Eva Tanguay was reported to be making $3,500 a week from her appearances.[46]

Tanguay chose a path in vaudeville in order to break free of her social and economic standing and in doing so achieved great wealth and fame. A turn-of-the-century newspaper featured an article on vaudeville that touted Eva Tanguay as "[a] woman [who] is as free and independent as a man. Generally she needs no protector, for she is usually able to take care of herself."[47] Vaudeville historian Douglas Gilbert's report of Eva Tanguay's act in Pittsburgh, in which "a bit of comedy introduced (a short 'blue' monologue about a chicken) was tossed out by the authorities," is telling of how some female performers defied social and cultural conventions of the day, becoming successful for their audacity. Tanguay purportedly responded to this criticism of her act being too "blue" in a subsequent performance, as she "gaily continued to shake her torso and wriggle her thighs, explosively shrieking 'I Love to Be Crazy.'"[48] Her performances signaled the new—both onstage and off—reflecting the spirit of the day as female vaudevillians became associated with the new women.

Eva Tanguay serves as a significant example of the class conflict of the new woman with middle-class reformers of the early twentieth century. Tanguay went from being a French-Canadian immigrant to making her mark at Hammerstein's Victoria Theater in 1901, and by 1905 Tanguay had become the "Queen of Vaudeville" all in just a few short years.[49] Florenz Ziegfeld featured Tanguay as his star attraction in the 1909 edition of the *Follies*, replacing the husband-and-wife team of Jack Norworth and Nora Bayes, who had been Ziegfeld's top audience draws until that point.[50] For the next twenty-five years Tanguay remained one of the biggest stars featured as an "eccentric comedienne" all through sheer force of will and a unique performance style.[51] As she declared in her signature song, "It's All Been Done Before but Not the Way I Do It."[52] Her financial success and her extravagant stage persona can be witnessed in 1910, one year after the Lincoln penny was issued, in which she appeared onstage in a coat covered with one-cent coins.[53] Another stage costume boasted a two-thousand-dollar dress encrusted with coral weighing forty-five pounds. These outfits were a far cry from the old umbrella that Tanguay's mother had fashioned into a stage dress for her twenty-four years earlier.[54]

Eva Tanguay's defiance of middle-class female decorum was characterized by Douglas Gilbert who notes, "The terrific Tanguay was an electrified hoyden, a temperamental terror to the managers, a riotous joy to her audiences. A singing and dancing comedienne, it is easy to analyze her act: it was assault and battery." She was characterized as mad, crazy, "the Cyclonic Comedienne," the "Evangelist of Joy," and, the most elusive title of all, an "eccentric" act. Breaking with B. F. Keith's Sunday School Circuit morality, Gilbert contends that she "got more sex into her shouted numbers than could be found in a crib street in a mining town."[55] According to Joe Laurie's vaudevillian memoirs, Tanguay, more than any other performer, "represented the true spirit of vaudeville."[56] "In Vaudeville," Tanguay pronounced that she was "second to none" and made sure that she was billed as "The Girl Who Made Vaudeville Famous."[57] At the height of her popularity, with little to recommend her save her dynamic personality, Eva Tanguay is quoted as saying about her own act, "[A]s a matter of fact, I am not beautiful, I can't sing, I don't know how to dance. I am not even graceful."[58] Regardless of her perceived talents, Tanguay defied the conventional description of the female voice and body using her unusual and "unfeminine" looks, singing, and movements in order to establish and redefine the notion of the new woman through her comic performances. As Douglas Gilbert further observes:

> It is virtually impossible to overestimate Tanguay's personality, or her influence in vaudeville. In the years she was tops this incredible woman alone jolted the maudlin period of the early 1900's away from its eye-dabbing with the vigor of unashamed sex. Precisely when the vaudeville public was listening to such treacle as "You'll Be Sorry Just Too Late," Tanguay was screaming "I Want Someone to Go Wild with Me."[59]

Describing "'The Queen of Perpetual Motion,'" popular entertainment historian Robert M. Lewis writes that "[Tanguay's] untamed nature, her wild extravagant, physical gestures, and her off-stage reputation for tempestuous love affairs" were essential to her success. And most significantly he concludes, "[Tanguay's] eccentricity made her the quintessential vaudeville star—the individual as the primary creative force, the performer as personality."[60] The nature of Eva Tanguay's eccentric act emphasizes the desire to be unique and indefinable in order to make a name in vaudeville. It also points to the need for the female performer of the modernist era to make a mark in a period where mass production of entertainment, and the industrialization of the worker, promoted the homogenous values and virtues of the newly minted middle class.

Tanguay also employed a self-deprecating model to reach her audience. As a reviewer noted in 1919, after having seen her ten years earlier in a "second class little theater tucked away almost behind a church,"[61] she mocked her own lack of singing, dancing, and acting skills. By this admission she stumped the critics by going against the traditional early-twentieth-century notions of refined female sex appeal and stage presence, making this the hallmark of her act. Tanguay's appeal, according to the *New York Dramatic Mirror*, was that:

> She thought out something different. Who ever heard an actress knock herself on the stage? She had been knocked by a great many critics so she said goodbye to the legitimate and framed up a vaudeville act and beat the knocking critics at their own game. She has made out of herself the biggest theatrical novelty the theater has ever known in the world.[62]

The *Dramatic Mirror* was certainly not alone in this assessment of Tanguay's unique performance style. In 1907, a Chicago newspaper confirmed that she was a "unique figure in the mimic world of today." In fact, she had "no counterpart, no imitators and is herself so original, so temperamental that there is not the slightest similarity between her work and that of any other performer on the stage."[63] Part of the reason for her success was Tanguay's cavalier onstage attitude. As one of her most popular routines declared:

> Some people say I think I'm it,
> But I don't care,
> They say they don't like me a bit,
> But I don't care;
> 'Cos my good nature effervescing,
> In one, there is no distressing,
> My spirit there is no oppressing,
> Just 'cos I don't care![64]

In 1905 Eva Tanguay appeared in a musical called *The Sambo Girl* that featured the song "I Don't Care." The narrative of the musical was really a series of vaudeville highlights of songs and dances for Tanguay. This number marked a turning point in her career that was to launch Tanguay into instant vaudeville fame. "I Don't Care" was a whirlwind of outrageous fun and nonconformity. It was an ideal number for her emerging talents. The song was coupled with others like it as well as comic sketches that appeared in her subsequent vaudeville touring repertoire.

Another popular part of her act, "I Want to Go Wild with Someone," depicted a woman who was liberated, sexually open, and in control of her own desires and needs. The perceived danger of her offensive onstage behavior came to the attention of the Keith circuit managers, who, in attempting to "clean up" her act, were met with a very strong willed performer who had the right to perform her act as she saw fit, as her popularity and paycheck boasted. As Tanguay herself sang to much notoriety and fame, "I don't care, what they may think of me!"[65] As a cultural critic for the *Atlantic* wrote of Eva Tanguay at the time, the blame could not necessarily be laid on "the 'unquiet women' [of] to-day," but rather on "the unquiet world."[66] The "unquiet world" that produced performers like Tanguay was a veiled reference to the shifting demographic of the United States and the advent of the immigrant underclass. Eva Tanguay and other "unquiet women" were thought to be a negative influence on the rise of the new women as evidenced by their lowbrow, burlesque-based performances that boasted that they did not care what anyone thought of them.

Eva Tanguay embraced the portrayal of the new woman who did not have to conform to the standards of innocence and attractiveness that had characterized the nineteenth-century female. Her originality fused the allure of the female form and the promise of forbidden sensuality. She contrasted this with an unfeminine braying voice, frenzied movements, overly tight costumes, and an untamable mane of hair. These visual markers embodied and professed her lack of confinement, refinement, and social decorum. The contour of the new woman as a wild woman, who uses ribald humor, sexual innuendo, and manic, uncontrollable stage energy, confirmed what reformers and critics feared most—that a woman's image of propriety, dignity, and social status was being contested and mocked in comic vaudeville routines.

The resistance to the new "wild" woman as new humorist was reflected in theatrical publications of the time. As an unidentified theater critic noted in 1902: "While heretofore the women in the casts of farcical productions have had to look prim and pretty and be satisfied with that... nowadays they... furnish food for risibility."[67] Audiences' desire for comic female vaudevillians became a lucrative profession for women with some popular performers making between $3,500 and $5,000 a week during the height of their careers and, as this same critic concludes, "with the demand came the supply. The funny girl has arrived."[68] The issue that the new female humorists presented as another reviewer put it was their "insinuating appeals to the senses, clever women do not hesitate to sacrifice all of the vanities of their sex—looks and grace—to evoke laughter from their audience."[69] This "sacrifice" on behalf of female vaudevillians was seen as an insult to womanhood by reformers and critics alike.

As the form evolved at the turn of the twentieth century, the tropes of the sexualized chorus girl and comic were closely related, and even crossed over in the case of Eva Tanguay, in much more integrated sensual/comic performances. Entertainment journalist John B. Kennedy for *Collier's* magazine conveyed this admixture of sex and comedy, writing:

> The pattern of the old shows was always the same. Opening chorus in which the girls appeared in knee-skirts. Then the comedians—an Irishman with a red nose, a Dutch comic with an enormous stomach and a Semite with an apostolic beard. These gentlemen immediately embroiled in a love tangle with a lady, usually an hour-glass soubrette referred to as "the lady widow." Each schemed to marry her. Each wore baggy clothes in contrast to the smart attire of the wise-guy or straight man who also paid court to the lady widow. The racial roughnecks punctuated their wooings with kicks fore and aft and coarse gibes, and were, in turn, punctuated by the ladies of the chorus who gamboled on in gradually minimized costumes, bawling popular songs.[70]

The female new humorists would forego the male comedians and take over these roles for themselves.

Early burlesque was dominated by producers like Weber and Fields, who sought to capitalize on the new humor found in sexual behavior and innuendo on the vaudeville stage. In the 1890s most of the singer/dancers were women, and most of the comedians, men. However, May Irwin and Eva Tanguay discovered that the sexualized body and the comic voice when combined by the female vaudevillian was a potent combination that pleased a wide variety of patrons both male and female. That combination of body and voice came under attack by Progressive reformers and social censors who were determined to remove the comic voice from female performers, and, by the 1920s, burlesque turned into nothing more than elaborate striptease acts, and comic vaudevillians were considered female "grotesques"—aberrations of femininity. Comic interludes were retained between the disrobing women, but they were often crude and sexually oriented jokes to keep the now mostly male audience's attention during the transition between the strippers. Women onstage were therefore bifurcated into two groups—the low-brow burlesque stripteasers and the highbrow Ziegfeld Girls—reduced to silent and statuesque models for the *Follies*.[71]

This separation of feminine beauty and comic masculine grotesque was a target of Progressive reformers to blunt the influences of tough girls on the vaudeville stage. Popular comic entertainments, particularly vaudeville, produced by mostly male entrepreneurs, attempted to remove the voice from comic female performers by focusing exclusively on the display of their bodies. The separation of the voice from the body produced silent females that would "Glorify the American Girl"[72] as witnessed in the choruses of the Ziegfeld *Follies*.[73]

Florenz Ziegfeld, Jr. was born into a middle-class German family in Chicago in 1868. As a young man he promoted performers like the strongman and bodybuilder Eugen Sandow for the 1892–93 Columbian Exposition in Chicago. After a stint touring Europe looking for more talent to promote, Ziegfeld was introduced to Anna Held, a Parisian singer.[74] Held had middling talents as a performer, but because of her exotic French background and beauty Ziegfeld promoted her as "the epitome of Gallic spice and naughtiness"—even though she was actually from a humble Polish Jewish heritage. Ziegfeld promoted her personality and sensuality rather than her stage skills by focusing on her "Parisian" mystique.[75]

He created the *Follies* beginning in 1907, starring Anna Held, with opulent sets and costumes and a chorus of women that would "glorify the American girl." Using the famous Parisian format for the *Folies Bergères* in combination with an American vaudeville model, the Ziegfeld *Follies* consisted of a series of scenes and interludes that featured singers, dancers, and comedians. However, to justify the higher ticket prices and distinguish the *Follies* from other Keith/Albee big-time vaudeville shows, Ziegfeld spared no expense when it came to spectacle; and one of the chief spectacles became the chorus girls. Ziegfeld would run his *Follies* until 1931 with such vaudeville headliners leading the bill as Fanny Brice, Eddie Cantor, W. C. Fields, Will Rogers, Eva Tanguay, Sophie Tucker, and Bert Williams.[76] Brice, Tucker, and Tanguay were considered comic grotesques—masculine women who could not be taken seriously. With impresarios like Ziegfeld, female comedians were intentionally presented as either overly sexualized bodies and burlesqued visions of ribald "broads" who were loud, brash, and unruly, or, conversely, as silent, pale, statuesque, and all-American mannequins used to decorate the stage.

Female performers defied Progressive-era reformers and producers like Ziegfeld, who sought to suppress women's voices as distinct from their bodies, through the characterization of their acts as "unruly," "wild," and "eccentric" new women of the comic vaudeville stage.[77] The rise of the new woman and the female comic vaudevillian, as evidenced by the reviews of their stage performances, shows the growing conflict between reformers and critics and the new women onstage during vaudeville's peak 1902–17 and the advent of World War I.

Reformers observed the social insurgency of the new humor in the nontraditional image of women displaying confrontational attitudes with regard to self-determination in their careers, sexual desires, and bombastic performances on the vaudeville stage. Because of their large bodies, unconventional looks, and ribald humor, they were perceived by middle-class reformers as grotesque versions of idealized American femininity and morality. These comic grotesques were seen as an affront to the serious place that women were trying to establish for themselves in American society. The new humor coupled with the new woman created an insurgency that undermined the efforts of reformers like Jane Addams and Frances Kellor.

Female new humorists because of their size and perceived masculine features and body types portrayed tough and boisterous ethnic immigrant characters that were neither traditional stage beauties nor respectable middle-class "ladies." They created a comedy category of "newcomers in grotesquerie," according to feminist performance scholar Susan A. Glenn.[78] As a vaudeville theater critic affirms, with their "insinuating appeal to the senses, [these] clever women do not hesitate to sacrifice all of the vanities of their sex—looks and grace—to evoke laughter from their audience."[79] The merger of the female/male persona for working-class immigrant women was itself a comic vision of womanhood enacted by new humorists. As popular entertainment historians Robert C. Allen, Susan A. Glenn, and M. Alison Kibler have observed, female performers in the first decades of the twentieth century were considered to represent "low others" through their association with prostitution, the lower body, or the working classes, and gained comic license largely because they were disenfranchised from middle-class society.

Theatrical reviewers and Progressive reformers pointed out the crude, lewd, and vulgar behaviors of the comic grotesque woman as a freakish and unsettling image that was to be condemned for its damaging influences, particularly with young female audience members who were presumably the most impressionable of all. The notion of bourgeois respectability meant a regulation and erasure of the ethnic heritage of recent immigrants and their American-born children. The female comic stage depicted women who were overbearing, brash, intelligent, and funny. Rejecting the refinements of the middle-class notions of the American family, with its harmonious clan where each member knew their place, was an impossibility given the realities of daily survival for the new immigrants and their families.

The shock for audiences and reformers alike was not simply the reversal of servant/master roles but rather the fact that a female comedian played the traditional role of the male eccentric comedian. They displayed characters of both the lower and upper classes as having a questionable moral code that left spectators either offended or intrigued. The ambivalent reception to the new woman as stage comedian can be witnessed with Marie Dressler. Consideration of Dressler as a new humorist points to the resistance of an overly simplistic division of the sensual feminized—demur, petite, and pretty—and the comic grotesque—manly, fat, and homely—body and voice.

Wild and unruly female performers were abided so long as their stage personas were filtered and diffused through a grotesque lens. For example, in 1913, one of producer B. F. Keith's managers described Marie Dressler's comedy in terms of the transgressive grotesque, reporting, "One hesitates to contemplate what would become of Miss Dressler's vocation if she ever lost her weight. She is just the same big, boisterous gross clown of yore and always bordering over the line. Nevertheless, she stirred up a riot of laughter and applause."[80] Equating Dressler's success as a "riot" of the "gross clown of yore," reinforced the notion of the grotesque created by and causing riotous behavior both on and offstage.

Born Leila Koerber in Cobourg, Canada, on November 9, 1869, Marie Dressler was the daughter of an itinerant musician who moved his family regularly from town to town. At the age of fourteen, she joined the Nevada Stock Company against the wishes of her parents and took the name of Marie Dressler from a favorite aunt. She moved from stock company to stock company, eventually arriving in New York, and singing at the Atlantic Garden on the Bowery, and Koster and Bial's Twenty-Third Street Theatre. Her first major stage achievement came with her role as Flo Honeydew of the Music Halls in an operatic comedy titled *The Lady Slavey*, which opened in Washington, DC, in September 1896. However, Dressler scored her biggest success when she introduced her character Tillie Blobbs, a comic inversion of the *Cinderella* character, in *Tillie's Nightmare*, at New York's Herald Square Theatre, May 5, 1910. As a result of the attention that the Tillie character brought her, she was hired by Mack Sennett to star in a 1914 feature-length comedy for Keystone Pictures in Hollywood. The film was to be called *Tillie's Punctured Romance*, co-starring a novice film comedian Charlie Chaplin, and the comedy film star Mabel Normand. Dressler also appeared in two less-successful sequels, *Tillie's Tomato* (1915) and *Tillie Wakes Up* (1917). But Marie Dressler's real triumph would be on the vaudeville stage, headlining in April 1919 at New York's Palace Theater for $1,500 per week. Her career stalled in the 1920s as the popularity of vaudeville waned and she could not get any traction in silent films. However, with the coming of sound pictures, Marie Dressler proved herself an accomplished actor working opposite Greta Garbo in Eugene O'Neill's screen adaptation of *Anna Christie*

(1930), and receiving the Academy Award for Best Actress in that same year for her performance in *Min and Bill.* She died shortly after in Santa Barbara, California, on July 28, 1934.[81]

In 1904, Marie Dressler joined up with vaudeville impresario and performer Joe Weber, touring with him for a number of years under the ignominious title of "Weber's Amazon."[82] Dressler starred in a successful Weber and Fields musical comedy, *Higgledy-Piggledy.* The musical was composed of a simplistic narrative as an excuse to feature vaudevillian episodes that included comic songs, dances, acrobatic routines, and sketches of humorous dialogue. The show highlighted "Weber's Amazon" singing what would become her signature number, "A Great Big Girl Like Me."[83] One of her first vaudeville appearances was at New York's Colonial Theatre in January 1907. This performance offered impersonations of Mrs. Leslie Carter and Blanche Bates, actresses from the legitimate stage, and Dressler's theme song from *Higgledy-Piggledy.*

Part of Marie Dressler's achievement can be attributed to her comic commentary capturing what a *Variety* critic noted as "the essence of her humor is its satire on insincerity and affectation."[84] Her act, according to the same review, consisted of "a howling travesty of the chesty elocutionist," and "an exquisite lampoon on the 'classy' prima donna"; the "beauty of her method" requiring "just enough accuracy and truth in her burlesques to make the picture ridiculously plain."[85] Ultimately, this at times canny review falls into the objectification of the grotesque female comedian, ending with the conclusion that "the Joe Weber amazon is a great big vaudeville hit."[86] Reduced to being Joe Weber's "amazon" the paradox of the truth of her performance is confronted with the suggestion that the real success of Dressler's comedy is her being tall, overweight, loud, and mannish. As another critic of the period observed, "[She] frankly abandons any ambition to be pretty or even attractive. The ludicrous is her aim, and in that object there is no sacrifice too great for her."[87] Descriptions of stage performances of many female comics during the early twentieth century reinforce the notion of how relative attractiveness and perceptions of the grotesque defined what was funny—and unnerving to reformers—about the new woman as female comedian.

Marie Dressler represented another vision of the new woman as comic vaudevillian. Through her skillful shifting back and forth from tough uncouth maid to immigrant "Big Mama," Dressler was able to comment on the stereotyped image of matronly working-class immigrant women as simple, soft-spoken caretakers, mothers, and servants who were only to serve their betters and not be heard from, as seen with her portrayal of Tillie Blobbs the overworked daughter a boardinghouse matron. After falling asleep from a long day of housework, while her mother and pretty sister have a night out on the town, Tillie has a dream about marrying a millionaire, moving to Paris, riding in an airship, and other fantasy sequences that would feature Dressler's comic talents. This dream sequence was a vehicle for a loose narrative structure supplied for the Weber and Fields comedy. Tillie Blobbs became a working girl's fantasy of freedom from a life of drudgery with the ultimate dream of escape. The most popular song in the show, which continued into her future vaudeville solo act, was "Heaven Will Protect the Working Girl."[88] This song also became linked with Dressler, as her comedy frequently championed a populist emphasis of the needs and concerns of the underclasses and marginalized women. Dressler would become a staunch defender of working women, particularly those of the vaudeville and Broadway stages. She personally led Broadway's chorus girls in the Actors' Equity strike of 1919, becoming the first president of the Chorus Equity Association, which demanded that Broadway's lowest-ranked women performers should share in the benefits of unionization. On and off the vaudeville stage, Dressler did her part to protect the "working girl."[89]

In contrast to the male assessment of women in comedy, Chicago critic Amy Leslie, who found Dressler's aggressive physicality "irresistible" and "amazing," claimed that this "rowdy [comic] knows nothing of delicacy or taste; she calls a spade a spade with the courage of a bad boy."[90] Marie Dressler herself is quoted in a 1910 interview where she argued that women were "natural comediennes." Several women currently performing in New York "could get right to the top in the comedy line if they would only stop trying to look pretty and to act funny at the same time," she espoused, but "dignity and comedy cannot go hand in hand."[91] When Dressler returned to vaudeville at the Palace in 1919 after her brief stint in Hollywood, she was greeted by audiences and critics alike as a beloved star and stage talent.

By 1919, after almost two decades of vaudeville success, Dressler was being touted as a comedy legend by the *New York Dramatic Mirror*:

> Marie Dressler, one of the greatest institutions of burlesque on the American stage—not of the ten-twenty-thirty standard, but of the strata that demands talent and brains—has returned to vaudeville... She was in all her cut-up glory, exactly like the old days of Weber and Fields. She satisfied everyone... the reason [for her success is] that she has always some[thing] to say that even college professors can understand as well as servant girls... Miss Dressler is a household name and she will be a big card for the two-a-day [first-tier vaudeville circuit] from the Atlantic to the Pacific.[92]

Dressler's comic grotesque appeal was a product of talents developed in "burlesque" and the "cut-up glory" of the vaudevillian. Her humor was accessible to various classes and levels of education and culture. The "ten-twenty-thirty standard" audiences—meaning patrons of the third-tier vaudeville houses who charged ten, twenty, or thirty cents maximum—as well as the well-healed audiences of the Palace Theater, could appreciate Dressler's unique comic voice and body equally. The female vaudevillian as comic grotesque was to take her rightful place as an institution of American popular entertainment with Marie Dressler.

The female spectators who purchased tickets for new humorists like May Irwin, Eva Tanguay, and Marie Dressler are of particular interest in understanding the new women in relationship to comedy. Without a codification of female behavior no control over civilizing women could be put in place. Anxiety over prescribed rank in society was of concern outside the home of these same women who refused class hierarchy and their place in it. Caroline Caffin mentions the ambivalent reactions of women in a vaudeville audience with regard to female acts writing, "I sat next to two dear little old Brooklyn ladies who were delighted with the audacities of Gertrude Vanderbilt because she 'looked so like dear Eloise.' On the other hand, she declares a visiting English singer to be a 'perfectly odious person. She distorts herself in such an unwomanly way.'"[93] This apprehension was already in evidence in the vaudeville audience as the more refined acts that focused on the middle classes were becoming less and less popular than acts that appealed to the cheap seats of the gallery. Caffin's remark about audience response to female acts is insightful as to how vaudeville—especially comedy—had to verge on the edge of being offensive even when trying to appeal to a diverse audience. Caffin continues noting,

> Now betwixt these contrasting elements—and the extremes are even greater than the [one] I have named—the programme must fill in the breach. There must be something for everyone and, though the fastidious may be a little shocked (the fastidious rather like to be shocked sometimes), they must not be offended, while the seeker for thrills must on no account be bored by too much mildness.[94]

Rather than merely being crude, lewd, and loud, performances by female new humorists attracted audiences who desired release and relief from the civilized restraints of bourgeois American society—especially for the new women. Vaudeville comedy, according to popular entertainment historian Henry Jenkins, reveals a conflict between the freedom of the comic fool's outbursts versus intrusions into polite society by the "dupes, killjoys, and counterfeits"[95] that are the models for "all that is stifling or corrupt in the social order."[96] Like their male counterparts, female comic acts capitalized on the new humor reflecting a world in social turmoil. They signaled a restructuring of values with significant emphasis on the vibrant, the fast, and the protean, and "with women cheering on boxing matches, 'hoi polloi' paying attention to literature, and the box patrons occasionally immersed in 'riots,' vaudeville theaters were sites in which patrons could test new freedoms and cross social boundaries."[97] Female comedians in particular reflected these sociocultural changes onstage as well as off.

Attempting to combat the dangers associated with the new humor and the new woman, the formidable entrepreneur B. F. Keith pronounced: "In many instances, indeed, [variety theaters] were offensive to the essentially wholesome and clean-minded American majority. I have endeavored to reform abuses at which I hint, by eliminating from my bills everything savoring of vulgarity or salaciousness."[98] Keith's battle to court decency—and audiences that included middle-class women and their children—often clashed with his very own acts, particularly the female new humorists. The new woman as comic performer challenged and broke through boundaries of class, ethnicity, and gender as set by reform standards of the time. The new women as new humorists established a place for themselves that directly challenged the male-dominated province of stage comedy. Reinventing the female image onstage with their songs, dances, improvisations, and sketches, they were able to successfully subvert the Anglo-American middle-class definitions of womanhood.

The success of these new humorists as social insurgents provoked an interesting conundrum in that audiences, reformers, and authorities simultaneously embraced and rejected women as comedians. By creating performances that defied Progressive-era reformers, critics, and authorities, these new humorists were able to destabilize the confinement of being labeled "wild women" and "tough girls." They worked to reunite the voice and body of the new women through their acts. Over a thirty-year period, the rising fame and popularity of women in comic vaudeville was proof that they had successfully challenged and unseated the attempted controls that Progressive-era reformers had advocated. Finding themselves in conflict with moral and cultural authorities as well as the press, female comic vaudevillians created new perceptions of women's voices and bodies in performance for future generations. The legacy of these social insurgents and the striking of "sex-o-clock" can be seen in the contemporary acts of Roseanne Barr, Ellen Degeneres, Tina Fey, Rosie O'Donnell, Bette Midler, Amy Poehler, Sarah Silverman, and Julia Sweeney, all of who owe a debt to these new humorists of the vaudeville stage.

Epilogue

The new humor of the early twentieth century concerned itself with the plight of the underclasses particularly of new immigrants and their families. Ethnic, family, and school acts focused on subjects of domestic urban life, verbal and physical misunderstandings, conflicts between ethnic groups vying for survival, the disparity between rich and poor, and the social climbing of the new middle class. In Brett Page's 1915 book, *Writing for Vaudeville*, he quotes a satirical stump speech in which a "German Senator" lays out the issues of the day:

> And when [the Statue of Liberty] stands there now, looking on the country the way it is and what she has to stand for, I tell you tears and tears must drop from her eyes. Well, to prove it—look at the ocean she filled up. And no wonder she's crying. Read the nuisance papers. See what is going on. Look at what the country owes... Nobody knows what we owe it for; and nobody ever sees what we have got for it; and if you go to Washington, the Capsule of the United States, and ask them, THEY don't even know THEMSELVES.[1]

The promise of the melting pot that embraces all newcomers with a chance at making a new life in a fair and democratic nation of tolerance and opportunity is belied by this next part of the speech:

> Statistics prove that the average wages of the workingman is one dollar a day. Out of that, he's got to spend fifty cents a day for food; fifty-five cents for rent; ten cents for car fare. And at the end of a hard day's work—he owes himself fifteen cents. Yet the rich people say that the poor people are getting prosperous. They say look at our streets. You see nothing but automobiles. You don't see half the poor people now that you used to. Certainly you don't. Half of them have already been run over and the other half are afraid to come out.[2]

It is difficult not to recognize the exaggerated inequality between the "rich and rest of us" that Tavis Smiley and Cornell West have written about in the early twenty-first century.[3] The Progressive-era reformers, critics, and authorities whose intentions were to bridge this disparity with regulations that focused on the strengthening of the middle class was challenged by the new humor. The "German Senator" act examined the realities of daily life including the gulf between classes, the high costs of living, and government corruption. The new humor was a forum for openly confronting injustices and provided solidarity through laughter for the underclasses of new immigrants and new women.

Progressive-era psychologist Max Eastman noted the significance between the laughter of the nineteenth century and the new humor of the early twentieth century. Eastman's book *The Sense of Humor* made a distinction between joking and having a "sense of humor," and with this sensibility came "the most original and most profound contribution of modern thought to the problem of the comic."[4] A 1907 article, "The Limitations of Humor," warned that the new humor was being taken too far and "humor, which should be relief and nothing more, is now an end in itself."[5]

However, the importance of the new humor for another psychologist of the period, Gilson Gardner, was that it created a mindset that "detects" and "repudiates" truth from falsehood, and reality from appearances.[6] The concept of detecting truth through the new humor can be witnessed when Chico Marx—attempting to prove that he can hypnotize another character by the name of Richman (Edward Metcalfe)—in a vaudeville routine from the Marx Brothers' revue *I'll Say She Is* (1923)—embraces its logic during the following dialogue:

> CHICO: You are a snake.
> RICHMAN: How do you snake?
> CHICO: Just like a worm, only more.
> *(Business of wriggling like a snake for Richman.)*
> CHICO: What a fat snake.
> RICHMAN: Yes, but I don't think I am a snake.
> CHICO: You don't, but I will give $1,000 to anyone who can prove that I don't think you are a snake.[7]

With Chico's line, "prove that *I* don't think you're a snake," he confirms the new humor's reasoning that reality has to be proven and that truth comes from whoever happens to be in authority. As with Groucho's admonition of why he should have to prove his citizenship and loyalty as an American while the Pilgrims and those of Anglo-American origins do not, being an American—like being a snake—is subjective to those who make the rules.

The backbone of the new humor was the lowbrow comedy of the new immigrant and the new woman. However during the mid-1910s and 1920s as entrepreneurs like Edward F. Albee and Florenz Ziegfeld focused on appealing to the middle and upper middle classes with their vaudeville spectacles in theater palaces, the padded Dutchman, the brawling "Irisher," and the grotesque foreigner were forced out and replaced by tuxedoed "sophisticated" comics and glamorous showgirls backed by cycloramas, elaborate scenery, and extravagant costumes that added to the pageantry but not to the comedy. As Albee's million-dollar theaters dominated vaudeville, they became too large, and ticket prices too high, to support the intimacy of the vaudeville comedians and their underclass audiences. The eccentric, boob, and nut comedians were pushed into the background as vaudeville foregrounded Americanization.

Some high-profile performers like Buster Keaton, the Marx Brothers, and Marie Dressler were absorbed into the film industry. And many new humorists reemerged in radio and television during the mid-twentieth century as former vaudevillians like Fred Allen, Fanny Brice, and Groucho Marx, who had second careers that extended their stage work in these new media formats.[8] Their legacy continues to influence the new humor of film, television, and now internet platforms like YouTube. The so-called dangers presented by the eastern and southern European new immigrants and the new women have been replaced by the new fears surrounding homosexuals, Muslims, and Mexicans. The new humor still responds to these new paradigm shifts as we begin the new millennium by confronting and satirizing these irrational anxieties caused by the decline of Anglo-Christian hegemony in the United States. Current new humorists including Dave Chappelle, Stephen Colbert, Larry David, Tina Fey, Assif Mandvi, Key and Peele, and

Sarah Silverman continue to scrutinize and destabilize what it means to be an American.

As Stephen Colbert states, mocking right-wing conservative pundits and journalists in an episode of *The Colbert Report*, "I know you watch this show to keep abreast of what to be scared and/or angry about."[9] Colbert reminds us not to be blinded by nationalism and media-generated fears from contemporary charlatans on "news" programs like Fox, CNN, and MSNBC. The court of public opinion and its reliance on "truthiness" (truth based on "gut" responses rather than critical thinking, the vetting of information, and actual experience) is questioned and dispelled in contemporary comedy continuing the "who are you going to believe, me or your own eyes?" philosophy of the new humor into the twenty-first century.

Notes

PREFACE

1. U.S. Immigration Commission, Vol. 1 (Washington, DC: General Printing Office, 1910), 13.
2. Woodrow Wilson, *A History of the American People*, Vol. 5 (New York: Harper & Brothers, 1902), 212–13.
3. Prescott Hall writing in 1897, quoted in Barbara M. Solomon, *Ancestors and Immigrants* (Chicago: University of Chicago Press, 1956), 111.
4. Edward Harrigan interview with Frank C. Drake, *New York World* (1909), n.p., qtd. in Douglas Gilbert, *American Vaudeville: Its Life and Times* (New York: Dover Publications, 1940), 111; also qtd. in Albert McLean, Jr., *American Vaudeville as Ritual* (Lexington, KY: University of Kentucky Press, 1965), 106.
5. The Immigration Restriction League had an umbrella organization called the National Association of Immigration Restriction Leagues created in 1896. Prescott Hall served as its general secretary from 1896 to 1921.
6. Harrigan qtd. in Gilbert, *American Vaudeville*, 111. The concept of the "new humor" is discussed in McLean, *American Vaudeville as Ritual*, 106–37.
7. Ellwood Cubberley, *Changing Conceptions of Education* (New York: Macmillan, 1909), 14–15.
8. Harrigan quoted in Gilbert, *American Vaudeville*, 111. It should be noted that another composer and collaborator of Harrigan's early musical comedies was David Braham.
9. David Savran, *Highbrow/Lowdown: Theater, Jazz, and the Making of the New Middle Class* (Ann Arbor, MI: University of Michigan Press, 2009), 2–3.
10. Mary Cass Canfield, "The Great American Art," *The New Republic* (November 22, 1922): 334–5.

1 AMERICANIZATION: PROGRESSIVE-ERA REFORMERS, CULTURAL CRITICS, AND POPULAR COMIC ENTERTAINMENTS

1. In 1923, the "Theatrical Agency" would become the opening of their Broadway musical revue hit *I'll Say She Is*.
2. The Four Marx Brothers, "Theatrical Agency," scene from *On the Balcony* (Library of Congress, February 1921); subsequently revised for *I'll Say She Is* (Library of Congress, November 19, 1924); and revised again for the movie trailer to *Monkey Business*, 1931, http://www.marx-brothers.org/marxology/story.htm; see also Glenn Mitchell, *The Marx Brothers Encyclopedia* (London: Titan Books, 2011), 154.
3. Quoted from Emma Lazarus, "The New Colossus," 1883. The inscription was engraved inside the pedestal of the Statue of Liberty in 1903.
4. Groucho Marx, "Europa Has a Rough Trip," *New York Times* (February 15, 1931), 18.
5. David Roediger, *Working Toward Whiteness: How America's Immigrants Became White* (New York: Basic Books, 2005), 11. For the relationship of the Progressive era to the industrial revolution and American culture at the turn of the twentieth century see also Patricia Bradley, *Making American Culture: A Social History, 1900–1920* (New York: Palgrave Macmillan, 2009); Richard Butsch, *The Making of American Audiences: From Stage to Television, 1750–1990* (Cambridge, UK: Cambridge University Press, 2000); Steven J. Diner, *A Very Different Age: Americans of the Progressive Era* (New York: Hill and Wang, 1998); Peter Gay, *Modernism: The Lure of Heresy* (New York and London: W.W. Norton & Company, 2008); Rob King, *The Fun Factory: The Keystone Film Company and the Emergence of Mass Culture* (Berkeley and Los Angeles: University of California Press, 2009); Jackson Lears, *Rebirth of a Nation: The Making of Modern America, 1877–1920* (New York: Harper Perennial, 2009); Michael E. McGerr, *The Decline of Popular Politics: The American North, 1865–1928* (New York and Oxford: Oxford University Press, 1986); Michael E. McGerr, *A Fierce Discontent: The Rise and Fall of the Progressive Movement in America, 1870–1920* (New York: Free Press, 2003).
6. US Immigration Commission, Vol. 1, 13.
7. Henry Cabot Lodge, "The Restriction of Immigration," *North American Review* 152 (1891): 32, 35.
8. Qtd. in John Whiteclay Chambers II, *The Tyranny of Change*, 3rd ed. (New York: Rutgers University Press, 2000), 2.
9. Benjamin Parke De Witt, *The Progressive Movement: A Non-Partisan Comprehensive Discussion of Current Tendencies in American Politics* (New Brunswick, NJ: Transaction Publishers, 2013[1915]), 14.

10. Ibid., 24–5.
11. Robert H. Wiebe, *The Search for Order, 1877–1920* (New York: Hill and Wang, 1967), 111.
12. E. A. Ross, *Sin and Society: An Analysis of Latter-Day Iniquity* (Boston: Houghton Mifflin, 1907), 45.
13. Herbert Croly, *The Promise of American Life* (New York: Macmillan, 1909), xiv.
14. Christopher Lasch, preface to *Randolph Bourne The Radical Will: Selected Writings 1911–1918*, ed. Olaf Hansen (Berkeley: University of California Press, 1977), 11.
15. Randolph S. Bourne, "Trans-National America," *Atlantic Monthly* 118 (July 1916): 86–97, reprinted in Bourne, *War and the Intellectuals, Collected Essays 1915–1919*, ed. Carl Resek (New York: Harper and Row, 1964), 107–23.
16. Bourne qtd. in introduction of *The Radical Will*, 59.
17. Ibid.
18. Ibid.
19. Randolph Bourne, "Pageantry and Social Art," in *Radical Will*, 516; original in *Dial* (November 1918), n.p.
20. Walter Lippmann, *Public Opinion* (New York: Macmillan, 1922), 79–81.
21. Walter Lippmann, *Drift and Mastery: An Attempt to Diagnose the Current Unrest* (New York: Mitchell Kennerley, 1914), 250.
22. Lippmann, *Public Opinion*, 85–6.
23. Edward Hale Bierstadt, "Untitled Review," *The New Republic* (June 1, 1921), 21.
24. Lippmann, *Public Opinion*, 90–1.
25. Ibid., 80.
26. Ibid., 81–2.
27. Ibid., 72.
28. See Wilfred M. McClay's introduction to Lippmann's *The Phantom Public* (New Brunswick, NJ: Transaction Publishers, 1993).
29. Excluding black Americans as Jim Crow segregation would be in place until the 1960s.
30. Sigmund Freud, *Jokes and Their Relation to the Unconscious*, trans. James Strachey (New York and London: W.W. Norton, 1960[1905]).
31. Frank Lloyd Wright, *Autobiography* (New York: Pomegranate Communications, 2005[1932]), 80.
32. Gertrude Stein, "Portraits and Repetition," in *Writing and Lectures, 1911–1945*, ed. Patricia Meyerowitz (London: Owen, 1967), 98–9.
33. Frederic Thompson, "Amusing the Million," *Everybody's Magazine* (September 1908), 6.

34. Edmund Wilson, "Gilbert Seldes and the Popular Arts" (1924), in *The Shores of Light: A Literary Chronicle of the Twenties and Thirties* (New York: Farrar, Straus, and Young, 1952), 163–4.
35. Lippmann, *Public Opinion*, 81.
36. Ibid., 82.
37. Stuart Hall, "Notes on Deconstructing 'the Popular,'" in *People's History and Socialist Theory*, ed. Raphael Samuel (London: Routledge and Kegan Paul, 1981), 227.
38. Ibid., 227–40.
39. Jane Addams, *The Spirit of Youth and the City Streets* (New York: Macmillan, 1909), 18–19.
40. Ibid.
41. Elizabeth Israels Perry, *Belle Moskowitz: Feminine Politics and the Exercise of Power in the Age of Alfred E. Smith* (New York: Oxford University Press, 1987), 41–57.
42. Ibid.
43. Belle Moskowitz, "Dance Problem," *Playground* 4 (October 1910): 244, 248, 249; see also, Louise Bowen, *Speeches, Addresses, and Letters of Louise deKoven Bowen* (Ann Arbor, MI: Edwards Brothers, 1937); Mary Kingsbury Simkhovitch, *The City Worker's World in America* (New York: Macmillan, 1917).
44. Michael M. Davis, *The Exploitation of Pleasure: A Study of Commercial Recreations in New York City* (New York: The Russell Sage Foundation, 1912), 33, 36.
45. Francis Bellamy, "The Pledge of Allegiance," *Illustrated American* (October 1892), n.p.
46. Bellamy's "Pledge" is still used in public schools in the United States as of the writing of this book.
47. R. L. Duffus, *Lillian Wald: Neighbor and Crusader* (New York: Macmillan, 1939), 147.
48. Peter Roberts, *The New Immigration* (New York: Macmillan, 1913), 306–7.
49. Ibid.
50. *Immigrants in America Review*, I (1915): 3–4, 15.
51. Ibid.; Frances Kellor and Joseph Mayper, *Recommendations for a Federal Bureau of Distribution Department of Labor* (Boston: Wright & Potter, 1914).
52. Daughters of the American Republic, *Report* (1905–06): 23; Sons of the American Revolution, *National Year Book* (1902): 174–80 and (1914): 137–8.
53. Sime Silverman, "Review of *Fun in Hi Skule*," *Variety* (February 24, 1912), 17.
54. Sime Silverman, "Review of Mae West," *Variety* (May 25, 1912), 16.

55. Edward F. Albee, "Twenty Years of Vaudeville," *Variety* 72, no. 3 (September 6, 1923): 18; *Theatre Magazine* 31 (May 1920): 408.
56. Louis Reeves Harrison, "Is 'Vodeveal' Necessary?" *The Moving Picture World* 8, no. 14 (April 9, 1911): 758–60.
57. Hartley Davis, "In Vaudeville," *Everybody's Magazine* 13 (August 1905): 233.
58. "The Decay of Vaudeville," *American Magazine* 69 (April 1910): 841.
59. Rob Wagner, "Smart-Crackers and Cheese," qtd. in *Rob Wagner's Script* 2, no. 5 (September 14, 1929): 1–2, 32.
60. "'Movie,' Manners and Morals," *Outlook* 113 (July 26, 1916): 694–5.
61. Thompson, "Amusing the Million," 1–9.
62. Ibid.; see also Mikail Bahktin on the "carnivalesque" in *Rabelais and His World*, trans. Helene Iswolsky (Bloomington and Indianapolis: Indiana University Press, 1984[1940]).
63. Thompson, "Amusing the Million," 1–9.
64. Ibid.
65. Ibid.
66. See Paul DiMaggio, "Cultural Entrepreneurship in Nineteenth-Century Boston: The Creation of an Organizational Base for High Culture in America," *Media, Culture and Society* 1 (January 1982): 33–50; Lawrence W. Levine, *Highbrow/Lowbrow: The Emergence of Cultural Hierarchy in America* (Cambridge, MA: Harvard University Press, 1988); Savran, *Highbrow/Lowdown*.

2 PUTTING IT OVER IN AMERICAN VAUDEVILLE

1. "In Vaudeville: A Short History of This Popular Character of Amusement," *Midway* (October 1, 1905), 27.
2. Ibid.
3. Albert F. McLean, Jr., *American Vaudeville as Ritual* (Frankfort, KY: University of Kentucky Press, 1965), 107. McLean capitalizes "New Humor" in his study.
4. Louis Bolard More, *Wage-Earners' Budgets: A Study of Standards and Costs of Living in New York City* (New York, 1907), 142; Annie M. MacLean, *Wage-Earning Women* (New York: Macmillan, 1910), 72.
5. Much of vaudeville's history, including its performers and acts, were researched from multiple sources including, but not exclusive to, archival research on specific performers, stage reviews, and critical articles of the period, as well as sociological data found in newspapers and publications, especially *the New York Clipper*, *Variety*, the *New York Daily Mirror*, the *New York Times*, and *Billboard*.

6. *Billboard Magazine*, 1915; cited in *From Travelling Show to Vaudeville: Theatrical Spectacle in America, 1830–1910*, ed. Robert M. Lewis (Baltimore, MD and London: The Johns Hopkins University Press, 2003), 328.
7. Edwin Milton Royle, "The Vaudeville Theatre," *Scribner's Magazine* (October 26, 1899), 489; cited in Lewis, *From Travelling Show to Vaudeville*, 322.
8. Will M. Cressy, "Putting It Over," *The Green Book Magazine* (March 1916): 547–52, in *Selected Vaudeville Criticism*, ed. Andrew Slide (Metuchen, NJ and London: The Scarecrow Press, 1988), 218–22.
9. Ibid.
10. Ibid.
11. Caffin, *Vaudeville*, 61–2.
12. Acts consisted of between two and ten performances on any given day. Five-a-day were an average number of performances.
13. Canfield, "Great American Art," 334–5.
14. Freud, *Jokes*, 117.
15. Caffin, *Vaudeville*, 15–16.
16. Ibid., 21–2.
17. Twentieth Century Club Drama Committee, *The Amusement Situation in Boston* (Boston 1910), 3 and 8.
18. Robert Lytell, "Vaudeville Old and Young," *New Republic* (July 1, 1925), 156.
19. Henry Jenkins, *What Made Pistachio Nuts?: Early Sound Comedy and the Vaudeville Aesthetic* (New York: Columbia University Press, 1992), 70.
20. Seminal texts in popular entertainments of the nineteenth century and their influence on the early-twentieth-century comic vaudeville stage include, Robert C. Allen, *Horrible Prettiness: Burlesque and American Culture* (Chapel Hill, NC and London: University of North Carolina Press, 1991); Gilbert, *American Vaudeville*; McLean, *American Vaudeville as Ritual*; David Nasaw, *Going Out: The Rise and Fall of Public Amusements* (New York: Basic Books, 1990); Robert C. Toll, *On with the Show: The First Century of Show Business in America* (New York: Oxford University Press, 1976).
21. Laurence Senelick, "Minstrel Shows," in *The Cambridge Guide to American Theatre*, 2nd ed., ed. Don B. Wilmeth (Cambridge: Cambridge University Press, 2007), 446.
22. Eric Lott, *Love and Theft: Blackface Minstrelsy and the American Working Class* (New York: Oxford University Press, 1995), 5–6.
23. More information on minstrelsy can be found in Senelick, *Cambridge Guide to American Theatre*, 446; Robert C. Toll, *Blacking Up: The Minstrel*

Show in Nineteenth-Century America (New York: Oxford University Press, 1974); Lott, *Love and Theft*. Two of the most recent books to address blackface minstrelsy and its complex history include *Burnt Cork: Traditions and Legacies of Blackface Minstrelsy*, ed. Stephen Johnson (Amherst, MA: University of Massachusetts Press, 2012) and Christopher J. Smith, *The Creolization of American Culture: William Sidney Mount and the Roots of Blackface Minstrelsy* (Champaign, IL: University of Illinois Press, 2013).

24. Toll, *Blacking Up*, 162–3.
25. Senelick, *Cambridge Guide to American Theatre*, 446–8.
26. Frank Cullen, *Vaudeville Old & New: An Encyclopedia of Variety Performers in America*, ed. Frank Cullen, with Florence Hackman and Donald McNeilly, Vol. 1 (New York: Routledge, 2007), 266–7.
27. My concern in this study is not with the racial components of blackface minstrelsy. For a comprehensive evaluation of minstrelsy and its racial and sociocultural implications during nineteenth-century America, I recommend Lott's *Love and Theft*, David Krasner's *Resistance, Parody and Double Consciousness in African American Theatre, 1895–1910* (New York: Palgrave Macmillan, 1997), and Toll's *Blacking Up*.
28. Robert Snyder, *The Voice of the City: Vaudeville and Popular Culture in New York* (New York and Oxford: Oxford University Press, 1989), 9.
29. Cullen, *Vaudeville Old & New*, 260–1.
30. "Origins of the Variety Show," *New York Herald* (September 3, 1883), 32.
31. "The Concert Saloons," *New York World* (April 25, 1862), 4.
32. M. B. Leavitt, *Fifty Years in Theatrical Management* (New York: Broadway Publishing, 1912), 209–10.
33. Junius Henry Browne, *The Great Metropolis: A Mirror of New York* (Hartford, CT: American Publishing Co., 1868), 327.
34. Ibid., 326–8.
35. Robert Grau, *The Business Man in the Amusement World* (New York: Broadway Publishing, 1910), 108.
36. Senelick, *Cambridge Guide to American Theatre*, 663.
37. Cullen, "Variety," *Vaudeville Old & New*, Vol. 2, 1150–2; Senelick, *Cambridge Guide to American Theatre*, 663; Lawrence E. Mintz, "Humor and Ethnic Stereotypes in Vaudeville and Burlesque," *MELUS* 21, no. 4, Ethnic Humor (Winter 1996): 19–28.
38. F. T. Marinetti, *Critical Writings*, ed. Günter Berghaus, trans. Doug Thompson (New York: Farrar, Straus and Giroux, 2006), 189.
39. Senelick, "Minstrel Shows," 663.
40. Allen, *Horrible Prettiness*, 30.
41. Ibid., 29.

42. Ibid., 28–9.
43. Ibid., 28.
44. Richard Grant White, "The Age of Burlesque," *Galaxy* (August 1869): 256–66.
45. Slide, ed., *The Encyclopedia of Vaudeville* (Westport, CT: Greendwood Press, 1994), 508–9.
46. "Sophie Tucker," *New York Dramatic Mirror* (September 11, 1909).
47. Ibid.
48. An excellent examination of Jewish performers using blackface in performance at the turn of the twentieth century can be found in Michael Rogin, *Blackface, White Noise: Jewish Immigrants in the Hollywood Melting Pot* (Berkeley and Los Angeles: University of California Press, 1996).
49. "Interview with Sophie Tucker," *New York Dramatic Mirror* (February 1, 1919).
50. Senelick, "Burlesque Shows," *Cambridge Guide to American Theatre*, 135.
51. Rowland Barber, *The Night They Raided Minsky's: A Fanciful Expedition to the Lost Atlantis of Show Business* (New York: Simon & Schuster, 1960), 201.
52. Jill Dolan, "'What, No Beans?' Images of Women and Sexuality in Burlesque Comedy," *Journal of Popular Culture* 18, no. 3 (Winter 1984): 39.
53. Andrew Davis, *Baggy Pants Comedy: Burlesque and the Oral Tradition* (New York: Palgrave Macmillan, 2011), 66.
54. It should be noted that the nineteenth-century popular entertainment forms discussed here often overlapped. Productions were ongoing throughout the early to late 1800s, often performing simultaneously. These entertainments continued on as discrete performance forms after they had informed vaudeville well into the twentieth century.
55. B. F. Keith, "The Vogue of Vaudeville," in *American Vaudeville As Seen by Its Contemporaries*, ed. Charles W. Stein (New York: Alfred A. Knopf, 1984), 17.
56. "Decay of Vaudeville," 846.
57. *Dramatic Mirror* (September 21, 1910); Richard Butsch, *Making of American Audiences*, 113.
58. "The Decay of Vaudeville," *American Magazine* 69 (April 1910): 840.
59. Gilbert, *American Vaudeville*, 243.
60. Frances Peck Smith, "In Vaudeville," *The Green Book Album* 8 (July 1912): 142.
61. George A. Gottlieb, "Psychology of the American Vaudeville Show from the Manager's Point of View," *Current Opinion* 60 (April 1916): 257.
62. McLean, *American Vaudeville as Ritual*, 17.

63. Robert Knopf provides one of the most complete examinations of Keaton's vaudeville years, although his primary focus is Keaton's later film work. Robert Knopf, *The Theater and Cinema of Buster Keaton* (Princeton, NJ: Princeton University Press, 1999), 36–7.
64. A "buster" here means one who bounces back from being thrown around on the stage and potentially "busted."
65. Buster Keaton, with Charles Samuels, *My Wonderful World of Slapstick* (New York: Da Capo Press, 1960), 18–19.
66. Ibid., 33.
67. Keaton, with Samuels, *Wonderful World of Slapstick*, 28.
68. Edward Bellamy, *Looking Backward: 2000–1887* (New York: New American Library, 2009[1888]).

3 THE NEW HUMOR: ETHNIC ACTS AND FAMILY ACTS

1. Joe Laurie, Jr., *Vaudeville: From the Honky Tonks to the Palace* (New York: Henry Holt, 1953), 20–170.
2. Ibid., 81.
3. Harrison Grey Fiske, *New York Dramatic Mirror* (July 29, 1895), 8.
4. Ibid.
5. Twentieth Century Club Drama Committee, *The Amusement Situation in Boston* (Boston 1910): 30–1.
6. Josiah Strong, *The Challenge of the City* (New York: Young People's Missionary Movement, 1907), 115.
7. Diner, *A Very Different Age*, 77.
8. Paul Klapper, "The Yiddish Music Hall," *University Settlement Studies* 2, no. 4 (1905): 20–1.
9. Kathy Lee Peiss, *Cheap Amusements: Working Women and Leisure in Turn-of-the-Century New York* (Philadelphia, PA: Temple University Press, 1986), 143.
10. Klapper, "The Yiddish Music Hall," 22; see also Butsch, *Making of American Audience*, 132–5.
11. John Murray Cuddihy, *The Ordeal of Civility: Freud, Marx, Levi-Strauss, and the Jewish Struggle with Modernity* (New York: Basic Books, 1974), 126.
12. Armond Fields and L. Marc Fields, *From the Bowery to Broadway: Lew Fields and the Roots of American Popular Theater* (New York and Oxford: Oxford University Press, 1993), 36–53.
13. Gilbert, *American Vaudeville*, 78.

14. This routine is recounted in Felix Isman, *Weber and Fields* (New York: Boni and Liveright, 1924), 148.
15. Bourne, "Trans-National America," 86–97.
16. Robert Benchley, "Review of Weber and Fields," *Life* (October 7, 1926), 9, Weber and Fields clippings file, Robinson Locke Collection of Theatrical Scrapbooks, Billy Rose Theatre Collection, New York Public Library for the Performing Arts.
17. H. L. Mencken, "A Plea for Comedy," in *The Collected Drama of H. L. Mencken: Plays and Criticism*, ed. S.T. Joshi (Lanham, MD: Scarecrow Press, 2012), 179.
18. Ibid., 181.
19. "Four Marx Brothers Offer Amusing Sketch at Palace," *Newark News* (August 5, 1919), n.p.
20. Gehring, *The Marx Brothers*, 41.
21. George S. Kaufman, *Animal Crackers* in *Kaufman & Co.: Broadway Comedies*, ed. Laurence Maslon (New York: Library of the Americas, 2004), 133–5. The text of *Animal Crackers* found in this Kaufman anthology, and cited here, is a combination of Sam Harris's 1928 Princeton University archival version, and the 1929 version found in the Groucho Marx papers at the Library of Congress.
22. Ibid., 138–9.
23. Ibid., 140. Note that in the original *Animal Crackers* manuscript of 1929, Abie the Fishman was referred to as Ivan Pidulski the Fish-Peddler. I have used Abie since it was used in the 1930 film version, as well as in the 1982 Arena Stage revival, and is the most common version.
24. Laurie, *Vaudeville*, 82.
25. Ibid., 144.
26. Ibid., 145.
27. Biographical and anecdotal background on Buster Keaton comes primarily from Keaton and Samuels, *Wonderful World of Slapstick*; Knopf, *Theater and Cinema of Buster Keaton*; and Edward McPherson, *Buster Keaton: Tempest in a Flat Hat* (New York: Faber and Faber, 2007).
28. Keaton with Samuels, *Wonderful World of Slapstick*, 12.
29. "In Vaudeville Houses," *New York Times* (May 21, 1903), n.p., Buster Keaton clippings file, Robinson Locke Collection of Theatrical Scrapbooks, Billy Rose Theatre Collection, New York Public Library for the Performing Arts.
30. "The Three Keatons," *New York Dramatic Mirror* (October, 30 1909), 19, Buster Keaton clippings file, Robinson Locke Collection of Theatrical Scrapbooks, Billy Rose Theatre Collection, New York Public Library for the Performing Arts.

31. "The Three Keatons," *New York Clipper* (July 20, 1901), 438, Buster Keaton clippings file, Robinson Locke Collection of Theatrical Scrapbooks, Billy Rose Theatre Collection, New York Public Library for the Performing Arts.
32. Keaton with Samuels, *Wonderful World of Slapstick*, 34–35.
33. *The Playhouse* in *Buster Keaton: The Short Films Collection 1920–1923*, DVD, written and directed by Buster Keaton and Eddie Kline (New York: Kino Lorber, 2011[1921]).
34. Keaton with Samuels, *Wonderful World of Slapstick*, 12–13.
35. C. McK, "The Keatons Again," *Syracuse Herald* (January 6, 1914), n.p., Buster Keaton clippings file, Robinson Locke Collection of Theatrical Scrapbooks, Billy Rose Theatre Collection, New York Public Library for the Performing Arts.
36. Cressy, "Putting It Over," 551.
37. *Who's Who in Music and Drama: An Encyclopedia of Biography of Notable Men and Women in Music and the Drama*, ed. Harry Prescott Hanaford and Dixie Hines (New York: H.P. Hanaford, 1914), 108.
38. Ibid.
39. Slide, *Encyclopedia of Vaudeville*, 158.
40. "The Elinore Sisters" (December 20, 1906), n.p., Elinore Sisters clippings file, Vol. 444, 61, Robinson Locke Collection of Theatrical Clippings, Billy Rose Theatre Collection, New York Public Library for the Performing Arts.
41. "Kate Elinore Without a Sister at the American," *New York Star* (September 11, 1909), n.p., Elinore Sisters clippings file, Vol. 444, 67, Robinson Locke Collection of Theatrical Scrapbooks, Billy Rose Theatre Collection, New York Public Library for the Performing Arts.
42. Caffin, *Vaudeville*, 211.
43. *New Orleans Item* (n.d.), box 3, Vol. 3, 10, Elinore Sisters' Vaudeville Act Papers, Department of Rare Books and Special Collections, University of Rochester Library.
44. "Elinore Sisters Review" (n.d.), n.p., box 3, Vol. 3, 9, Elinore Sisters' Vaudeville Act Papers, Department of Rare Books and Special Collections, University of Rochester Library.
45. "The Theater: Breezy Kate Elinore; She Discusses Her Unique Rigs; Wagers Made as to Whether She Is Man or Woman" (n.d.), n.p., box 3, Vol. 3, 4, Elinore Sisters' Vaudeville Act Papers, Department of Rare Books and Special Collections, University of Rochester Library.
46. Robert Speare, "Plenty Doing at the Alhambra," *New Jersey Telegraph* 28 (May 28, 1908), n.p., Elinore Sisters clippings file, Vol. 444, 65, Robinson Locke Collection of Theatrical Clippings, Billy Rose Theatre Collection, New York Public Library for the Performing Arts.

47. Keith/Albee Collection, Report Book (1902–3), 324, Special Collections Department, University of Iowa Library.
48. Maurice E. McLaughlin, *The Irish 400* (1897), n.p., box 1, folder 11, Elinore Sisters' Vaudeville Act Papers, Department of Rare Books and Special Collections, University of Rochester Library.
49. Ibid.
50. Eugene Ellsworth, *The Adventures of Bridget McGuire* (n.d.), box 1, folder 10, 101–16, Elinore Sisters' Vaudeville Act Papers, Department of Rare Books and Special Collections, University of Rochester Library.
51. Ibid., 115.
52. Ibid., 116.
53. Keith/Albee Collection, Report Book 1, 65, Special Collections Department, University of Iowa Library.
54. Caffin, *Vaudeville*, 211–12.
55. Ibid., 212.
56. Ibid.
57. Hall, "Deconstructing the 'Popular,'" 227–40.

4 THE MARX BROTHERS GO TO SCHOOL

1. For my analysis of the Marx Brothers' vaudeville performances, I am working from Groucho and Harpo's memoirs as well as reviews of their acts from the period. The anecdotal citations are admittedly potentially unreliable, but I have made every effort to corroborate any anecdotal citations with Joe Adamson's thoroughly researched biography *Groucho, Harpo, Chico, and Sometimes Zeppo: A History of the Marx Brothers and a Satire on the Rest of the World* (New York: Simon and Schuster, 1983), which utilizes extensive interviews with Marx Brothers' collaborators and witnesses to their live performances in the 1910s and 1920s.
2. The Society for the Prevention of Cruelty to Children.
3. Keaton with Samuels, *Wonderful World of Slapstick*, 33.
4. Edgar Gardner Murphy, *Problems of the Present South: A Discussion of Certain of the Educational, Industrial and Political Issues in the Southern States* (New York: Macmillan, 1904), 72–4.
5. An example of this would be the Theater Guild that Groucho Marx would satirize in the 1928 stage and 1930 film version of *Animal Crackers*.
6. Ellwood Cubberley, *Changing Conceptions of Education* (New York: Macmillan, 1909), 14–15.
7. Woodrow Wilson, "Americanism," address to the Citizenship Convention, Washington, DC, July 13, 1916, included in W. Talbot, ed., *Americanization* (New York: H.W. Wilson, 1920), 28–31.

8. E. A. Ross, *Social Control: A Survey of the Foundations of Order* (New York: Macmillan, 1901), 428.
9. Anna Garlin Spencer in American Sociological Society, *Papers and Proceedings, Third Annual Meeting*, 198; Juvenile Court of the City and County of Denver, *The Problem of the Children and How Colorado Cares for Them* (Denver 1904), 22.
10. Joseph F. Kett, *Rites of Passage: Adolescence in America: 1790 to the Present* (New York: Basic Books, 1977), 215–44.
11. Ross, *Social Control*, 166.
12. McGerr, *A Fierce Discontent*, 110.
13. John Dewey, *The Child and the Curriculum and the School and Society* (Chicago: University of Chicago Press, 1956[1906]), 15.
14. Quotation from Hal S. Barron, *Mixed Harvest: The Second Great Transformation in the Rural North, 1870–1930* (Chapel Hill, NC: University of North Carolina Press, 1997), 71.
15. Dewey, *Child and the Curriculum*, 15.
16. Addams, *Spirit of Youth*, 102–3.
17. Ibid.
18. Eric C. Schneider, *In the Web of Class: Delinquents and Reformers in Boston, 1810s–1930s* (New York: New York University Press,1992), 132–8.
19. Gummo Marx states in an interview from *The Marx Bros. Scrapbook* that the core trio of Chico, Harpo, and Groucho were "unquestionably" the true comic soul of the Marx Brothers, and that he and Zeppo served as interchangeable straight men. Gummo and Zeppo were easily replaced by other actors, and were eventually superseded by a straight woman, Margaret Dumont, beginning with *The Cocoanuts* in 1925. In Groucho Marx and Richard J. Anobile, *The Marx Bros. Scrapbook* (New York: Darien House), 16.
20. Groucho Marx in his autobiography quotes the act's name as "the Larong Trio." Groucho Marx, *Groucho and Me* (New York: Bernard Geis, 1959), 57.
21. Ibid., 57; see also Adamson, *Groucho*, 43–8; Crichton, *The Marx Brothers*, 55–77.
22. Ibid., 55.
23. Ibid., 59.
24. Ibid., 60.
25. Gehring, *Marx Brothers*, 12.
26. The Three Nightingales went on to include additional performers, replacing Mabel O'Donnell, such as Lou Levy and Janie O'Riley, as the third nightingale, see Gehring, *Marx Brothers*, 13–18.
27. Four shows in one day.
28. Groucho Marx, *The Groucho Phile* (New York: Simon and Schuster, 1977), 32.

29. Anonymous review, qtd. in *Groucho Phile*, 39.
30. Harpo Marx, *Harpo Speaks!*, 17.
31. Ibid., 18–19.
32. Ibid., 427.
33. Ibid., 428.
34. Jenkins, *Pistachio Nuts?*, 42.
35. "*School Days*," *The Citizen*, Brooklyn, NY (October 16, 1927), n.p.
36. Ibid.
37. Harrigan's comments are discussed in chapter 1 in this book when defining the new humor.
38. The misspelling of "Hi Skule" was meant to signal the student's lack of ability to be educated.
39. It is worth noting that the Marx Brothers had no real formal education except a few years of grammar school between them. Unsigned *Variety* review, qtd. in *Marx Bros. Scrapbook*, 33.
40. Gehring, *Marx Brothers*, 26.
41. Sime Silverstein, "*Fun In Hi Skule*," *Variety* (February 24, 1912), 17.
42. Originally they were billed as "The Four Marx Brothers," which included Gummo who was then replaced by Zeppo.
43. "*Home Again*" by Al Shean, *Utah Democrat* (March 9, 1917), n.p.
44. From Verdi's opera, *Rigoletto*, 1850.
45. Marx, *Harpo Speaks*!, 117–18.
46. Ibid., 154.
47. Letter from Alfred Zimmern to his Mother, October 20, 1911 in Zimmern Papers, Bodleian Library, Oxford University, quoted in Desmond King, *Making Americans: Immigration, Race, and the Origins of Diverse Democracy* (Cambridge, MA and London: Harvard University Press, 2000), 89.
48. Marx, *Harpo Speaks!*, 121.
49. The fourth brother referred to at this point would be Gummo later replaced by Zeppo.
50. Dean Cornwell cartoon for performances at the Colonial Theater in 1914.
51. Groucho interviewed by Charlotte Chandler in *Hello, I Must Be Going* (New York: Doubleday, 1978).
52. "*Mr. Green's Reception*," *Kalamazoo Gazette* (January 12, 1913), n.p.
53. "New Acts," *Variety* (February 7, 1919), n.p.
54. "*Home Again*," 16.
55. Groucho initially still appeared as Mr. Green in the show, but pretty soon he was renamed Henry Hammer. After the sinking of *Lusitania* on May 7 1915, all German allusions disappeared overnight and thus Groucho's character became Henry Jones.

56. Al Shean, *Home Again*, from the "Marxology" website at http://www.marx-brothers.org/marxology/home.htm.
57. Ibid.
58. Marx, *Harpo Speaks!*, 122.
59. Henry B. Chamberlain, "Recreation and Crime," *New York Times* (May 28, 1922), qtd. in Arthur Evans Wood, *Community Problems* (New York: The Century Co., 1928), 280.
60. The Marx Brothers, *Duck Soup*, DVD, dir. Leo McCarey, writ. Bert Kalmar and Harry Ruby (Paramount Studios, 1933; Universal Home Video, Silver Screen Collection, 2004).
61. Chico received his nickname from "chasing the chickens" (women).
62. Adamson, *Groucho*, 17.
63. Gehring, *Marx Brothers*, 20; Crichton, *Marx Brothers*, 130.
64. Marx, *Harpo Speaks!*, 116–17.
65. *"Mr. Green's Reception," Kalamazoo Gazette* (January 12, 1913), n.p.
66. Marx, *Harpo Speaks!*, 27–34.
67. Interview with Groucho Marx qtd. in *Marx Bros. Scrapbook*, 16.
68. This act is repeated in his Broadway and film performance in *Animal Crackers*; Broadway, 1928; film version, 1930. In *Harpo Speaks!*, 142.
69. Ibid., 142.
70. Kaufman, *Animal Crackers*, 172.
71. Marx, *Groucho and Me*, 139.
72. Harpo Marx, *Harpo Speaks!*, 111–12.
73. It should be noted that *Mr. Green's Reception* was a transition school act between *Fun In Hi Skule* and *Home Again*.
74. As recounted by Harpo in *Harpo Speaks!*, 110.
75. Gehring, *Marx Brothers*, 63.
76. The Marx Brothers, *Horse Feathers*, DVD, dir. Norman McLeod, writ. Burt Kalmar, Harry Ruby, and S. J. Perelman (Paramount Pictures, 1932; Universal Home Video, Silver Screen Collection, 2004).
77. Marx Brothers, *Horse Feathers*, DVD.
78. Ibid.
79. This ending was shot but not used in *Horse Feathers*. It does not appear in the Final Script, only in the Tentative Script (February 11, 1932), in Special Collections, Margaret Herrick Library, Academy of Motion Picture Arts and Sciences, Beverley Hills, California; as noted in Gehring, *Marx Brothers*, 64–5, 103; Mikael Uhlin, from the "Marxology" website at http://www.marx-brothers.org/marxology/horse.htm.
80. Harry Ruby and Bert Kalmar, *Horse Feathers*, Tentative Script (February 11, 1932), L9.
81. Ibid.

82. Ibid.
83. *Animal Crackers* was staged on Broadway in 1928 and the film version released in 1930.
84. Kaufman, *Animal Crackers*, 182; The Marx Brothers, *Animal Crackers*, DVD, dir. Victor Sheekman. writ. Morrie Ryskind (Paramount Studios, 1930; Universal Home Video, Silver Screen Collection, 2004).
85. Bradley, *Making American Culture*, 12.

5 THE NEW WOMAN AND THE FEMALE COMEDIAN AS SOCIAL INSURGENT

1. Jeffrey P. Moran, "'Modernism Gone Mad': Sex Education Comes to Chicago, 1913," *Journal of American History* 83 (September 1996): 481–513.
2. Lynn Linton, "The Wild Woman as Social Insurgent," *Nineteenth Century* (October 1891), 596.
3. "'Comedian' Girls Jump to the Front" (June 8, 1902), n.p., Eva Tanguay clippings file, Vol. 450, Robinson Locke Collection of Theatrical Scrapbooks, Billy Rose Theatre Collection, New York Public Library for the Performing Arts.
4. Andrew L. Erdman, *Queen of Vaudeville: The Story of Eva Tanguay* (Ithaca and London: Cornell University Press, 2012), 8.
5. Adelda Rogers St. Johns, "The Private Life of Marie Dressler: Part One–The Ugly Duckling," *Liberty* 10, no.19 (May 13, 1933): 20–5.
6. Florencemae Waldron, "The Battle Over Female (In)Dependence: Women In New England Québécois Migrant Communities, 1870–1930," *Frontiers: A Journal of Women Studies* 26, no. 2 (2005): 158–205.
7. Allen, *Horrible Prettiness*, 30.
8. M. Alison Kibler, *Rank Ladies: Gender and Cultural Hierarchy in American Vaudeville* (Chapel Hill and London: University of North Carolina Press, 1999), 23.
9. Constant Coquelin, "Have Women a Sense of Humor?" *Harper's Bazaar* (January 1901): 67.
10. Robert Burdette, "Have Women a Sense of Humor?" *Harper's Bazaar* (July 1902): 598.
11. Grau, *Business Man in the Amusement World*, 82–3.
12. "May Irwin" (n.d.), May Irwin clipping, ser. 5, pt. 2 reel 38, 373, Daniel Blum Scrapbooks, Wisconsin State Historical Society.
13. "Courted into Court" (ca. 1897), n.p., May Irwin clippings file, Vol. 297, 11, Robinson Locke Collection of Theatrical Clippings, Billy Rose Theatre Collection, New York Public Library for the Performing Arts.

14. Cullen et al., *Vaudeville Old & New*, 555.
15. Ibid., 266–7.
16. Slide, *Encyclopedia of Vaudeville*, 262–3; Cullen et al., *Vaudeville Old & New*, 554–6.
17. Charles E. Trevathan, "May Irwin's Frog Song" (White-Smith Music Publishing, 1896); JScholarship website, Johns Hopkins University, https://jscholarship.library.jhu.edu/handle/1774.2/16096.
18. "Review of *The Widow Jones*," *New York Times* (September 17, 1895), n.p.
19. Qtd. in William C. Young, ed., *Actors and Actresses on the American Stage: Documents of the American Theater*, Vol. 1 (New York: R.R. Bowker, 1975), 564–5.
20. Ibid.
21. Ibid.
22. Not unlike the notion of the "carnivalesque" that Mikhail Bakhtin would discuss in his assessment of medieval comedy decades later in *Rabelais and His World.*
23. "Now Ain't Dat Scand'lous" (n.d.), May Irwin clippings file, Vol. 297, 90, Robinson Locke Collection of Theatrical Clippings, Billy Rose Theatre Collection, New York Public Library for the Performing Arts.
24. "May Irwin, the Jolly," *Criterion* (December 25, 1897), n.p., May Irwin clippings file, Vol. 297, 20, Robinson Locke Collection of Theatrical Clippings, Billy Rose Theatre Collection, New York Public Library for the Performing Arts.
25. Cullen et al., *Vaudeville Old & New*, 185.
26. "May Irwin, Ragtime, and the Cakewalk" (February 15, 1902), n.p., May Irwin clippings file, Vol. 297, 85, Robinson Locke Collection of Theatrical Clippings, Billy Rose Theatre Collection, New York Public Library for the Performing Arts.
27. "Chase's—May Irwin Heads Good Bill," *Washington Post* (January 14, 1908): 5.
28. Armond Fields, *Women Vaudeville Stars* (Jefferson, NC: McFarland, 2006), 149–50.
29. Peiss, *Cheap Amusements*, 163.
30. Addams, *Spirit of Youth*, 99.
31. Czitrom, *Media and the American Mind*, 46–7.
32. Mara L. Keire, "The Committee of Saloon Reform in New York City, 1905–1920," *Business and Economic History* 26, no. 2 (Winter 1997): 573.
33. "'Comedian' Girls Jump to the Front."
34. McGerr, *A Fierce Discontent*, 94.
35. Josiah Strong, *Religious Movements for Social Betterment* (New York: Baker and Taylor, 1900), 48.

36. Albion Small "The Relations of Social Diseases to the Family," in American Sociological Society, *Papers and Proceedings, Third Annual Meeting* (Chicago 1909), 192.
37. Ibid.
38. "Cheap amusements" refers to the title of Kathy Peiss's study of working women and leisure in turn-of-the-century New York, and how working-class women were stigmatized by encouraging, participating in, and being able to only afford a degraded form of popular entertainment; Kathy Peiss, *Cheap Amusements.*
39. Jane Addams, qtd. in Paul R. Gorman, *Left Intellectuals and Popular Culture in America* (Chapel Hill: University of North Carolina Press, 1996), 45.
40. Thomas H. Dickinson, *The Insurgent Theatre* (New York: Benjamin Blom, 1972[1917]), 228.
41. Addams, *Spirit of Youth*, 89.
42. Ibid., 83.
43. Peiss, *Cheap Amusements*, 34–41.
44. Erdman, *Queen of Vaudeville*, 30–2.
45. Ibid., 47.
46. McLean, *Vaudeville as Ritual*, 54.
47. "Vaudeville and Variety Miscellaneous" file, no publication cited (1900), n.p., Harvard Theatre Collection, Houghton Library, Harvard University.
48. Gilbert, *American Vaudeville*, 328.
49. Ibid., 329.
50. Erdman, *Queen of Vaudeville*, 140–5.
51. Ibid.; also in Slide, *Encyclopedia of Vaudeville*, 146–8.
52. Erdman, *Queen of Vaudeville*, 198–9.
53. Sime Silverman, "Eva Tanguay," *Variety* (September 24, 1910), n.p. Eva Tanguay spent most of her subsequent career in vaudeville starring in only two silent films, *Energetic Eva* (1916) and *The Wild Girl* (1917).
54. Although Tanguay was a wealthy woman by the 1920s, she reportedly lost $2,000,000 in the Wall Street crash of 1929. In 1947, relatively broke, although aided by friends like fellow vaudevillian Sophie Tucker, Tanguay died in Hollywood while working on her autobiography. Three excerpts from this appeared in Hearst newspapers, which was to be entitled *Up and Down the Ladder*; Erdman, *Blue Vaudeville*, 128.
55. Gilbert, *American Vaudeville*, 327.
56. Laurie, *Vaudeville*, 58.
57. Gilbert, *American Vaudeville*, 329.
58. Ibid.
59. Ibid., 328.

60. Lewis, *From Traveling Show to Vaudeville*, 319.
61. "Higgins," *New York Dramatic Mirror* (April 29, 1919): 636.
62. Ibid.
63. *Chicago Inter-Ocean* (March 21, 1907), n.p., qtd. in Erdman, *Queen of Vaudeville*, 9.
64. References to the script of *The Sambo Girl* are based on a manuscript in the Eva Tanguay Collection, Benson Ford Research Center; "West End—The Sambo Girl," Eva Tanguay clippings file, Vol. 450, Robinson Locke Collection of Theatrical Scrapbooks, Billy Rose Theatre Collection, New York Public Library for the Performing Arts. The song "I Don't Care!" is from the musical *The Sambo Girl*, Book and Lyrics by Harry B. Smith, Music by Gustav Kerker (Broadway premiere October 16, 1905).
65. Ibid.
66. Earl Barnes, "The Economic Independence of Women," *Atlantic Monthly* (August 1912): 262–3.
67. "The Day of the Lady Comedian" (1902), n.p., Eva Tanguay clippings file, Vol. 450, Robinson Locke Collection of Theatrical Scrapbooks, Billy Rose Theatre Collection, New York Public Library for the Performing Arts.
68. Ibid.
69. "'Comedian' Girls Jump to the Front."
70. John B. Kennedy, "Revised Version," *Collier's* 90, no. 20 (November 12, 1932): 45–7.
71. Allen, *Horrible Prettiness*, 221–32.
72. Bradley, *Making American Culture*, 25.
73. Mack Sennett with Cameron Shipp, *King of Comedy* (Garden City, NY: Doubleday, 1954), 165.
74. Slide, *Encyclopedia of Vaudeville*, 571–3.
75. Kathy Lee Peiss, *Hope in a Jar: The Making of America's Beauty Culture* (New York: Metropolitan Books, 1998), 98; Erdman, *Queen of Vaudeville*, 138; Slide, *Encyclopedia of Vaudeville*, 571.
76. Erdman, *Queen of Vaudeville*, 137–9.
77. Kibler, *Rank Ladies*, 12–14; Gilbert, *American Vaudeville*, 327–31.
78. Glenn, *Female Spectacle*, 46.
79. "Comedian' Girls Jump to the Front."
80. Report Book 15, 161, Keith/Albee Collection, Special Collections Department, University of Iowa Library; reprinted in Allen, *Horrible Prettiness*, 282.
81. Victoria Sturtevant, *A Great Big Girl Like Me: The Films of Marie Dressler* (Urbana and Chicago: University of Illinois Press, 2009), 1–29; Slide, *Encyclopedia of Vaudeville*, 141–3.
82. St. Johns, "Private Life of Marie Dressler: Part One—The Ugly Duckling," 20–5.

83. Qtd. in Victoria Sturtevant, *A Great Big Girl Like Me: The Films of Marie Dressler* (Urbana and Chicago: University of Illinois Press), 5. The song "A Great Big Girl Like Me!" is from the Weber and Fields Music Hall production of *Higgledy-Piggledy*, Book and Lyrics by Edgar Smith, Music by Maurice Levi (Broadway premiere October 20, 1904).
84. Alfred Greason—"Rush," *Variety* (April 25, 1908): 14.
85. Ibid.
86. Ibid.
87. Qtd. in Roberta Ann Raider, "A Descriptive Study of the Acting of Marie Dressler," Ph.D. diss. (University of Michigan, 1970), 117.
88. References to the script of *Tillie's Nightmare* from Tams-Witmark Collection, Mills Music Library, University of Wisconsin-Madison, 14–15. The song "Heaven Protect the Working Girl" is from *Tillie's Nightmare*, Book and Lyrics by Edgar Smith, Music by A. Baldwin Sloane (Broadway premiere May 5, 1910).
89. Adelda Rogers St. Johns, "The Private Life of Marie Dressler: Part Two—The Rising Star," *Liberty* 10, no. 20 (May 20, 1933): 10–15.
90. *Chicago News* (April 1905), n.p., Marie Dressler clippings file, Vol. 163, Robinson Locke Collection of Theatrical Scrapbooks, Billy Rose Theatre Collection, New York Public Library for the Performing Arts.
91. *Leslie's Weekly* (June 23, 1910), n.p., Marie Dressler clippings file, Vol. 164, Robinson Locke Collection of Theatrical Scrapbooks, Billy Rose Theatre Collection, New York Public Library for the Performing Arts.
92. "Higgins," *New York Dramatic Mirror* (April 8, 1919): 531.
93. Caffin, *Vaudeville*, 17–18.
94. Ibid., 18.
95. Jenkins, *Pistachio Nuts?*, 232.
96. Ibid., 221–2.
97. Kibler, *Rank Ladies*, 54.
98. B. F. Keith qtd. in Royle, "The Vaudeville Theatre," n.p.

EPILOGUE

1. Aaron Hoffman, "The German Senator," qtd. in Brett Page, *Writing for Vaudeville* (Springfield, MA: The Writer's Library, 1915), 435–43.
2. Ibid.
3. Tavis Smiley and Cornell West, *The Rich and the Rest of Us: A Poverty Manifesto* (New York: Smiley Books, 2012).
4. Max Eastman, *The Sense of Humor* (New York: Scribner's, 1921), 168.
5. "The Limitations of Humor," *Living Age* CCLIV (August 1907): 560–4.
6. Gilson Gardner, "Why Is a Joke Funny?" *Putnam's* III (October 1907): 55–61.

7. The Marx Brothers and Tom Johnstone, *I'll Say She Is* (from the Library of Congress manuscript, 1923), online at http://www.marx-brothers.org/marxology/home.htm.
8. For a comprehensive examination of the mid-twentieth-century vaudeville resurgence in radio and television in relationship to current new humorists Larry David, Tina Fey, Stephen Colbert, and Dave Chappelle, see Rick DesRochers, *The Comic Offense: From Vaudeville to Contemporary Comedy—Larry David, Tina Fey, Stephen Colbert, Dave Chappelle* (New York: Bloomsbury Academic Publishing, 2014).
9. Stephen Colbert, "The Word–Docu–Drama," *The Colbert Report*, April 26, 2010, http://www.colbertnation.com/the–colbert–report–videos/308060/april–26–2010/the–word–docu–drama.

Bibliography

MANUSCRIPTS AND ARCHIVES

Harvard Theatre Collection, The Houghton Library, Harvard University, Cambridge, Massachusetts.

Library of Congress, Rare Book and Manuscript Division, Washington, DC, Groucho Marx papers and manuscripts special collection.

New York Public Library Rare Book and Manuscript Division, New York City.

Robinson Locke Collection of Theatrical Scrapbooks, Billy Rose Theatre Collection, New York Public Library for the Performing Arts, New York City.

Marie Dressler clippings file.
The Elinore Sisters clippings file.
May Irwin clippings file.
Buster Keaton clippings file.
The Marx Brothers clippings file.
Eva Tanguay clippings file.
Joe Weber and Lew Fields clippings file.

University of Iowa Library, Special Collections Department, Iowa City, Iowa. Keith/Albee Collection.

University of Rochester Library, Department of Rare Books and Special Collections, Rochester, New York.
The Elinore Sisters's Vaudeville Act Papers.

Wisconsin State Historical Society, Madison, Wisconsin.

NEWSPAPERS AND PERIODICALS

Atlantic Monthly, 1912–16
Billboard, 1915–32
Dial, 1900–18
Criterion, 1900–01
Harper's Bazaar, 1901–32

Life Humor Magazine, 1923–26
Midway, 1905
Moving Picture World, 1911
New Jersey Telegraph, 1908
New Republic, 1921–25
New York Clipper, 1901–32
New York Daily Mirror
New York Dramatic Mirror, 1909–19
New York Herald, 1883
New York Star, 1909
New York Times, 1903–49
New York World, 1862–1909
Newark News, 1919
Nineteenth Century, 1891
Variety, 1907–19

PRIMARY SOURCES

Addams, Jane. *The Spirit of Youth and the City Streets*. New York: Macmillan, 1909.

Albee, Edward F. "Twenty Years of Vaudeville." *Variety* 72, no. 3 (September 6, 1923): 18; *Theatre Magazine* 31 (May 1920): 408.

Bellamy, Edward. *Looking Backward: 2000–1887*. New York: New American Library, 2009[1888].

Bellamy, Francis. "The Pledge of Allegiance." *Illustrated American* (October 1892).

Chaplin, Charles. *My Autobiography*. New York: Simon and Schuster, 1964.

Freud, Sigmund. *Jokes and Their Relation to the Unconscious*. Trans. James Strachey. New York and London: W.W. Norton, 1960[1905].

Kaufman, George S. *Animal Crackers* in *Kaufman & Co.: Broadway Comedies*, ed. Laurence Maslon. New York: Library of the Americas, 2004.

Keaton, Buster. *The Playhouse* in *Buster Keaton: The Short Films Collection 1920–1923*, DVD, written and directed by Buster Keaton and Eddie Kline. New York: Kino Lorber, 2011[1921].

Keaton, Buster with Charles Samuels. *My Wonderful World of Slapstick*. New York: Da Capo Press, 1982[1960].

Kellor, Frances and Joseph Mayper. *Recommendations for a Federal Bureau of Distribution Department of Labor*. Boston: Wright & Potter, 1914.

Laurie, Jr., Joe. *Vaudeville: From the Honky-Tonks to the Palace*, New York: Henry Holt, 1953.

Lewis, Robert M., ed. *From Traveling Show to Vaudeville: Theatrical Spectacle in America, 1830–1910*. Baltimore, MD: Johns Hopkins University Press, 2003.

Lodge, Henry Cabot. "The Restriction of Immigration." *North American Review* 152 (1891): 27–36.

Marinetti, F. T. *Critical Writings*, ed. Gunter Berghaus, trans. Doug Thompson. New York: Farrar, Straus, Giroux, 2006.

Marx Brothers, The (1930). *Animal Crackers*, DVD, dir. Victor Sheekman, writ. Morrie Ryskind. Paramount Studios, 1930. Universal Home Video, Silver Screen Collection, 2004.

——— (1933). *Duck Soup*, DVD, dir. Leo McCarey, writ. Bert Kalmar and Harry Ruby. Paramount Studios. Universal Home Video, Silver Screen Collection, 2004.

———. *Fun In Hi Skule* (from the Library of Congress manuscript, 1921) on the "Marxology" website. http://www.marx-brothers.org/marxology/balcony.htm.

——— (1932). *Horse Feathers*, DVD, dir. Norman Z. McLeod, writ. Bert Kalmar, Harry Ruby, S. J. Perelman, Will B. Johnstone. Paramount Studios. Universal Home Video, Silver Screen Collection, 2004.

——— (1935)., *A Night at the Opera*, DVD, dir. Sam Wood, writ. George S. Kaufman and Morrie Ryskind. MGM Studios. Warner Home Video, 2004.

Marx Brothers, The and Tom Johnstone, *I'll Say She Is* (from the Library of Congress manuscript, 1923). http://www.marx-brothers.org/marxology /home.htm.

Marx, Groucho. *Groucho and Me*. New York: Bernard Geis, 1959.

———. *The Groucho Phile*. New York: Simon and Schuster, 1977.

Marx, Groucho and Richard J. Anobile. *The Marx Bros. Scrapbook*. New York: Darien House, 1973.

Marx, Harpo. *Harpo Speaks!* New York: Limelight Editions, 2008[1961].

Moskowitz, Belle. "Dance Problem." *Playground* 4 (October 1910): 244, 248, 249.

Murphy, Edgar Gardner. *Problems of the Present South: A Discussion of Certain of the Educational, Industrial and Political Issues in the Southern States*. New York: Macmillan, 1904.

Ross, E. A. *Sin and Society: An Analysis of Latter-Day Iniquity*. Boston: Houghton Mifflin, 1907.

———. *Social Control: A Survey of the Foundations of Order*. New York: Macmillan, 1901.

Sennett, Mack with Cameron Shipp. *King of Comedy*. Garden City, NY: Doubleday, 1954.

Shean, Al. *Home Again*. "Marxology" website. http://www.marx-brothers.org /marxology/home.htm.

Simkhovitch, Mary Kingsbury. *The City Worker's World in America*. New York: Macmillan, 1917.

Small, Albion. "The Relations of Social Diseases to the Family" in American Sociological Society, *Papers and Proceedings, Third Annual Meeting*, 192. Chicago 1909.

Smith, Edgar. Book and Lyrics. Music, Maurice Levi. *Higgledy-Piggledy*, Broadway premiere, October 20, 1904.

———. Book and Lyrics. Music, A. Baldwin Sloane. *Tillie's Nightmare* in Tams-Witmark Collection, Mills Music Library, University of Wisconsin-Madison, Broadway premiere, May 5, 1910.

Smith, Harry B. Book and Lyrics. Music, Gustav Kerker. "I Don't Care!" from the musical *The Sambo Girl*, Broadway premiere, October 16, 1905.

Solomon, Barbara M. *Ancestors and Immigrants*. Chicago: University of Chicago Press, 1956.

Stein, Charles W., ed. *American Vaudeville as Seen by Its Contemporaries*. New York: Alfred A. Knopf, 1984.

Stein, Gertrude. "Portraits and Repetition." *Writing and Lectures, 1911–1945*, ed. Patricia Meyerowitz. London: Owen, 1967.

Strong, Josiah. *The Challenge of the City*. New York: Young People's Missionary Movement, 1907.

———. *Religious Movements for Social Betterment*. New York: The Baker and Taylor Company, 1900.

Thompson, Frederic. "Amusing the Million." *Everybody's Magazine* (September 1908): 1–9.

Trevathan, Charles E. "May Irwin's Frog Song" (White-Smith Music Publishing, 1896); JScholarship website, Johns Hopkins University, https://jscholarship.library.jhu.edu/handle/1774.2/16096.

US Immigration Commission, Vol. 1. Washington, DC: General Printing Office, 1910.

Wilson, Woodrow. "Americanism," address to the Citizenship Convention, Washington, DC, July 13, 1916, in *Americanization*, ed. W. Talbot. New York: H.W. Wilson, 1920.

———. *A History of the American People*. New York: Harper & Brothers, 1902.

Wood, Arthur Evans. *Community Problems*. New York: The Century, 1928.

Wright, Frank Lloyd. *Autobiography*. New York: Pomegranate Communications, 2005[1932].

SECONDARY SOURCES

Adamson, Joe. *Groucho, Harpo, Chico, and Sometimes Zeppo: A History of the Marx Brothers and a Satire on the Rest of the World*. New York: Simon and Schuster, 1983.

Allen, Robert C. *Horrible Prettiness: Burlesque and American Culture*. Chapel Hill and London: University of North Carolina Press, 1991.

Anderson, Ann. *Snake Oil, Hustlers, and Hambones: The American Medicine Show*. Jefferson, NC: McFarland, 2000.

Bakhtin, Mikhail. *Rabelais and His World*, trans. Helene Iswolsky. Bloomington and Indianapolis: Indiana University Press, 1984[1940].

Barber, Rowland. *The Night They Raided Minsky's: A Fanciful Expedition to the Lost Atlantis of Show Business*. New York: Simon & Schuster, 1960.

Barron, Hal S. *Mixed Harvest: The Second Great Transformation in the Rural North, 1870–1930*. Chapel Hill, NC: University of North Carolina Press, 1997.

Bourdieu, Pierre. *Distinction: A Social Critique of the Judgment of Taste*, trans. Richard Nice. Cambridge, MA: Harvard University Press, 1984.

Bourne, Randolph S. *Randolph Bourne The Radical Will: Selected Writings 1911–1918*, ed. Olaf Hansen, preface by Christopher Lasch. Berkeley: University of California Press, 1977.

———. "Trans-National America." *Atlantic Monthly* 118 (July 1916): 86–97.

———. *War and the Intellectuals, Collected Essays 1915–1919*, ed. Carl Resek. New York: Harper and Row, 1964.

Bowen, Louise. *Speeches, Addresses, and Letters of Louise deKoven Bowen*. Ann Arbor, MI: Edwards Brothers, 1937.

Bradley, Patricia. *Making American Culture: A Social History, 1900–1920*. New York: Palgrave Macmillan, 2009.

Browne, Junius Henry. *The Great Metropolis: A Mirror of New York*. Hartford, CT: American Publishing, 1868.

Butsch, Richard. *The Making of American Audiences: From Stage to Television, 1750–1990*. Cambridge, UK: Cambridge University Press, 2000.

Caffin, Caroline. *Vaudeville*. New York: M. Kennerie, 1914.

Canfield, Mary Cass, "The Great American Art," *New Republic* (November 22, 1922): 334–5.

Chambers II, John Whiteclay. *The Tyranny of Change*, 3rd ed. New York: Rutgers University Press, 2000.

Chandler, Charlotte. *Hello, I Must Be Going*. New York: Doubleday, 1978.

Canfield, Mary Cass. "The Great American Art." *New Republic* (November 22, 1922): 334–5.

Colbert, Stephen. "The Word–Docu–Drama." *The Colbert Report*, April 26, 2010. http://www.colbertnation.com/the-colbert-report-videos/308060/april-26-2010/the-word-docu-drama.

Croly, Herbert. *The Promise of American Life*. New York: Macmillan, 1909.

Cressy, Will M. "Putting it Over." *Green Book Magazine* (March 1916): 547–52.

Critchley, Simon. *On Humour*. London and New York: Routledge, 2002.

Crichton, Kyle Samuel. *The Marx Brothers*. Garden City, NY: Doubleday, 1950.

Cubberley, Ellwood. *Changing Conceptions of Education*. New York: Macmillan, 1909.

Cuddihy, John Murray. *The Ordeal of Civility: Freud, Marx, Levi-Strauss, and the Jewish Struggle with Modernity*. New York: Basic Books, 1974.

Cullen, Frank with Florence Hackman and Donald McNeilly, eds. *Vaudeville Old & New: An Encyclopedia of Variety Performers in America*. Vols. 1–2. New York: Routledge, 2007.

Czitrom, Daniel J. *Media and the American Mind: From Morse to McLuhan*. Chapel Hill, NC: University of North Carolina Press, 1982.

Dale, Alan. *Comedy Is a Man in Trouble: Slapstick in American Movies*. Minneapolis: University of Minnesota Press, 2000.

Daughters of the American Republic, *Report* (1905–06): 23.

Davis, Andrew. *Baggy Pants Comedy: Burlesque and the Oral Tradition*. New York: Palgrave Macmillan, 2011.

Davis, Hartley. "In Vaudeville." *Everybody's Magazine* 13 (August 1905): 233.

Davis, Michael M. *The Exploitation of Pleasure: A Study of Commercial Recreations in New York City*. New York: The Russell Sage Foundation, 1912.

"The Decay of Vaudeville." *American Magazine* 69 (April 1910): 840–6.

de Francesco, Grete. *The Power of the Charlatan*. New Haven: Yale University, 1939.

DesRochers, Rick. *The Comic Offense: From Vaudeville to Contemporary Comedy—Larry David, Tina Fey, Stephen Colbert, Dave Chappelle*. New York: Bloomsbury Academic Publishing, 2014.

Dewey, John. *The Child and the Curriculum and the School and Society*. Chicago: University of Chicago Press, 1956[1906].

De Witt, Benjamin Parke. *The Progressive Movement: A Non-Partisan Comprehensive Discussion of Current Tendencies in American Politics*. New Brunswick, NJ: Transaction Publishers, 2013[1915].

Dickinson, Thomas H. *The Insurgent Theatre*. New York: Benjamin Blom, 1972[1917].

Dickstein, Morris. *Dancing in the Dark: A Cultural History of the Great Depression*. New York: W.W. Norton, 2009.

DiMaggio, Paul. "Cultural Boundaries and Structural Change: The Extension of the High Culture Model to Theater, Opera, and the Dance, 1900–1940." *Cultivating Differences: Symbolic Boundaries and the Making of Inequality*, ed. Michele Lamont and Marcel Fournier. Chicago: University of Chicago Press, 1992.

———. “Cultural Entrepreneurship in Nineteenth-Century Boston: The Creation of an Organizational Base for High Culture in America.” *Media, Culture and Society* 1 (January 1982): 33–50.

Dimeglio, John E. *Vaudeville U.S.A.* Bowling Green, OH: Bowling Green University Popular Press, 1973.

Diner, Steven J. *A Very Different Age: Americans of the Progressive Era*. New York: Hill and Wang, 1998.

Dolan, Jill. “‘What, No Beans?’ Images of Women and Sexuality in Burlesque Comedy.” *Journal of Popular Culture* 18, no. 3 (Winter 1984): 37–47.

Donahue, John D. and Richard Zeckhauser. “The Tummler’s Task: A Collaborative Conception of Port Protection.” *Ports in a Storm: Public Management in a Turbulent World*, ed. John D. Donahue and Mark H. Moore. Washington, DC: Brookings Institution Press, 2012.

Duffus, R. L. *Lillian Wald: Neighbor and Crusader*. New York: Macmillan, 1939.

Eastman, Max. *The Sense of Humor*. New York: Scribner’s, 1921.

Erdman, Andrew L. *Blue Vaudeville: Sex, Morals and the Mass Marketing of Amusement, 1895–1915*. Jefferson, NC and London: McFarland, 2004.

———. *Queen of Vaudeville: The Story of Eva Tanguay*. Ithaca, NY and London: Cornell University Press, 2012.

Erdman, Harley. *Staging the Jew: The Performance of an American Ethnicity, 1860–1920*. New Brunswick, NJ: Rutgers University Press, 1997.

Erenberg, Lewis. *Steppin’ Out: New York Nightlife and the Transformation of American Culture, 1890–1930*. Westport, CT and London: Greenwood Press, 1981.

Eyles, Allen. *The Marx Brothers Their World of Comedy*. New York: A.S. Barnes, 1969.

Fields, Armond and L. Marc Fields. *From the Bowery to Broadway: Lew Fields and the Roots of American Popular Theater*. New York and Oxford: Oxford University Press, 1993.

———. *Women Vaudeville Stars*. Jefferson, NC: McFarland, 2006.

Flanagan, Maureen A. *America Reformed: Progressives and the Progressivisms, 1890s–1920s*. New York and Oxford: Oxford University Press, 2007.

Forbes, Camille F. *Introducing Bert Williams: Burnt Cork, Broadway, and the Story of America’s First Black Star*. New York: Basic *Civitas* Books, 2008.

Gardner, Gilson. “Why Is a Joke Funny?” *Putnam’s* III (October 1907): 55–61.

Gay, Peter. *Modernism: The Lure of Heresy*. New York and London: W.W. Norton, 2008.

Gehring, Wes D. *The Marx Brothers: A Bio-Bibliography*. New York: Greenwood Press, 1987.

Gilbert, Douglas. *American Vaudeville: Its Life and Times.* New York: Dover, 1940.

Glenn, Susan A. *Female Spectacle: The Theatrical Roots of Modern Feminism.* Cambridge, MA: Harvard University Press, 2002.

Gorman, Paul R. *Left Intellectuals and Popular Culture in Twentieth-Century America.* Chapel Hill and London: University of North Carolina Press, 1996.

Gottlieb, George A. "Psychology of the American Vaudeville Show From the Manager's Point of View." *Current Opinion* 60 (April 1916): 257.

Grau, Robert. *The Business Man in the Amusement World.* New York: Broadway Publishing, 1910.

Hall, Stuart. "Notes on Deconstructing 'the Popular.'" *People's History and Socialist Theory*, ed. Raphael Samuel. London: Routledge and Kegan Paul, 1981.

Hamilton, Marybeth. "*When I'm Bad, I'm Better": Mae West, Sex, and American Entertainment.* Berkeley and Los Angeles: University of California Press, 1996.

Hanaford, Harry Prescott and Dixie Hines, eds. *Who's Who in Music and Drama: An Encyclopedia of Biography of Notable Men and Women in Music and the Drama.* New York: H.P. Hanaford Publishing, 1914.

Higham, John. *Strangers in the Land: Patterns of American Nativism, 1860–1925.* East Rutherford, NJ: Rutgers University Press, 2002.

Huyssen, Andreas. *After the Great Divide: Modernism, Mass Culture, Post-modernism.* Bloomington and Indianapolis: Indiana University Press, 1986.

Immigrants in America Review, I (1915): 3–4, 15.

Isman, Felix. *Weber and Fields.* New York: Boni and Liveright, 1924.

Jenkins, Henry. *What Made Pistachio Nuts?: Early Sound Comedy and the Vaudeville Aesthetic.* New York: Columbia University Press, 1992.

Johnson, Stephen, ed. *Burnt Cork: Traditions and Legacies of Blackface Minstrelsy.* Amherst, MA: University of Massachusetts Press, 2012.

Keire, Mara L. "The Committee of Saloon Reform in New York City, 1905–1920." *Business and Economic History* 26, no. 2 (Winter 1997): 573.

Kett, Joseph F. *Rites of Passage: Adolescence in America: 1790 to the Present.* New York: Basic Books, 1977.

Kibler, M. Alison. *Rank Ladies: Gender and Cultural Hierarchy in American Vaudeville.* Chapel Hill and London: University of North Carolina Press, 1999.

King, Desmond. *Making Americans: Immigration, Race, and the Origins of Diverse Democracy.* Cambridge, MA and London: Harvard University Press, 2000.

King, Rob. *The Fun Factory: The Keystone Film Company and the Emergence of Mass Culture.* Berkeley and Los Angeles: University of California Press, 2009.

King, Rob and Tom Paulus, eds. *Slapstick Comedy*. New York and London: Routledge, 2010.

Klapper, Paul. "The Yiddish Music Hall." *University Settlement Studies* 2, no. 4 (1905): 20–1.

Knopf, Robert. *The Theater and Cinema of Buster Keaton*. Princeton, NJ: Princeton University Press, 1999.

Krasner, David. *Resistance, Parody and Double Consciousness in African American Theatre, 1895–1910*. New York: Palgrave Macmillan, 1997.

Lears, Jackson. *Rebirth of a Nation: The Making of Modern America, 1877–1920*. New York: Harper Perennial, 2009.

Leavitt, M. B. *Fifty Years in Theatrical Management*. New York: Broadway Publishing, 1912.

Levin, Harry. *Playboys and Killjoys: An Essay on the Theory and Practice of Comedy*. New York and Oxford: Oxford University Press, 1987.

Levine, Lawrence W. *Highbrow/Lowbrow: The Emergence of Cultural Hierarchy in America*. Cambridge, MA: Harvard University Press, 1988.

"The Limitations of Humor." *Living Age* CCLIV (August 1907): 560–4.

Lippmann, Walter. *Drift and Mastery: An Attempt to Diagnose the Current Unrest*. New York: Mitchell Kennerley, 1914.

———. *The Phantom Public*. New Brunswick, NJ: Transaction Publishers, 1993.

———. *Public Opinion*. New York: Macmillan, 1922.

"London Hippodrome" program (April 1904): 10.

Lott, Eric. *Love and Theft: Blackface Minstrelsy and the American Working Class*. New York: Oxford University Press, 1995.

Lynd, Robert S., and Helen Merrell. *Middletown: A Study in American Culture*. New York: Harcourt, Brace & World, 1929.

MacLean, Annie M. *Wage-Earning Women*. New York: Macmillan, 1910.

Make 'Em Laugh: The Funny Business of America, Episode Three: The Knockabouts. Public Broadcasting Service, DVD, Ghost Light Films; Thirteen/WNET.org; Rhino Entertainment, 2008.

May, Lary. *The Big Tomorrow: Hollywood and the Politics of the American Way*. Chicago and London: The University of Chicago Press, 2000.

———. *Screening Out the Past: The Birth of Mass Culture and the Motion Picture Industry*. Chicago: University of Chicago Press, 1983.

McGerr, Michael E. *The Decline of Popular Politics: The American North, 1865–1928*. New York and Oxford: Oxford University Press, 1986.

———. *A Fierce Discontent: The Rise and Fall of the Progressive Movement in America, 1870–1920*. New York: Free Press, 2003.

McLean, Jr., Albert F. *American Vaudeville as Ritual*. Frankfort, KY: University of Kentucky Press, 1965.

McNamara, Brooks. *The New York Concert Saloon*. Cambridge, UK: Cambridge University Press, 2002.

McNamara, Brooks. *Step Right Up*, rev. ed. Jackson, MS: University of Mississippi Press, 1995.

McPherson, Edward. *Buster Keaton: Tempest in a Flat Hat.* New York: Faber and Faber, 2007.

Mencken, H.L. *The Collected Drama of H.L. Mencken: Plays and Criticism*, ed. S. T. Joshi. Lanham, MD: Scarecrow Press, 2012.

Mintz, Lawrence E. "Humor and Ethnic Stereotypes in Vaudeville and Burlesque." *MELUS* 21, no. 4, Ethnic Humor (Winter 1996): 19–28.

Mitchell, Glenn. *The Marx Brothers Encyclopedia.* London: Titan Books, 2011.

Moran, Jeffrey P. "'Modernism Gone Mad': Sex Education Comes to Chicago, 1913." *Journal of American History* 83 (September 1996): 481–513.

Mordden, Ethan. *Ziegfeld: The Man Who Invented Show Business.* New York: St. Martin's Press, 2008.

More, Louis Bolard. *Wage-Earners' Budgets: A Study of Standards and Costs of Living in New York City.* New York: Henry Holt, 1907.

"'Movie,' Manners and Morals." *Outlook* 113 (July 26, 1916): 694–5.

Murdock, Edward P. "Ethnocentrism." *Encyclopedia of the Social Sciences*, ed. Edwin A. Seligman and Alvin Johnson, Vol. 5, 613. New York: Macmillan, 1931.

Nasaw, David. *Going Out: The Rise and Fall of Public Amusements.* New York: Basic Books, 1990.

Nelson, T.G.A. *Comedy: An Introduction to Comedy in Literature, Drama, and Cinema.* New York and Oxford: Oxford University Press, 1990.

Page, Brett. *Writing for Vaudeville.* Springfield, MA: The Writer's Library, 1915.

Painter, Nell Irvin. *Standing at Armageddon: The United States, 1877–1919.* New York and London: W.W. Norton, 1987.

Pease, Otis, ed. *The Progressive Years.* New York: George Braziller, 1962.

Peiss, Kathy Lee. *Cheap Amusements: Working Women and Leisure in Turn-of-the-Century New York.* Philadelphia, PA: Temple University Press, 1986.

———. *Hope in a Jar: The Making of America's Beauty Culture.* New York: Metropolitan Books, 1998.

Perry, Elizabeth Israels. *Belle Moskowitz: Feminine Politics and the Exercise of Power in the Age of Alfred E. Smith.* New York: Oxford University Press, 1987.

Piott, Steven L. *American Reformers, 1870–1920: Progressives in Word and Deed.* Lanham, MD and New York: Rowman & Littlefield, 2006.

Raider, Roberta Ann. "A Descriptive Study of the Acting of Marie Dressler." Ph.D. diss., University of Michigan, 1970.

Riis, Thomas. *Just Before Jazz: Musical Theater in New York, 1890–1915.* Washington, DC: Smithsonian Institute Press, 1989.

Roberts, Peter. *The New Immigration*. New York: Macmillan, 1913.

Roediger, David. *Working Toward Whiteness: How America's Immigrants Became White*. New York: Basic Books, 2005.

Rogin, Michael. *Blackface, White Noise: Jewish Immigrants in the Hollywood Melting Pot*. Berkeley and Los Angeles: University of California Press, 1996.

Royle, Edwin Milton. "The Vaudeville Theatre." *Scribner's Magazine* 26 (October 1899): 489.

Rudlin, John. *The Commedia dell'arte in the Twentieth-Century*. London: Routledge, 1994.

St. Johns, Adelda Rogers. "The Private Life of Marie Dressler: Part One—The Ugly Duckling." *Liberty* 10, no. 19 (May 13, 1933): 20–5.

———. "The Private Life of Marie Dressler: Part Two—The Rising Star." *Liberty* 10, no. 20 (May 20, 1933): 10–15.

Savran, David. *Highbrow/Lowdown: Theater, Jazz, and the Making of the New Middle Class*. Ann Arbor, MI: University of Michigan Press, 2009.

Schechter, Joel, ed. *Popular Theatre: A Sourcebook*. London and New York: Routledge, 2003.

Schneider, Eric C. *In the Web of Class: Delinquents and Reformers in Boston, 1810s–1930s*. New York: New York University Press, 1992.

Seldes, Gilbert. *The 7 Lively Arts*. New York: Sagamore Press, 1957.

Senelick, Laurence. "Minstrel Show," in *The Cambridge Guide to American Theatre*, 2nd ed., ed. Don B. Wilmeth (Cambridge: Cambridge University Press, 2007), 446.

———. "Variety into Vaudeville: The Process Observed in Two Manuscript Gagbooks." *Theatre Survey* (May 1978): 1–15.

Slide, Anthony, ed. *The Encyclopedia of Vaudeville*. Westport, CT: Greenwood Press, 1994.

———, ed. *Selected Vaudeville Criticism*. Metuchen, NJ and London: The Scarecrow Press, 1988.

Smiley, Tavis and Cornell West. *The Rich and the Rest of Us: A Poverty Manifesto*. New York: Smiley Books, 2012.

Smith, Christopher J. *The Creolization of American Culture: William Sidney Mount and the Roots of Blackface Minstrelsy*. Champaign, IL: University of Illinois Press, 2013.

Smith, Frances Peck. "In Vaudeville." *The Green Book Album* 8 (July 1912): 142.

Snyder, Robert. *The Voice of the City: Vaudeville and Popular Culture in New York*. New York and Oxford: Oxford University Press, 1989.

Sollors, Werner. *Beyond Ethnicity: Consent and Descent in American Culture*. New York and Oxford: Oxford University Press, 1986.

Sons of the American Revolution. *National Year Book* (1902): 174–80; (1914): 137–8.

Spencer, Anna Garlin. American Sociological Society, *Papers and Proceedings, Third Annual Meeting*, 198; Juvenile Court of the City and County of Denver, *The Problem of the Children and How Colorado Cares for Them*. Denver 1904.

Staples, Shirley. *Male-Female Comedy Teams in American Vaudeville, 1865–1932*. Ann Arbor, MI: UMI Research Press, 1984.

Stott, Andrew. *Comedy*. New York and London: Routledge, 2005.

Strong, Josiah. *The Challenge of the City*. New York: Young People's Missionary Movement, 1907.

———. *Religious Movements for Social Betterment*. New York: Baker and Taylor, 1900.

Sturtevant, Victoria. *A Great Big Girl Like Me: The Films of Marie Dressler*. Urbana and Chicago: University of Illinois Press, 2009.

Sypher, Wylie, ed. *Comedy: "An Essay on Comedy" by George Meredith and "Laughter" by Henri Bergson*. Baltimore, MD: Johns Hopkins University Press, 1956.

Toll, Robert C. *Blacking Up: The Minstrel Show in Nineteenth-Century America*. New York: Oxford University Press, 1974.

———. *On with the Show: The First Century of Show Business in America*. New York: Oxford University Press, 1976.

Twentieth Century Club Drama Committee. *The Amusement Situation in Boston* (Boston 1910): 3, 8, 30–1.

Wagner, Rob. "Smart-Crackers and Cheese." *Rob Wagner's Script* 2, no. 5 (September 14, 1929): 1–2 and 32.

Waldron, Florencemae. "The Battle Over Female (In)Dependence: Women in New England Québécois Migrant Communities, 1870–1930," *Frontiers: A Journal of Women Studies* 26, no. 2 (2005): 158–205.

Wertheim, Arthur Frank. *Vaudeville Wars: How the Keith-Albee and Orpheum Circuits Controlled the Big-Time and Its Performers*. New York: Palgrave Macmillan, 2009.

White, Richard Grant. "The Age of Burlesque." *Galaxy* (August 1869): 256–66

Wiebe, Robert H. *The Search for Order, 1877–1920*. New York: Hill and Wang, 1967.

Williams, Raymond. *The Sociology of Culture*. Chicago: University of Chicago Press, 1981.

Wilmeth, Don B., ed. *The Cambridge Guide to American Theatre*, 2nd ed. Cambridge: Cambridge University Press, 2007.

Wilson, Edmund. *The Shores of Light: A Literary Chronicle of the Twenties and Thirties*. New York: Farrar, Straus and Young, 1952.

Wilson, James. *Bulldaggers, Pansies, and Chocolate Babies: Performance, Race, and Sexuality in the Harlem Renaissance.* Ann Arbor: University of Michigan Press, 2010.

Young, William C., ed. *Actors and Actresses on the American Stage: Documents of the American Theater*, Vol. 1. New York: R.R. Bowker, 1975.

Index

GPSR Compliance
The European Union's (EU) General Product Safety Regulation (GPSR) is a set of rules that requires consumer products to be safe and our obligations to ensure this.

If you have any concerns about our products, you can contact us on

ProductSafety@springernature.com

In case Publisher is established outside the EU, the EU authorized representative is:

Springer Nature Customer Service Center GmbH
Europaplatz 3
69115 Heidelberg, Germany

www.ingramcontent.com/pod-product-compliance
Ingram Content Group UK Ltd.
Pitfield, Milton Keynes, MK11 3LW, UK
UKHW041629190726
13854UKWH00006B/2389

* 9 7 8 1 3 4 9 4 7 0 7 4 7 *